Researching Young People's Lives

Researching Young People's Lives

Sue Heath, Rachel Brooks, Elizabeth Cleaver
and Eleanor Ireland

Los Angeles • London • New Delhi • Singapore • Washington DC

SAGE Publications Ltd
1 Oliver's Yard
55 City Road
London EC1Y 1SP

SAGE Publications Inc.
2455 Teller Road
Thousand Oaks, California 91320

SAGE Publications India Pvt Ltd
B 1/I 1 Mohan Cooperative Industrial Area
Mathura Road
New Delhi 110 044

SAGE Publications Asia-Pacific Pte Ltd
33 Pekin Street #02-01
Far East Square
Singapore 048763

Library of Congress Control Number: 2008932441

British Library Cataloguing in Publication data

A catalogue record for this book is available from the
British Library

ISBN 978-1-4129-1055-2
ISBN 978-1-4129-1056-9 (pbk)

Typeset by C&M Digitals (P) Ltd, Chennai, India
Printed in Great Britain by the MPG Books Group
Printed on paper from sustainable resources

Mixed Sources
Product group from well-managed
forests and other controlled sources
www.fsc.org Cert no. SGS-COC-2953
© 1996 Forest Stewardship Council
FSC

Contents

Acknowledgements

This book almost didn't happen: huge thanks are due to Rachel Brooks, Liz Cleaver and Eleanor Ireland for ensuring that it did – and also for ensuring that it was a much better book than a sole-authored version would have been! I would also like to thank Patrick Brindle and Claire Lipscomb at Sage for encouraging me to keep going with the project and for generally being supportive as the original deadline drifted further into the past. Thanks, too, to Fiona Devine, Wendy Bottero, Derek McGhee, Traute Meyer, Graham Crow, Rose Wiles, Alison Fuller, Andy Cullis, Danna Molony, Mel King, Mel Nind and Lindsey Williams for their friendship over the last few years. Finally, a big thank you to my partner Jayne Williams, for all sorts of things, including her (mostly) quiet insistence on back-ups, but most of all for her patience and encouragement during the writing of this book. The allotment will now get a lot more attention, I promise!

Sue Heath

1 Researching Young People's Lives: An Introduction

Young people's lives are a source of curiosity and intrigue within contemporary societies, as indeed they have been for a very long time. Open any newspaper and you will encounter any number of familiar and regularly recycled storylines relating to 'the youth of today': be it the nation's latest 'youngest mum', the brave young survivor of cancer, the one-person juvenile crime wave, the youthful academic prodigy, the teenaged sporting hero … the list goes on. Taken as a measure of what society might look like in the future as successive cohorts reach adulthood, the attitudes and experiences of younger generations are constantly picked over and subjected to close scrutiny, with regular pronouncements then made about both the current state of the nation and its prospects for the years ahead. Following the spate of teenage shootings in London in early 2007, for example, the leader of the UK Conservative Party, David Cameron, proclaimed, 'That's what our society's now come to: teenagers shooting other teenagers in their homes at point-blank range. I think what we need is to recognise our society is badly broken and we need to make some big changes, starting now' (Owen, 2007). Young people's lives are then frequently held up as a 'social barometer' of wider societal change (Jones and Wallace, 1992), whether for good or ill, and as such are constantly in the spotlight.

Social researchers are by no means exempt from this fascination with young people's lives. Over the last 100 years, social scientists from a diverse range of disciplinary backgrounds have attempted to explain society's fascination with youth as a life stage, have provided detailed descriptive accounts of different facets of young people's lives and have advanced various theoretical frameworks for understanding their experiences. Key to these processes has been the development and implementation of effective strategies for researching youth. Given the scale of this endeavour, there are surprisingly few current textbooks which focus exclusively on the specific methodological challenges of conducting youth research. McLeod and Malone (2000) and Bennett et al. (2003) are notable exceptions, both entitled *Researching Youth* and both providing fascinating insider accounts of issues of method arising from specific examples of youth research. Other books in this field, though, have tended to conflate the challenges of youth research with those of childhood research (e.g., Fraser et al., 2003; Kellett et al., 2003; Best, 2007). Amy Best's edited collection *Representing Youth: Methodological Issues in Critical Youth Studies*, for example, is an important and valuable contribution to the field, yet the book includes as many chapters on research with young children as it does on youth research. Best justifies this coverage on the basis of the degree of commonality between childhood and youth research. We would not deny that there are indeed important areas of methodological overlap between the two traditions, nor that youth researchers and childhood researchers might not have much to learn from each other. Nonetheless, as we argue below, we still want to insist on the distinctiveness of youth research, not just because of its distinct histories, theoretical perspectives, methods and key literatures, but also due to what we believe to be young people's distinctive position within society relative to all other groups – including relative to children.

In this book we seek to make a contribution to filling this void by presenting an overview of some of the key methodological challenges associated specifically with researching young people's lives and by providing an introduction to a broad repertoire of methods which are particularly well suited to youth-orientated research. Our book is targeted primarily at novice researchers, in particular students studying and researching in the broad area of youth studies, including those pursuing specialist youth studies-related degree programmes and youth work qualifications, as well as students opting for individual youth-related units of study or conducting youth-related dissertations within broader social science degree programmes. We hope that it will also appeal to practitioners engaged in the evaluation of service provision to young people, as well as to established youth researchers who might wish to explore the potential of using a different set of methods to those with which they are already familiar. Throughout the book we place an emphasis on research *in practice*, drawing on examples of recent youth research from a wide range of disciplines and substantive areas, and from a range of both UK and non-UK contexts.

A book of this kind is timely given that recent years have seen a rekindled interest in the academic study of young people's lives. In part, this has been spurred on by a renewal of theoretical debate within youth studies, concerning issues as diverse as the ongoing relevance or otherwise of subcultural theory, the validity of the individualisation thesis in understanding young people's lives in late modernity, the extent to which certain risk behaviours have been 'normalised' amongst contemporary youth and the increasingly blurred boundaries between youth and adult-hood. In the UK context, this rekindling of interest has also been fuelled by New Labour's focus over the last decade on youth intervention strate-gies as a key tool for tackling social exclusion and promoting wider social inclusion. Strategies such as Connexions, the New Deal for Young People, and policies such as those which seek to reduce teenage preg-nancy rates or to lower the incidence of various forms of anti-social behaviour have all generated considerable interest amongst youth researchers, and have provided many opportunities for both official and unofficial policy evaluation.

In parallel with this resurgence of substantive and theoretical interest within youth studies, there has also been a renewed interest in the spe-cific methods by which young people's lives can be researched, as well as a broadening of the range of methods now commonly used by youth researchers. Whilst tried and tested methods such as interviews and sur-veys remain widely used, there is also a much greater willingness amongst youth researchers to draw on a more diverse repertoire of methods of data collection and approaches to analysis, not least those made possible by advances in new technologies. This broadened reper-toire includes, then, the use of visual approaches, such as photo elici-tation, spatial mapping techniques and video diaries (often used within broader ethnographic studies); 'mobile methods', such as research 'walkabouts'; internet-based methods, such as web surveys, email inter-viewing, and discourse and conversation analysis of website/chat room content; participatory and peer-led approaches to youth research; the growing use of narrative and biographical interviewing and techniques of analysis; longitudinal qualitative approaches and the re-use of exist-ing qualitative data; and a developing interest in comparative methods. Whilst methods and approaches such as these are by no means unique to researching the experiences of young people, we argue that their deployment within the context of youth research does nonetheless raise a wide range of methodological issues which *are* specific to research-ing young people as opposed to other groups, not least because of the very specific contexts within which much youth research is conducted. Our book then is timely in reflecting upon the applicability to youth research of more general methodological developments within the social sciences.

A crucial issue in making the case for the distinctiveness of youth research relates to our working definition of this life stage and the degree to which it is possible to draw a clear distinction between child-hood and youth on the one hand, and youth and adulthood on the other. Many social scientists argue – as we do – that each of these life stages is both a culturally- and historically-specific construction. Some argue for the existence of a new life stage between childhood and youth populated by a group popularly referred to as 'the tweenies', and there is strong evidence for the parallel emergence of 'young adult-hood' as a distinct new life stage between youth and adulthood (e.g., Heath and Cleaver, 2003; Arnett, 2004). Most social scientists would almost certainly point to the difficulties of aligning these different life stages with specific age-based boundaries. Nonetheless, in our view it remains important to distinguish between these different life stages wherever possible – not least because young people themselves tend to be acutely aware of these distinctions and of the extension or with-drawal of the rights and privileges which attend them. In practical terms, then, this book sets out to focus on issues which are broadly rel-evant to the conduct of research with young people in their mid-teens to mid-twenties, although these boundaries should by no means be seen as fixed nor impermeable. Incidentally, such a focus is broadly in line with the United Nation's definition of youth in terms of those aged 15 to 24 years old. When we draw comparisons throughout the book with research on *children*, we are generally referring to research involv-ing individuals younger than this specific age group.

We acknowledge that this nonetheless represents a broad age group-ing, and that a 15 year old and a 24 year old might have very little in common beyond the label of 'youth'. However, in the context of ongo-ing debates concerning the consequences of 'delayed' transitions to adult-hood, the lives of many young people in their early to mid-twenties remain characterised by a relative freedom from many of the traditional markers of 'adult' status, such as permanent employment, settling down with a long-term partner, parenthood and independent housing arrangements. Some writers claim further that many twenty-somethings deliberately seek to distance themselves from the concept of adulthood and instead cling to the distinctiveness of youth (du Bois-Reymond, 1998; Côté, 2000; Arnett, 2004).

The distinctiveness of youth research

In certain respects, many of the methodological issues and choices facing youth researchers are no different from those facing any group of social researchers. All researchers have to grapple with the challenges of gain-ing access, selecting an appropriate sample, choosing the most appropri-ate research method, and working out how best to analyse their research data. However, there are a number of features which are unique to the conduct of youth research as opposed to other forms of research – includ-ing childhood research – and which in combination create a case for the distinctiveness of youth research. This section explores four key contex-tual factors. First, young people's lives are structured by a range of age-specific contexts and institutions, such as educational institutions, training programmes, and leisure activities and subcultures targeted specifically at young people. Second, their lives are framed by age-specific policies, such as an age-regulated social security regime and various other government initiatives which target specific age groups. Third, youth is constructed as a critical time of transition and individual development within the life course, and as such there is widespread societal concern with the monitoring of young people's lives. Finally, and by no means of least importance, young people are a relatively powerless group within the research process for reasons which are often specific to their life phase, and which therefore necessitate particular attention during the research process. Each of these factors has important implications for the specific nature of youth research as opposed to other forms of research, and we consider each in turn.

The age-specific institutional and spatial contexts of young people's lives

Young people experience many aspects of their lives in highly age-segregated contexts, contexts which separate them out from other age groups. This is a feature of the 'institutionalisation' of the lives of different age groups, whereby individuals spend large amounts of time in age-structured institutions which serve to reinforce distinctions between those different age groups, and which often construct young people as marginal to 'adult' concerns. Educational institutions such as schools and colleges, for instance, are central to the lives of many young people, with chronological age being a key organisational feature. Students typically progress through educational institutions according to increasing age rather than achievement per se, whilst privileges such as the relaxation of strict uniform codes or access to common room space are also often attached to increasing age. With the rapid expansion of higher education amongst young people over the last 15 years or so, many universities and colleges of higher education have also become more homogeneous in terms of age than perhaps used to be the case.

Outside of these formal institutions, young people may spend large amounts of their time in leisure sites which, whether intentionally or by default, are also structured by age, such as youth clubs, student pubs and nightclubs. They may participate in junior leagues of sports clubs, play in youth orchestras, read books and magazines targeted specifically at young people, sign up to youth-dominated social networking websites such as MySpace, holiday with companies such as Club 18–30, participate in the youth organisations of various religious groups, take part in age-specific developmental activities such as the Duke of Edinburgh Award Scheme or the Millennium Volunteers, seek advice from age-specific one-stop-shops, and join age-specific organised groups such as the Venture Scouts or the Air Cadets, or the youth sections of political parties and pressure groups. The living arrangements of young people who have left the parental home may also be marked by a high degree of age homogeneity, whether living in halls of residence, peer shared households, local authority care homes, foyers, hostels, young offenders' institutions or military barracks.

Young people, then, spend very large amounts of time with other young people, and often develop a stronger allegiance to their peer groups than to more age-diverse social groupings. Children's lives are of course also strongly shaped by their involvement in age-specific institutions, but child-centred institutions tend to segregate them from most of the institutions referred to above: in other words, children and young people tend not to occupy the *same* institutional spaces. Even within secondary schools, which have the greatest potential for the blurring of divisions between different age groups, pupils spend most of their time corralled into classroom spaces according to their specific age. Not only do child-centred institutions and spaces tend to be distinct from those serving older groups, children also spend far more of their time under the direct supervision of adults, whether those adults are professionals of various kinds or family members. In all of these ways, age differences are constantly reinforced, and often by young people themselves.

The policy contexts of young people's lives

Young people's lives are also circumscribed by age-specific policies and laws which mark them out as belonging to a separate category of the population to both adults and children and which serve to legitimate their differential treatment. As Mizen has noted, 'the simple fact of possessing a certain biological age brings with it differential access to social power, while age also provides the means through which young people are brought into a more or less common relationship with many of the central institutions of modern life' (2003: 9). Their status as 'not yet adult' is strongly linked to the widespread view that young people are 'citizens in the making' and as such do not deserve equal treatment in policy terms. For example, the UK's social security system does not treat most young people as fully adult, and hence eligible for higher rates of benefit, until the age of 25. Similarly, minimum wage legislation is not universally applied to all young workers, but is based on distinctions between different groups of workers according to age. Connexions has been targeted at young people aged 13 to 19, whilst government training schemes such as Apprenticeships and the New Deal for Young People are targeted at those aged 16 to 24 and 18 to 24 respectively.

Furthermore, young people in their mid-to-late teens are specifically targeted by various government initiatives aimed at tackling social exclusion 'in the bud', including anti-truancy measures, measures to tackle school exclusions, and policies targeted at reducing teenage pregnancies.

More generally, age-related legislation with respect to the attainment of various rights and responsibilities is also complex, with young people treated as adults for different purposes at different ages. For example, in the UK a young person is allowed to work part-time at 13, can enter a public house but not drink alcohol at 14, is legally permitted to drink alcohol and have sex at 16, can go to war and obtain a licence to drive most vehicles at 17, can vote, buy cigarettes and tobacco, buy alcohol in a bar and get a tattoo at 18, and can stand for election to Parliament at 21. The lives of young people in their mid-teens to mid-twenties are, then, arguably subject to far greater levels of state regulation and control than the lives of younger children – and possibly the lives of older groups, too.

The monitoring of youth transitions

The degree to which young people's lives are circumscribed by age-specific policies is not unrelated to broader societal concerns regarding the need to monitor their transitions to adulthood. Youth is constructed both in popular and in much academic discourse as a key period of transition and change, marked by individual development from the status of 'child', through 'youth', and onwards towards 'adulthood'. As a buffer zone between childhood and adulthood, youth as a life stage has taken on a special status, as a time when young people are regarded as being particularly vulnerable to risk-taking and negative influences. Developmental psychologists often characterise this phase as being marked by 'storm and stress' and various manifestations of more or less acceptable experimentation, representing what Erik Erikson famously referred to as the 'psychosocial moratorium' of adolescence. As such, young people are deemed to require special guidance and protection from adults, on the back of which a vast industry of youth intervention agencies has emerged over the years: educational and developmental psychologists, careers advisers, Connexions personal advisers, youth workers, counsellors, youth offending teams, mentors, teachers, social workers – all concerned in one way or another with monitoring the lives of young people and with ensuring that, as far as possible, they are able to remain upon the straight and narrow during a key transitional period of their lives.

Young people are popularly regarded, then, as important less because of who they are in the here and now but because of *who or what they may or may not become* in the future. Wyn and White sum this up in the following terms: 'if youth is the state of "becoming", adulthood is the "arrival". At the same time, youth is also "not adult", a deficit of the adult state' (1997: 11). Youth is consequently constructed as a make or break developmental stage, thereby justifying the high levels of intervention within the lives of many young people. Researchers do not stand outside of this circle of observation and surveillance, but by definition are unavoidably complicit in its perpetuation, a point to which we return in the final section of this chapter.

The relative powerlessness of young people

Finally, youth research is distinctive because of the relative powerlessness of young people within the research process itself when compared with other groups. In this respect, youth research does indeed share much in common with childhood research. For example, and as we explore in Chapter 2, the involvement of under-16 year olds in research is subject to various legal considerations, whilst research access to youth-oriented institutions is invariably governed by gatekeepers of various kinds rather than by young people themselves. Young people are likely to have less informed knowledge of the nature of research involvement than older people, yet at the same time might be more amenable to requests to participate, even though it may not always be in their interests to do so. They may be coerced into research, whether directly by institutional gatekeepers or unscrupulous researchers, or more subtly as a consequence of the power dynamics which attend most youth-oriented research, whereby research is invariably conducted by someone older than the research participant. Moreover, specific efforts might be made by researchers to make the research an enjoyable rather than a boring experience through the use of 'youth-friendly' research methods, or young people might be offered payment for their involvement, yet even these well intentioned strategies might be construed as subtle forms of coercion. These concerns are by no means absent from research with other groups, but they are arguably amplified in the context of research with younger participants.

Partly in response to an increased awareness of the imbalance of the power dynamics which attend relationships between adults and young people, there has been a growing emphasis in recent years on the importance of respecting and indeed foregrounding young people's autonomy and social agency, both in the realm of social research and in the realm of youth policy. Whilst critical youth researchers have been highlighting these concerns for many years (see for example Griffin, 1993; Cohen, 1996), the dramatic rise of the new sociology of childhood has brought these concerns to the fore for a new generation of researchers, and this has in turn impacted upon the conduct of youth research. The discursive shift within childhood studies from viewing children as 'objects' of research towards a view which stresses their competency and agency, often as co-participants in the research process, grants 'central and autonomous conceptual status' (Christiansen and Prout, 2002: 481) to children and refuses to take pre-existing distinctions between adults and children for granted. Such a perspective compels researchers to reject notions of children's essential vulnerability and/ or incompetence, and to enter into 'a dialogue that recognises commonality but also honours difference' (2002: 480). Similar concerns face researchers working with young people, many of whom seek to challenge young people's relative powerlessness within their own research practice by attempting to 'democratise' the research process (France, 2004). Some of the ways in which researchers might seek to engage with these concerns within their own research practice are discussed in detail in Chapter 4.

In sum, then, youth research is distinctive from research on other groups. It tends to be conducted in youth-specific contexts from which both children and adults are often excluded, is affected by and is often related to young people's experiences of youth-specific policies and interventions, is implicated in the broader scrutiny of their lives at an important transitional and developmental moment, and places young people in a relatively powerless position in relation to the research process. Young people's lives and experiences are of course hugely diverse, and are differentiated by characteristics such as social class, gender, ethnicity, sexuality, health status and geographical location. Nonetheless, these four broad factors, which determine the contexts in which young people live their lives, are more or less universally shared. Given this distinctiveness, and not least the well established nature of youth studies as an academic tradition, it is surprising to us that there are so few textbooks currently available which focus exclusively on researching youth. In contrast, the relatively new field of childhood studies has generated a plethora of methodologically-orientated textbooks specifically focused on research with children (e.g., Christensen and James, 2000; Lewis and Lindsay, 2000; Kellett et al., 2003; Lewis et al., 2004; Hogan and Greene, 2004). In our view, it is time that youth studies caught up with childhood studies in this respect. Given the multidisciplinary nature of youth research, it is certainly not for want of researchers with important and interesting things to say about methodological issues, as the many examples drawn upon in this book will illustrate.

Traditions of youth research

Youth studies is a broad church; it embraces research on all aspects of young people's lives, and youth researchers are to be found across all social science disciplines. Nonetheless, it is possible to identify a number of distinct research traditions and disciplinary perspectives within that broad church, each to some extent also characterised by distinct methodological traditions.

Developmental psychology

There is a long tradition of research on young people's lives within developmental psychology, from G. Stanley Hall's 'discovery' of adolescence in the early twentieth century, Erik Erikson's work on identity in the 1950s, through to contemporary research on the changing nature of youth and adolescence (e.g., Apter, 2001; Bradford Brown et al., 2002; Mortimer and Larson, 2002; Arnett, 2004). Developmental psychologists tend to refer to 'adolescence' rather than 'youth' as a central concept in their work, and their focus is on the importance of this phase in young people's social and psychological development. Much research within this tradition draws upon survey methods and experimental design, although recently there has been a shift towards the adoption of a more critical and more qualitatively-orientated approach, including the use of methods drawing on narrative and psychoanalytic approaches (see Hollway and Jefferson, 2000; Richardson, 2002; Camic et al., 2003). Notwithstanding this more critical tradition, there is a general tendency to focus on adolescence as a potentially problematic period within this body of research, including a concern with the identification of risk factors which enable psychologists and others to identify young people most at risk from particular problems or behaviours. Key journals publishing research from within this tradition include the *Journal of Adolescence, Journal of Youth and Adolescence, Journal of Research on Adolescence, Journal of Adolescent Research* and *Youth and Society.*

Educational research

Educational research is a multidisciplinary endeavour with a common focus on educational experiences and processes within both institutional and non-institutional settings. Unsurprisingly, much educational research has a direct or indirect focus on the lives of young people, whether as formal or informal learners, as members of school-based youth subcultures, as those experiencing the sharp end of educational reforms, as agents of educational choice, or as the focus of any number of other educationally-orientated topics. Reflecting the diverse disciplinary backgrounds represented within the educational research community, there is no one dominant methodology in use. Rather, educational researchers interested in exploring young people's lives have traditionally drawn upon a wide repertoire of research tools (see Cohen et al., 2007). Educational research can, however, be justifiably proud of its rich tradition of ethnographic studies of school life, an approach which in recent years has had much to contribute to broader youth studies debates concerning youth and identity, including in relation to sexuality, masculinities and femininities, ethnicity and class, and the various intersections between them (e.g., Mac an Ghaill, 1994; Ball et al., 2000; Gordon et al., 2000). Educational research is published in a vast array of journals, although some of the best youth-focused research is located in journals such as the *British Journal of Sociology of Education, Gender and Education* and the *Journal of Education and Work*.

Cultural studies

The origins of the field of cultural studies lie within youth-orientated research. In the USA, cultural studies has its roots in the traditions of the Chicago School, which pioneered some of the classic ethnographic studies of 'deviant youth' in the last century (e.g., Thrasher, 1927; Shaw, 1930). In the UK, cultural studies is associated with the Centre for Contemporary Cultural Studies (CCCS) at the University of Birmingham, which emerged in the late 1960s and early 1970s with a series of mostly abstract studies of working class male youth subcultures (e.g., Hall and Jefferson, 1976). These more theoretical accounts were supplanted from the mid-1980s onwards by a return to a more ethnographically-orientated tradition (Bennett, 2002), including more recently the growing use of internet-based methods such as the observation of chat rooms, blogs and other social networking sites. The predominant focus of youth research from within the cultural studies tradition has centred on various forms of popular culture, including young people's engagement with music, the media, new technologies and other leisure pursuits. Recently, however, there has been a shift away from the language of youth 'subcultures' towards the alternative language of 'scenes', '(neo)tribes' and 'lifestyles', a shift which has also highlighted the blurring of the age boundaries formerly associated with various subcultural pursuits. Nonetheless, music-based subcultures remain a popular theme within cultural studies-influenced youth research (e.g., Bennett and Kahn-Harris, 2004). Youth research from within this tradition is published in a broad range of journals, including *Young: The Nordic Journal of Youth Research, Journal of Youth Studies* and *Youth Studies Australia*, as well as mainstream journals such as *Leisure Studies, Cultural Studies* and the *European Journal of Cultural Studies*.

Youth transitions research

Youth transitions research represents a dominant – some would argue hegemonic – strand of youth research. Largely conducted by sociologists, educational researchers, social policy researchers and economists, this is a policy-orientated approach which has traditionally focused predominantly on school-to-work transitions and, to a lesser extent, domestic and housing transitions. More recently, researchers such as MacDonald and Marsh (2005) have incorporated parallel transitions focused on, for example, drug careers or criminal careers. Youth transitions research has its origins in the collapse of the youth labour market in the late 1970s and early 1980s and is often concerned with mapping the structural contexts of young people's changing transitions to adult-hood. There is a strong strand of research within this tradition based upon the quantitative secondary analysis of large scale data sets, including longitudinal analysis of cohort study data such as the Youth Cohort Study and the 1970 British Cohort Study (BCS70). There is also a more qualitatively-orientated strand linked to this approach, and in recent years transitions researchers have made increasing use of both narrative/biographical and qualitative longitudinal approaches (e.g., Henderson et al., 2006a). Research associated with the youth transitions tradition is regularly published in journals such as the *Journal of Youth Studies, British Journal of Sociology of Education, Journal of Education and Work, Youth and Policy,* and *Youth Studies Australia.*

Social and cultural geography

Over the last decade an exciting new strand of youth research has emerged from the work of social and cultural geographers, much of it with a quali-tative focus (e.g., Skelton and Valentine, 1998; Malbon, 1999; Chatterton and Hollands, 2003; Panelli et al., 2007). A growing body of work has focused on the broad theme of youth and spatiality, embracing issues as diverse as place, space and youth identity; rural youth; young people's leisure spaces, including virtual leisure spaces; the gendering of youth space; and contested youth space. The impact of this new focus on 'geographies of youth' has been felt outside of the discipline through a growing focus in youth research more generally on the significance of place, space and time in young people's lives, and through the adoption of new research techniques such as spatial mapping exercises and the use of 'interviews on the move' (see Chapters 5 and 7). Specialist geography journals which publish youth research from within this tradition include *Children's Geographies* and *Children, Youth and Environment.*

Feminist youth research and 'girl studies'

Much early youth research took as its primary focus the lives of young men, sometimes referred to as 'the gangs of lads' model of youth research. In their now famous critique of this trend, McRobbie and Garber (1976) attempted to explain the marginalisation of young women within youth research and issued a call to arms for researchers to foreground the lives of young women. Christine Griffin's *Typical Girls* (1985) was a landmark study in this regard, a feminist riposte to classic boy-centred studies such as Paul Willis's *Learning to Labour* (1977). In the years since, there has been a consistent feminist critique of 'malestream' youth research, although it is still the case that studies specifically focusing on young women's lives remain relatively few and far between. Feminist youth researchers can be located across all of the traditions highlighted above, although much of this work has come together in recent years under the umbrella of 'girl studies' (see for example Harris, 2004), including a considerable amount of work coming from the perspectives of either cultural studies or critical social psychology (e.g., Best, 2000; McRobbie, 2000; Walkerdine et al., 2000). Feminist youth research, like feminist research more generally, tends to be qualitative in its methodological focus, and is often explicitly concerned with the empowerment of young women as a research outcome, incorporating action research and various participatory approaches to achieve this aim (see Chapter 4). Key outlets for feminist youth research include *Feminism and Psychology*, *Gender and Education* and *Feminist Review*.

Youth researchers are also located within other disciplines and fields of study, including criminology, social policy, health research, social history, political science and anthropology: each with their own distinct methodological traditions and preferences. Youth research is, then, characterised by a wide diversity of approaches, a diversity which embraces a variety of methodological and disciplinary traditions, and which we seek to do justice to in the many research examples we draw upon within this book. Increasingly there are moves towards interdisciplinarity and methodological pluralism in the conduct of youth research, a point to which we will return in the conclusion to this chapter. Regardless of approach, however, there remains a central dilemma for youth researchers which we deal with in the following section.

The youth researcher's dilemma: research as objectification

Many, if not most, researchers who choose to work in the area of youth studies do so at least in part out of a strong sense of commitment to challenging the ways in which young people's lives are popularly (mis)represented, and possibly out of a hope that by so doing they might contribute to the improvement of their lives. Much youth research is hence concerned with giving voice to young people and to promoting a better understanding of their worlds. Most researchers would probably seek to take their responsibilities to young people in this regard very seriously and as such would endorse the exhortations of Stephen and Squires, that youth researchers should neither portray young people as 'victims or dupes to structure' nor 'erroneously celebrate them as completely free actors' for ideological purposes: instead, that 'we must simply listen to what young people themselves have to say when making sense of their own lives' (2003: 161). Dwyer and Wyn (2001) make a similar point when they caution youth researchers to avoid the polarised and equally unhelpful positions of either demonising or romanticising young people's lives.

Part of this manifest concern with giving young people a voice is linked to a desire amongst many youth researchers to empower young people, in a context where so many aspects of their lives are objectified and held up to (often negative) scrutiny. Nonetheless, a central dilemma remains for youth researchers: namely the ever-present danger that their own research endeavours have the unintended consequence of further objectifying young people's lives, bringing them under yet another manifestation of the expert's gaze. Peter Kelly has written widely on this theme (see for example Kelly, 2003 and 2006) and has argued that the discourse of academic youth research, even in seeking the promotion of a 'better understanding' of their worlds, is as complicit in the objectification, control and governance of young people as any other expert discourse:

> This constantly growing research literature promises to develop more 'sophisticated' ways of identifying populations of young people with regard to various community and policy concerns ... In this sense, Youth Studies, as a diverse, heterogeneous, but recognisable institutionally located intellectual activity, emerges as such so that Youth, in all its variety, can be made knowable in ways that promise to make the government of Youth possible. (Kelly, 2003: 169)

By making young people's lives 'knowable' in these ways, youth researchers – who so often are concerned with exposing the extent to which young people's lives are subject to the control of various external forces – instead find themselves contributing to the governance of young people's lives alongside various other youth 'experts' and professionals. Griffin (2001) has argued that such forms of knowledge also tend to inadvertently reinforce popular notions of young people as either 'troubled' or 'in trouble'. Her earlier identification of mainstream versus radical traditions of youth research (Griffin, 1993) made an important and timely point concerning the significance of the specific motivations and political ideologies underpinning the work of different groups of youth researchers throughout the 1980s and early 1990s. However, the implication of Kelly's argument is that the consequences for young people may well be indistinguishable in terms of effectively laying bare the lives of young people for others to pick over.

Best has noted that 'despite being the subject of nearly a century of research', for much of that time young people have been 'largely excluded from the very social processes through which knowledge about them is collected' (2007: 14). One way in which youth researchers have attempted to circumvent these specific difficulties has been to seek the replacement of research *on* young people by research *with* young people through the promotion of various forms of participatory and action research. France (2004) refers to the rise of approaches which hand over control of the research process to young people in this way as a 'new orthodoxy' within youth research; one which has emerged in parallel with a growing emphasis within government policy on youth participation. Whilst there are many strengths and benefits associated with this approach, many of which are discussed in Chapter 4, the emphasis on giving voice to young people can nonetheless still be used in ways which can, albeit unwittingly or unintentionally, further reinforce the objectification of young people's lives – paradoxically, achieved by the actions of young people themselves. Writing about what she refers to as a 'new watchfulness in youth research, policy and popular culture', Harris (2004), for example, has noted the extent to which young people are now subject not only to the 'perpetual everyday observation' of their lives by various groups of youth experts, but are also themselves actively engaged in forms of 'self-monitoring'. This is not just about the emergence of a new social obligation for young people to make their views known through forms of self-governance. Rather, it is as much about a requirement within societies which are increasingly subject to the forces of individualisation that young people should view their lives as unique biographical projects (see for example du Bois-Reymond, 1998):

> (Young people) are not only obliged to manage their own life trajectories, but are enticed to display this management for the scrutiny of experts and observers. The obligation for youth to become unique individuals is therefore constructed as a freedom, a freedom best expressed through the display of one's choices and projects of the self. The current focus on placing young people in schools, workplaces and appropriate recreational centers [sic], and in hearing from them, for example, in youth citizenship debates, can be understood as related to this trend toward exhibition of one's biographical project. (Harris, 2004: 6)

All of these points need to be taken very seriously by youth researchers, and in the light of such arguments it is important that we reflect upon our motivations for engaging in youth research, both as a profession and as individual researchers. We do not, however, see this as a counsel of despair, or regard youth research as a lost cause. Youth research remains an important enterprise, contributing to a greater understanding of broader processes of social change and, critically, providing important opportunities for young people, if we allow them to set the agenda in a context within which their voices are all too often ignored or underplayed. We need, then, to view youth research as a fundamentally political enterprise; to do less is to do a disservice to the young people with whom we seek to work.

Structure of the book

To repeat our central aim: in this book we seek to present an overview of some of the key methodological challenges associated specifically with researching young people's lives and to provide an introduction to a broad repertoire of methods which are particularly well-suited to youth-orientated research. The rest of the book is split into two parts. In Chapters 2 to 4 we consider some broad methodological and contextual concerns of relevance to the design and conduct of youth research. Chapter 2 focuses on the ethical imperatives which should underpin research involving young people, and in particular considers the significance of informed consent, anonymity and confidentiality to the process of youth research. We highlight the importance of respecting young people's agency and competency within this process, which in practice is not always easy to achieve given the specific contexts within which much youth research is conducted. In Chapter 3 we explore a range of issues in relation to the conduct of youth research 'across difference', including a consideration of the impact on the research process of a researcher's individual identity, such as the significance of their gender, ethnicity, sexuality and age, and some of the challenges associated with conducting research amongst groups of young people who are effectively 'hidden' or difficult to access. Finally, Chapter 4 focuses on the ways in which youth researchers can involve young people as active participants in the research process, not just in terms of ensuring that their voices and perspectives are included as research data, but in the organisation and conduct of the research process more generally.

The second part of the book focuses on the use of specific research methods in the conduct of youth research. Chapter 5 is concerned with the use of interviews in youth research, perhaps the most widely used method within youth studies. Chapter 6 explores the contribution of ethnographic studies to youth research, focusing specifically on the use of participant and non-participant observation as a research tool, whilst Chapter 7 explores some of the possibilities afforded by the increasingly widespread use of visual research methods in researching young people's lives. Chapter 8 focuses on the use of surveys in youth research, another very commonly used research method. Chapter 9 considers the possibilities of using existing data sources in youth research, including the use of official statistics, large scale survey data and archived qualitative data, whilst Chapter 10 considers the potential for using the internet in youth research, both as a means of gathering data and as a source of data in its own right.

The chapters in Part Two of the book undeniably give greater weight to qualitative approaches to youth research, but this should be viewed as a reflection of the field of youth studies, rather than a statement on our part about the relative merits of different methodological traditions. In practice, a great deal of youth research utilises a mixed methods approach (Bryman, 2006; Creswell and Plano Clark, 2006), drawing on a variety of different methods in order to explore a particular research question. Often this will involve a mixture of different qualitative approaches – the use of observation, interviews and visual methods within the same study, for example – but may equally involve a combination of quantitative and qualitative methods, such as a questionnaire survey deployed alongside focus groups. A mixed methods approach may sometimes privilege data generated by one method over another, for example by using focus groups principally to highlight potential themes for inclusion in a large scale survey, or by using statistical data sources as a backdrop to an essentially qualitative study. On other occasions, researchers might seek to integrate different methods in more imaginative ways, and Mason (2006) provides a useful discussion of some of the ways in which this task might be conceptualised.

It should be noted, however, that the various methods which we highlight in this book are subject to various – and often disputed – claims concerning their *epistemological* underpinnings, which for many researchers carry implications for the ways in which methods can, if at all, be legitimately 'mixed and matched'. Epistemology is a branch of philosophy concerned with the validity of our assumed knowledge of the social world, including the status of the knowledge which specific methods are able to generate. It is concerned with claims about what counts as *valid* knowledge of the social world, and is related to debates about the applicability or otherwise to the *social* sciences of methods for generating knowledge which are derived from the *natural* sciences. Two epistemological positions which are commonly invoked in these debates are those of *positivism* and *interpretivism*. Positivism views the methods of the natural sciences as entirely appropriate for use in social scientific research and thus tends to emphasise the importance of the tangible measurement of 'facts' in developing our knowledge of the social world, whilst interpretivism eschews the idea that the methods of the natural sciences can be applied to the social world and instead emphasises the subjective meaning of social action. Quantitative research methods are often associated with the former position (by qualitative researchers, if not by quantitative researchers themselves), and qualitative methods tend to be associated with the latter, although Bryman (1988) has questioned the extent to which these are *necessary* associations. Nonetheless, for some researchers these assumed associations place qualitative and quantitative approaches in conflict and render problematic their use in combination within a mixed methods research design. These debates, which until relatively recently tended to dominate discussions concerning mixed methods, have often been referred to as 'the paradigm wars' between qualitative and quantitative approaches. Whilst the issues underpinning these discussions are still very important ones, in recent years there has been a move away from the epistemological debate about the validity of mixed approaches towards a more practically-oriented debate, and for many researchers the greatest challenge is now seen to lie in working out how, in practical terms, different methods can be best combined in pursuit of social scientific knowledge (Bryman, 2006; Creswell and Plano Clark, 2006).

Finally, readers should note that it is not our intention to provide a straightforward 'how to' guide to the use of specific methods, nor to enter into detailed discussions of their epistemological underpinnings, although we do nonetheless provide pointers and guidance along the way. Rather, we seek to highlight a range of issues which are particularly relevant to the use of these various methods in the context of youth research. There is a vast array of both general and specialist introductory research methods textbooks which provide a much better introduction to all of these issues than we are able to do within the remit of this book, and at the end of each chapter we provide references to some of the best of these. Our hope is that our book will not only inspire you to find out more about the various methodological issues we discuss, but that it will also give you the confidence to gain first hand experience of researching young people's lives within a research project of your own.

Suggestions for further reading

Bennett, A., Cieslik, M. and Miles, S. (2003) *Researching Youth*, Basingstoke: Macmillan. This is a fascinating edited collection based on insider accounts of issues of method arising from specific examples of British youth research.

Bryman, A. (2004) *Social Research Methods*, Oxford: Oxford University Press. This is a comprehensive introductory text on all aspects of the research process, including epistemological issues, and probably the best general introduction currently available. This book also has a publisher-supported website containing links to a very broad range of methods-related resources: www.oup.com/uk/orc/bin/9780199264469/

Furlong, A. and Cartmel, F. (2007) *Young People and Social Change*, Buckingham: Open University Press. This provides an excellent overview of many current issues in youth studies, grounded in a critique of Beck's individualisation thesis.

France, A. (2007) *Understanding Youth in Late Modernity*, Buckingham: Open University Press. This is another insightful introduction to key themes in youth studies, including a good historical overview.

McLeod, J. and Malone, K. (2000) *Researching Youth*, Hobart: Australian Clearinghouse for Youth Studies. This is another engrossing edited collection, this time based on examples of youth research from Australia.

PART ONE

THE CONTEXT OF YOUTH RESEARCH

2 Ethical Practice in Youth Research

Introduction

What counts as 'good' youth research? In considering a response to this important question, at the very outset we would want to argue for the centrality of ethical practice. According to Barnes, ethical decisions arise 'when we try to decide between one course of action and another not in terms of expediency or efficiency but by reference to standards of what is morally right or wrong' (1979: 16). Ethical practice cannot, then, be divorced from broader questions of morality and in the context of social research is concerned with the need to act with due care and regard towards all those who are involved in our research, and at all stages of the research process. The ethical conduct of a research project is not sufficient *of itself* to necessarily constitute good quality research, as a research project might be ethically designed and deployed, yet data collection might nonetheless be sloppy, or analysis poorly conducted. We would, though, certainly want to argue that *un*ethical youth research is, by definition, research of dubious value, with question marks hanging over the credibility of its claims to knowledge.

Developing this theme, Ramcharan and Cutcliffe (2001) have explored the following assertions: first, that a poorly designed study is by definition unethical; and second, that not every well-designed project is, purely by virtue of being well-designed, ethical. The first of these statements seems relatively uncontentious. It is the responsibility of all researchers to ensure that their research is well conceived and designed. We agree that this is as much an ethical issue as it is a technical issue, as the implementation of a poorly designed study risks exposing potential participants to unnecessary and possibly harmful intrusion into their lives to no useful end. The second statement is perhaps more debateable, as one might argue that a research design which has not given due consideration to ethical concerns is, by definition, *not* well designed. Nonetheless, one can conceive of a situation where a great deal of thought has been put into the technical design of a project, which will have the capacity to generate a wealth of fascinating and important data, yet which is let down by the neglect of ethical considerations.

The classic example which is often cited in this regard is *The Tearoom Trade* (1975) by Laud Humphreys. This study undoubtedly generated extraordinary and important insights into the lives of men who had sex with other men in the 'tearooms' – the public toilets – in the parks of a large US city, and who for the most part, it transpired, were married with children and did not self-identify as homosexual. Yet the methods used by Humphreys were dubious in the extreme: acting as 'watch queen' in the tearooms, then taking down the men's car licence plate numbers, which were subsequently run through police records in order to locate their addresses, with Humphreys then turning up at their homes with a changed appearance some time later to interview these men purportedly as part of a study of men's health. Laud Humphreys's approach was condemned for being unethical in design at virtually every turn of the study, although he himself defended it in terms of the ends justifying the means.

Thankfully, youth research is not associated with such glaringly controversial research examples, but youth researchers nonetheless need to attend to the temptation to prioritise the collection of data over ethical considerations: a 'my data, right or wrong' sort of approach. In other words, not all research data is fair game, regardless of the originality of the insights thus gained or the brilliance of its methods of data collection. Valerie Hey's utilisation as data of the discarded notes exchanged in classrooms between girls in her study of female friendships, *The Company She Keeps* (1997), provides a good illustration of this point. Although the notes undoubtedly provided a wonderful source of naturally occurring data, Hey grappled with the issue of whether it was ethically appropriate to fish these notes out of the bins into which they had been thrown and to then use them as research evidence, (initially) without the girls' knowledge. She concluded somewhat ambivalently that it was legitimate to use them, and subsequently some of the girls even handed their notes directly to Hey, but other researchers might well have reached rather different conclusions depending on their personal code of ethics.

This example highlights a distinction that is often drawn within debates on research ethics between a *rules-based* approach and an approach which is grounded within an understanding of the specific context within which a piece of research is being conducted: what is often referred to as *situated* ethics. The rules-based approach is based on a notion of ethical absolutes in relation to classic concerns such as informed consent, avoidance of harm, and guarantees of confidentiality and anonymity. An approach based on situated ethics, in contrast, emphasises the importance of making judgements based on the very specific context of any given ethical dilemma: in other words, there are very few, if any, absolute rights and wrongs in relation to ethical practice. A rules-based approach to Hey's dilemma, for example, would probably lead a researcher to reject the use of the notes on the basis that data gathered without informed consent are always and without exception off-limits, whereas an approach based on situated ethics might lead a researcher to argue – as Hey did – that in the specific context of her study the ends (fascinating research data contributing to a better understanding of girls' friendships) justified the means and that little if any harm was done to the young women by the use of their (anonymous) notes within her research.

In our experience, youth researchers are more likely than not to argue that some form of a situated approach to research ethics represents an appropriate response to the sorts of ethical dilemmas that are often faced in the conduct of research with young people. We would support such a position, and would also agree with those who call for a greater emphasis on an 'ethic of care' as a governing principle of research practice (see for example Glen, 2000; Miller and Bell, 2002), not least within research involving young people. Nonetheless, we would not want to throw the baby out with the bath water, and believe that the criteria for good ethical practice which are often cited within a rules-based approach provide an important and useful starting point for thinking through some of the ethical dilemmas that we are likely to face in the conduct of youth research. Accordingly, this chapter focuses primarily on some of these traditional concerns, including informed consent, anonymity and confidentiality, before considering the ethics of using incentives in youth research. An abiding theme within the chapter relates to the significance to these concerns of 'gatekeepers' – individuals who have the power to grant or withhold access to research participants and research sites, a situation which, given the institutionalisation of young people's lives, is not uncommon in the context of youth research.

Throughout the chapter, we draw frequently on examples provided by youth researchers who were involved in an ESRC-funded project on the negotiation of informed consent in social research involving potentially vulnerable groups (Wiles et al., 2007). The project was directed by Rose Wiles, Graham Crow and Sue Heath, a co-author of this book, and most of the fieldwork was conducted by Vikki Charles. Some of the examples appear in other publications, and where this is the case this is indicated, but others appear for the first time in this book.

Gaining informed consent

Informed consent is widely regarded as a key strand of ethical research practice across the social sciences. The ethical guidelines of the British Educational Research Association, for example, define informed consent as 'the condition in which participants understand and agree to their participation without any duress, prior to the research getting underway', and state unequivocally that the attainment of informed consent 'is considered the norm for the conduct of research' (BERA, 2004: 6). The BERA definition is similar to a range of others used across the social sciences, including those contained within the ethical guidelines of the British Sociological Association, the British Psychological Society and the Social Research Association. The process of gaining informed consent from young people involved in research is, then, generally viewed as a critical stage in any research project.

The British Sociological Association's definition is particularly helpful in flagging up the scope of what is involved in the gaining of informed consent, referring to the process as 'a responsibility on the sociologist to explain as fully as possible, and in terms meaningful to participants, what the research is about, who is undertaking and financing it, why it is being undertaken and how it is to be disseminated' (BSA, 2002: 3). Before considering how this might be achieved in practice, we would note that it is questionable whether a researcher is ever able to *genuinely* secure fully informed consent given the difficulties of explaining the exact nature of the research process and its likely outcomes to any research participants, unless they happen to be experienced researchers themselves. Indeed, some commentators have argued that informed consent is a largely unworkable process given that researchers – let alone participants – can rarely if ever know the full extent of what participation may entail, or predict in advance all the possible outcomes of participation (see, for example, Jossellson, 1996; Hollway and Jefferson, 2000; Mauthner et al., 2002). Smythe and Murray (2000) argue further that traditional formulations of informed consent arise from a 'data source' model of research which prioritises a pre-ordained, inflexible research design, which they consider to be particularly impractical in the context of negotiated, processual forms of research, an approach which is common within youth research.

Notwithstanding these criticisms, many researchers argue that it remains important that the principle of informed consent be retained within youth research (e.g., Alderson and Morrow, 2004; France, 2004), placing an onus on youth researchers to ensure that young people are as fully informed as is possible about the nature of the specific research project in which they are invited to be involved as well as the uses to which their involvement may be put. In adopting this position, the concepts of agency and competency are very much to the fore, based on an understanding that young people are able to express their own agency within the research process, arising from their competency at decision making. This includes not only their competency to engage with a project's specific research methods, but also their competency to make informed decisions as to whether or not to participate in the first place. As general principles, these are regarded as important safeguards governing young people's research participation, necessitating ready access to adequate information about the research process and the uses that might be made of the data generated by their involvement.

In practical terms, researchers are faced with important questions concerning how much information to provide to young people about a project, the form in which that information should be provided, and when it should be provided. Not surprisingly, the answers to these questions are rarely straightforward. In the aforementioned investigation by Wiles and colleagues (2007) into the specifics of how different groups of researchers negotiate informed consent in practice, one respondent provided an example of a study of young people's drug use which involved a complex multi-stage research design. The first stage of this study was based on short interviews with young people within the chill-out zone of a large night club. However, the study included several further stages of fieldwork in addition to the initial contact in the night club, and the sheer amount of information about these various stages led the researchers to conclude that it would be inappropriate to describe the project in detail within the club setting. Instead, they decided to ask for consent at each stage of the research, rather than seeking consent for participation across the project as a whole, a process which they felt would have alienated most potential participants from the outset: they had come to the club for a good night out, not for a lecture on research design! Moreover, given that many of the young people they were interviewing were likely to have been under the influence of either alcohol or drugs, it was judged unlikely that they would anyway be capable of remembering what they were told (which in turn raises an important ethical question of whether they were competent to give their consent in the first place).

A further issue highlighted by this example, and one which is of relevance to discussions of young people's competency and agency to participate in research, is the notion of 'process consent', a term used to describe the idea of consent as an ongoing concern within the research process. Process consent acknowledges not only that research participants have the right to express their agency by withdrawing at any time, but that consent should be negotiated on an ongoing basis, and not be assumed on the basis of initial consent only. This means that young people need to feel able to exercise some degree of control over their involvement in research, for example through being empowered to express a desire to opt out of some or all elements of a project despite having already agreed to participate. We know of researchers, for example, who give red cards to young people which they are encouraged to hold up during interviews if they wish to 'pass' on a particular question. In practice, though, few young people are likely to feel completely comfortable exercising such a right, given the inherent power inequalities between researchers and respondents. Researchers involved in longitudinal research with young people may also feel uncomfortable repeatedly returning to participants to seek their ongoing consent. Nonetheless, process consent provides a useful mechanism for updating participants involved in studies which have an emergent research design, and allows existing participants to decide whether or not to remain involved.

The provision of project information sheets, often using attention-grabbing graphics, is an increasingly common practice in youth research. Information sheets tend to provide details such as the identity of the researcher and who is funding the research, what the research is about and what participation will involve, as well as information on the uses to which the research might be put. It is critical that information sheets are appropriate for their target audience, neither patronising in tone nor assuming too much prior knowledge, and strike a balance between too little and too much information: the former can be misleading, the latter may be offputting. Provision of an information sheet can also ensure that young people are able to remember the details of the project after they have participated. This is particularly important given the enthusiasm with which some young people enter into a research project, to the point that they might attempt to circumvent the information-giving process. A researcher quoted in Wiles et al., for example, noted that 'we do what we can just to hold back young people's enthusiasm for taking part because on the whole most young people are very keen to take part and to be listened to ... we as researchers can be sort of overwhelmed by young people's enthusiasm and just think "yeah they understand, fine, let's get on"' (2007: section 3.4).

It is also increasingly common practice, fuelled by the growing emphasis on the formal regulation and governance of social research, to seek young people's written consent to participate in research. A consent form might simply consist of a general statement of a person's agreement to take part, or might include a range of optional clauses, allowing participants to give or withhold their consent in relation to various aspects of the project. For example, while a young person might be happy in general terms to participate, they might not want their data to be archived for the future use of other researchers, an increasing expectation in relation to research funded by major funding bodies such as the UK's Economic and Social Research Council. Many youth researchers nonetheless express some unease with the move towards signed consent as a default position, not least in light of persuasive arguments that the gaining of signed consent is often designed to protect the interests of researchers rather more than those of research participants (Homan, 1991). There are also many circumstances in which attempts to gain signed consent may be considered inadvisable. In the context of research involving, for example, young runaways, or young people involved in criminal behaviour, potential participants may fear that they will be identifiable if they provide a signature, and insistence might result in an understandable reluctance, if not a refusal, to take part. Additionally, the need to obtain a signature makes the consent process a very formal one, which might also be off-putting to some young people, including to those with poor levels of literacy. The question of whether to obtain written consent is, then, another good example of the importance of a situated rather than a rules-based approach to research ethics, even though there may be considerable external pressure exerted on researchers to secure written consent.

Legal considerations in research involving under-16 year olds

A key issue in relation to informed consent in youth research relates to the question of young people's competency to make up their own minds concerning their potential involvement in a research project. In legal terms, it is assumed that in the absence of any specific incapacities, such as a severe physical disability or a learning difficulty, anyone aged 16 or over is competent to give consent on their own behalf under UK law. However, research involving under-16 year olds, who are regarded in UK law as minors, is a rather greyer area. In England, Wales and Northern Ireland, the capacity of a legal minor to give or withhold their own consent is judged according to what has become known as 'Gillick competency', named after the appellant in a controversial High Court case in the 1980s involving the rights of under-16 year olds to be pre-scribed or advised regarding birth control. Gillick competency is based on the assumption that an under-16 year old with 'sufficient under-standing' can provide consent in their own right, and that under such circumstances a parent has no right to override their child's wishes. Although this ruling relates specifically to medical interventions, it is regarded as applicable to all other areas unless other legislation applies, including social (but not clinical) research. In Scotland, the relevant legis-lation governing research participation is contained within the *Children* (Scotland) Act 1995 and the Age of Legal Capacity (Scotland) Act 1991, and neither Act precludes the possibility of a more mature under-16 year old taking part in research without first seeking parental permission.

In reviewing the legal frameworks relevant to consent, Masson (2004) concludes that researchers should not be at risk under UK common law of legal proceedings brought by parents merely by virtue of involving a consenting under-16 year old in social research without having first sought parental permission. A researcher would, however, be at risk if the young person themself made a claim of harm. The weight of opinion therefore suggests that it is technically lawful to invite under-16 year olds to choose for themselves whether to participate in research without first seeking parental consent. An interesting example is provided in the Market Research Society's guidelines on conducting research with young people, where it is noted that 'it is possible to interview 14 and 15 year olds on the street or in a public place without parental permission'. However, a 'thank you letter stating what has taken place, why and by whom must be handed to the child to pass onto their parents' (www.mrs.org.uk/standards/children.htm). Whether or not the young person does so is of course outside of the control of the researcher in this context.

There is, however, considerable debate as to what might constitute the 'sufficient understanding' that is required to establish Gillick competency amongst under-16 year olds, which may be of particular relevance when conducting research in locations such as schools, youth clubs and other institutional settings. Whilst the Gillick ruling is firmly grounded in an individually-based assessment of competency, gatekeepers in youth-oriented institutional settings may be inclined to prioritise age over individual development, effectively equating competency with age. It might, for example, be considered appropriate for older age groups to be given the opportunity to participate in a research project whilst excluding younger age groups, regardless of the individual competency of young people in those groups. Of course, this may be largely due to organisational convenience: it is obviously much easier within a school context, for example, to direct a researcher to one particular year group rather than arranging access to and seeking consent from equally competent pupils across a range of year groups.

Regardless of individual levels of competency, it is not unusual for gatekeepers of youth-oriented institutional settings to insist upon parental consent before allowing under-16 year olds to participate in a research project. This may arise out of an understandable wish to avoid a negative reaction if parents were to discover that their child had been involved in research without their knowledge. It is also not uncommon for research sponsors to insist on parental consent, either in isolation or alongside young people's own consent. The Department for Children, Schools and Family's guidance for parents on research contact procedures in DCSF-sponsored research in schools, for example, explains that

> research organisations carrying out research on behalf of the Department contact the parents by letter in advance explaining the research and that they are acting on behalf of the Department and giving the parents the option to refuse to participate ... Face-to-face interviews with school age children are only carried out with parents' or schools' permission. (www.dcfs.gov.uk/research)

In practice, then, the seeking of parental consent is often viewed as a necessary complement to an under-16 year old's own consent – and in some institutional settings may even be extended to young people *over* the age of 16. Conversely, under-16 year olds have no legal powers to prevent their parents from providing personal information about them for research purposes, even though they may be unhappy about such information being given. Neither is it unusual for personal information concerning (identifiable) young people to be provided to researchers by employees within institutional settings – by teachers or social workers, for example – without first gaining their consent.

In practice, youth researchers are unlikely to be able to exert much of an influence on an organisation's insistence or otherwise on first gaining parental consent, despite any personal misgivings they might have concerning the appropriateness, not to mention the legality, of so doing, and may consequently feel themselves to be complicit in the denial of young people's rights to give or withhold consent on their own behalf. Heath et al. (2007) provide the example of a researcher employed by a voluntary sector organisation who was acutely aware of the tension that existed between her own personal commitment to young people's rights and the insistence within many of the institutions where her organisation conducted research that parental consent be sought in addition to that of the young people themselves. The researcher was particularly troubled by this scenario as most of her research with young people was directly concerned with young people's civil and political rights and their engagement in social action, and she felt that the insistence on parental consent undermined young people's autonomy.

The appropriateness or otherwise of seeking parental consent is also likely to be particularly contentious for researchers exploring sensitive research topics such as drug use and sexual behaviour, where young people do not always want their parents to know about their involvement nor, we would argue, should parents necessarily be expected to know. Heath et al. (2007), for example, note the experiences of a doctoral student who planned to explore young gay men's experiences of schooling via interviews conducted at youth clubs for lesbian, gay and bisexual young people. The student's university research ethics committee had insisted that consent must be gained from parents first, without appearing to demonstrate any awareness that this could potentially create more ethical dilemmas than it would solve given that the young men may not have been 'out' to their parents. The student rightly refused to go down this route, and the decision of the committee – based on a rules-based approach to ethics – meant that an opportunity to explore an important topic was lost through an insensitive approach, one which not only demonstrated a lack of understanding of the specific research context, but also of the broader ethical issues involved in researching young people's sexuality (see, for example, Valentine et al., 2001). Horrocks and Blyth (2003) faced similar difficulties in their evaluation of a young person's counselling service. In a number of cases it was considered inappropriate to seek parental consent for the participation of under-16 year olds, as some parents were not aware that their child was undergoing counselling. In these particular cases, individual counsellors were asked to give consent by proxy, although importantly neither parental nor counsellors' consent was seen as being a substitute for the young person's own consent.

In addition to not wanting to compromise young people's privacy, there may be other good reasons for not wishing to involve parents in the consent process, related for example to a desire to empower young people and to respect their autonomy. One of the authors of this book is supervising a doctoral student, Claire Long, who is conducting an ethnographic study of a youth club, focusing on the experiences of working class young women growing up in a marginalised community. On the basis of her experience of working with 14 and 15 year olds in the club in her dual role as part-time youth worker, her view is that the young people – although technically 'under age' – are more than capable of forming their own views regarding whether or not they take part in the study, and that to insist on parental consent would be to deny their individual agency. As she noted in her submission to the university research ethics committee, 'furthermore, my aim to engage in participatory research with the group is hoped to aid in the democratisation of the research process, and encourage their empowerment as "co-participants"'. This justification was accepted as valid by the committee, but by no means all research ethics committees will be as sympathetic to this stance.

A final issue to flag up in relation to legal concerns in UK-based youth research is the requirement of many organisations that researchers obtain clearance from the Criminal Records Bureau (CRB) in the form of a CRB 'disclosure'. Criminal records checks are a legal requirement for all individuals whose paid employment or voluntary activities bring them into contact with children or vulnerable adults, including as researchers. 'Children' are defined by the Criminal Justice Court Service Act as under-18 year olds, or under-16 year olds if they are no longer in education (i.e., research involving 16 and 17 year olds who are no longer in education does *not* require a CRB check, unless they can also be defined as 'vulnerable adults' for other reasons). This implies that all researchers working with young people up to the age of 16 need to apply for a CRB check, regardless of the context, as do those working with under-18 year olds who are still in education. In addition, a CRB check will be required for youth researchers working with any over-18 year old who can be considered as 'vulnerable' under the terms of the Criminal Justice Court Service Act, i.e., if they are dependent upon others in the performance of basic physical functions, have a severe impairment in their ability to communicate with others, or are unable to protect themselves from assault, abuse or neglect. CRB checks are conducted free for volunteers, but otherwise at the time of writing cost either £31 or £36, depending on the level of disclosure. The time it takes for a check to be conducted on researchers who are currently without a CRB check will need to be factored into the design of a research project.

Working with gatekeepers

As we have already indicated, a great deal of youth research is conducted in settings such as educational institutions, youth organisations and welfare agencies, where the gaining of research access is often dependent on the goodwill of institutional gatekeepers. These contexts can present a significant challenge to ethical research practice, whether due to inequalities in age and status between gatekeepers, researchers and participants, or attributable to the organisational constraints of specific youth research settings where young people are often in a subordinate relationship to adults. We have already discussed the frequent denial of young people's rights to give or withhold consent on their own behalf under such circumstances. As noted in Chapter 1, these power dynamics are characteristic of the institutionalisation of young people's lives, whereby large amounts of their time are spent in age-structured institutions which separate them from 'adult' society and construct them as marginal to 'adult' concerns.

Within such settings, adult gatekeepers are frequently charged with the responsibility for making decisions on behalf of the young people in their care, including whether or not to grant access to researchers. Whilst this is rightly designed to protect those within their care, Alderson (2004) points out that at times it may also silence and exclude them, by conflating the gatekeeper's right to give or withhold access to an institution with young people's own individual rights to give or withhold consent, despite gatekeepers having no legal powers to make this decision on their behalf. Of course, gatekeepers have a legitimate and important role in protecting their charges from unnecessary and inappropriately intrusive research. We would be the first to argue that not all youth research is worth doing and that the use of young people's time in pursuit of pointless, trivial or badly conducted research is in itself unethical. However, whether or not the decision to give or withhold access is always best made by gatekeepers alone might be open to dispute, particularly when that decision might on occasions be influenced rather more by factors such as pressures of time and institutional inconvenience, a reluctance to expose quasi-private worlds to public scrutiny, or even paternalism and over-protectiveness, rather than the genuine interests of young people. As we discuss in Chapter 4, a more

participatory approach to youth research would instead stress the importance of consulting with young people themselves.

Homan (2001) has argued that *assumed* consent is another potential
problem within institutional settings where access is controlled by gatekeepers. He uses this term to refer to a situation whereby a gatekeeper,
having granted access to the research site, assumes that the consent of
young people has been given within what follows, with or without
parental consent; or that consent is based only on partial knowledge of
the research topic and what it might entail, and is therefore not fully
informed. It is not unusual, for example, for youth researchers to find that
they are being given insufficient (or even no) time to explain the purpose
of their research and what it will involve. Under such circumstances,
although young people may be allowed to choose for themselves whether
or not to participate, their subsequent participation will not be based on
informed consent, as a researcher may not have been able to fully explain
the nature of involvement. Alderson and Morrow (2004) refer to such
instances as the obtaining of *assent* only – a passive acceptance or non-
refusal, rather than genuinely informed *consent*. A researcher cited in
Heath et al. (2007), for example, spoke of the frustrations of conducting
research in youth clubs without being given sufficient time to explain the
research aims or to give young people time to think carefully about
whether or not to get involved (she nonetheless went ahead with the
research). In another example cited in the same paper, a school sought
parental consent for the involvement of pupils in a research-related attainment test, but had not allowed sufficient time for consent forms to be
returned before the test was conducted. In the event, all pupils took the
test, and the data on pupils for whom consent was not subsequently
secured were excluded from the analysis.

As this last example suggests, youth research conducted in educational contexts tends to be particularly susceptible to these sorts of practices. It is common for young people not only to be expected to
participate in classroom-based research, but for data collection to be carried out under examination conditions, or within contexts where they
are expected to participate as part of the pedagogical process (see David
et al., 2001; Strange et al., 2003). Completion of a questionnaire might,
for example, form the centrepiece of a classroom activity, and might be
indistinguishable from other routine classroom assignments. Indeed, in
some instances students may not even know that they are contributing
to a research project rather than to an 'ordinary' classroom activity. All
students in a group might then be expected to participate, with little
opportunity to express 'informed *dis*sent' (Edwards and Alldred, 1999)
other than through grudging participation or, for example, the spoiling
of a questionnaire, activities which might get a student into trouble with
teachers for being non-cooperative. The ethical issues raised specifically
by the conduct of surveys in educational contexts are discussed further
in Chapter 8.

While most youth researchers probably feel uneasy when they are faced with assumed consent and its attendant practices, and might try hard to promote young people's rights to opt out, the pressures to gain access to research settings and to maximise response rates within them mean that many researchers might feel that they have little choice but to work with the institutional constraints imposed upon them. Indeed, France (2004) makes the important observation that researchers rarely challenge the consent practices of gatekeepers, however much they might disapprove of them. A researcher cited in Heath et al. (2007) captured this tension well, noting that she felt simultaneously both pleased and disappointed whenever young people declined to take part in her research: pleased because it meant they felt able to opt out, but disappointed because of the negative impact on response rates. Even where young people are given a choice as to whether or not to participate, it can be a brave act on their part to say 'no' within an institutional context. Under such circumstances, 'consent' may be based on little more than a desire to please, or a fear of the consequences of not being seen to be cooperative.

Researchers might choose to adopt various practical strategies in order to address these issues. These might include respecting the rights of young people to write 'nonsense' in questionnaires as a way of exercising dissent, or allowing them to remain silent in focus group discussions. There may, however, as Leonard (2007) points out, be a fine line in the latter case between allowing for dissent and taking account of the possibility that the dynamics of the focus groups are such that certain young people are effectively being silenced by other participants (see Chapter 5 for more on this theme). Another practice that we are aware of is the inclusion of alternative activities within questionnaires so that young people can choose to complete these instead of the survey questions, thus ensuring that their teachers will not necessarily know whether they are opting in or out of the research. Furthermore, some young people might agree to take part in research primarily in order to get out of classroom-based activities or in response to peer pressure and are therefore at best ambivalent about research involvement. Some researchers will respond to this by providing newspapers and magazines for respondents to read for the allotted period of time, whilst other researchers will give respondents the opportunity to talk about anything they wish if it becomes apparent that they are reluctant to engage with the research will topic. Nonetheless, these practical solutions might be considered to be instances of locking the stable door after the horse has bolted, whilst they might also be construed as encouraging duplicity on the part of young people.

Anonymity and confidentiality

Alongside the principle of informed consent, guarantees of anonymity and confidentiality are two other key strands of a rules-based approach to research ethics. In general terms, these are important principles to uphold, but we would argue that they are by no means unproblematic in the context of research involving young people. Importantly, although these terms are often used interchangeably, they are not synonymous. Anonymity refers to the protection of the specific identities of individuals involved within the research process, whereas confidentiality refers to promises not to pass on to others specific details pertaining to a person's life: a 'between you and me' sort of approach. However, one might reasonably argue that the passing on to others of specific details pertaining to other people's lives is an integral element of social research! So, when confidentiality is offered in the context of social research, what is often meant is something rather different. Indeed, what is being offered is more akin to a promise of anonymity; in other words, 'I will report the details of your life, but without letting anyone know that the details relate specifically to *you*'. However, this in itself may breach the promise of anonymity, as the specificities of young people's lives may render them very easily identifiable within any research outputs.

Anonymity is usually the default position in research, even though individual research participants might state that they would like their own names to be used within a report. However, some youth researchers argue that this position denies young people the right to assert their own identity if they so choose: if a young person is happy to make their views known under their own name, then what right does a researcher have to stand in their way? This is a strong argument, and depending on the specific context might be a compelling one. However, researchers need to attend to the consequences for a young person of 'going public' in this way. One might, for example, envisage a piece of research aimed at evaluating young people's views on youth service provision in which individual teenagers might make critical comments concerning individual youth workers. Although one would hope that their views would be respected, it might equally create problems for a young person if their views are publicly attributed to them. This example also highlights how anonymity might facilitate a greater freedom of response; it is likely to be easier for a young person to be honest about their views if they are offered anonymity, so a disregard for anonymity could well compromise the quality of the data that are generated. One might also argue that anonymity provides a carte blanche to say whatever one likes without regard for the consequences, and that this might not always be a good thing.

Researchers need then to make judgements about the pros and cons of allowing young people's real names to be used in research outputs, based on their greater knowledge of the likely harm that might be caused to a young person if their real names are indeed used, and should advise them accordingly. It is, however, difficult to use real names for some young people but not for others, as the use of just one real name might make it possible to work out the identity of other young people involved in a research project. As a consequence, for the most part researchers working with young people tend to use pseudonyms as a substitute for real names, often giving some control of this process to those involved in their research by allowing young people to choose their own pseudonyms (with the result that some research studies are populated by participants with names reminiscent of celebrities who happen to be in vogue at the time!). Youth research based on the use of visual methods, such as photographs and video diaries, presents particular challenges in relation to issues of anonymity, and these are discussed in Chapter 7.

Assurances of confidentiality are equally fraught with difficulties in youth research. This is particularly so in research involving young people under the age of 16, where in the UK researchers have a duty of care under the 1989 Children Act to report instances where they have reason to believe that a young person is in danger from others or is likely to cause danger *to* others. Research on young people's family life might, for example, reveal evidence suggestive of sexual or physical abuse, and under such circumstances researchers have a responsibility to pass on this information to a responsible adult. Depending on the context of the research, this person might for instance be a social worker, a parent, a teacher, or a youth worker. This is, of course, a highly sensitive area for researchers to enter into, and the onus is on research teams to be aware of the likelihood of such instances arising and to have procedures in place for dealing with such instances. The possibility of a breach of confidentiality should also inform the consent process in research where such issues might potentially arise (although such accounts could well arise within the context of research on any topic, of course). Youth researchers have the responsibility to inform a young person that under such circumstances they will be obliged to breach their promise of confidentiality. Providing this information in itself might be sufficient to prevent a young person from disclosing relevant information. Whilst this might let the researcher off the hook, the young person may still remain in a dangerous situation, in itself a major ethical dilemma.

More generally, confidentiality might be difficult to protect where a very specific set of circumstances is being described in research outputs and which might make it clear to at least some readers who is involved. Under such circumstances, a researcher might decide to withhold specific pieces of information in order to protect the identity of an individual as much as possible, or might choose to fudge the details slightly or alter the characteristics of key players to throw people off the scent. This in turn raises questions concerning the salience of those characteristics to the situation being researched, and whether it is legitimate to change details in this way. Is it ever appropriate, for example, to change details such as someone's gender, their age, or other key characteristics for reporting purposes, when these characteristics might be important variables for analysis? Nonetheless, it remains important to protect identities as far as one is able to do so. Stephen and Squires (2003), for example, conducted research on behalf of Sussex Police with young men involved in vehicle offending, in order to gain a better understanding of their motivations for car crime. Although access was gained via youth workers as well as in some cases by direct access, all of the young men were well known to the authorities. In order, therefore, to protect their identities the researchers decided against using any descriptors – such as their specific age, or their previous criminal record – when presenting the young men's experiences in their final report: 'we were concerned to eliminate any possible means of identification, or even opportunity to "second guess" who participated in this stage of the project' (2003: 149).

Leonard (2007) raises a further set of concerns relating to the limits of guaranteeing confidentiality in the specific context of focus groups with young people, noting that a researcher's promises are largely meaningless given their inability to control what members of the focus group might subsequently reveal to others outside of the group. She also provides an example of a blatant breach of confidentiality in the context of classroom-based survey research. Leonard was left to supervise a group of pupils whilst they completed a questionnaire on participation in term-time employment. When the teacher returned towards the end of the session he walked over to a particular pupil, picked up his completed questionnaire and began to read it: 'The boy in question had a term-time job in a pub, and the teacher expressed surprise at this revelation in the following way: "Well, well, I didn't think anybody as lazy as you would have a part-time job. So that's why you're always falling asleep during lessons"' (2007: 145). Leonard notes that this experience left her feeling 'extremely uneasy' about her inability to guarantee confidentiality in such settings. It is also worth noting the views of young people themselves that survey administration in schools should be done by outsiders in order to minimise influence and censorship, whether perceived or real (Stafford et al., 2003; see also Barker and Weller, 2003) – and presumably to minimise the possibility of incidents such as this.

The use of incentives

It is becoming increasingly common in youth research to offer some form of material benefit to young people in return for their participation in research. Common strategies include the exchange of cash, a voucher of some kind, entry into a prize draw, or even course credits in the context of research involving university students (see for example Johnson and White, 2004; Wierda-Boer and Ronka, 2004). Many researchers regard this as an appropriate way of expressing their gratitude to participants.

McDowell (2001), for example, made the following not untypical argument in relation to the cash payments she made to young men involved in her research on masculinities:

> I strongly believe it is important to recompense the individuals who are prepared to answer what must often seem like intrusive questions from social scientists. As these young men were all from relatively low income households and many of them held casual jobs whilst still at school, a small sum for participation seemed both an adequate reward and hopefully a way of encouraging their participation over the course of a year or so. (McDowell, 2001: 90)

However, what one researcher might regard as a legitimate way of saying 'thank you' might be regarded by another as an inappropriate bribe to encourage participation, which might be regarded as a particularly unscrupulous practice in the context of research with materially disadvantaged young people. The exchange of material benefits is, then, a practice currently lacking consensus amongst youth researchers, and provides another example of an area of research practice where researchers are divided as to the merits of a rules-based or situated approach to ethical practice.

There does, however, seem to be a world of difference between an upfront offer of a payment sufficiently large to be regarded as unduly influencing participation and the offer of a relatively modest and tokenistic 'thank you', although to a young person with few resources even a small sum could be regarded as inappropriately persuasive. Some researchers get round this by proffering some form of thank you only *after* a young person has participated in their research although, depending on the context, word of the exchange may well get round fairly quickly! Equally, the promise of entry to a prize draw seems relatively benign, given that very few participants are likely to benefit. Importantly, all of these strategies indicate that we should take young people's time seriously and not take their participation for granted. It may even be the case that young people have come to expect payment for research participation. Whilst we might want to resist the spread of this 'something for something' culture to our own research practice, it may well be the reality within which youth researchers increasingly have to operate. In their research on young people's views on consultation, for example, Stafford et al. note that the possibility of payment was mentioned 'in a half embarrassed way' in two of their focus groups:

> They did not want to seem grasping, and did not feel they should be bribed, but felt that a slight financial incentive might help 'because everyone's always skint'. They thought this might be successful in drawing in a wide variety of young people, including those who are usually reluctant to take part. (2003: 366)

Summary

This chapter has introduced readers to some of the key criteria traditionally associated with good ethical practice in youth research. We have considered the centrality of the gaining of informed consent to these concerns, and the role played by legal considerations as well as by gatekeepers in this process. The importance of guaranteeing anonymity and confidentiality has also been discussed, alongside some of the problems associated with protecting the identities of young people within research. Finally, we have considered the appropriateness of using incentives in youth research. Throughout this chapter we have sought to highlight the importance of context in ethical decision-making, and have noted that the practice of most youth researchers tends to be guided by a situated approach to research ethics rather than strict adherence to a rigid set of predetermined codes. Having reached the end of this chapter, this is by no means the end of our concern with ethics. The importance of ethical practice is embedded in all of the chapters that follow, with ethical quandaries specific to particular research methods raised as we go along. Many ethical quandaries also relate to the negotiation of sameness and difference between researchers and their participants, and this is the focus of the next chapter.

Suggestions for further reading

Alderson, P. and Morrow, V. (2004) *Ethics, Social Research and Consulting with Children and Young People*, Barkingside: Barnardo's. This publication provides a detailed introduction to many of the issues raised in this chapter, and includes lots of examples.

Homan, R. (1991) *The Ethics of Social Research*, Harlow: Longman. This is a classic and enduring introductory text on the ethics of social research.

Israel, M. and Hay, I. (2006) *Research Ethics for Social Scientists*, London: Sage. This is a thorough overview of a range of ethical issues in the conduct of social scientific research, with a strong international dimension.

Social Research Association (2003) *Social Research Association Ethical Guidelines*, www.the-sra.org.uk/ethical.htm The SRA guidelines provide an exhaustive, thoughtful and non-prescriptive overview of a range of ethical issues that all researchers should consider in the conduct of their research.

3 Researching Across Difference

Introduction

This chapter is concerned with some of the challenges of researching across difference in youth research. There are two main issues explored in this chapter. First, we consider the impact on the research process of a researcher's individual identity. This is a hotly contested issue in social research more generally, with debate often focusing on whether or not one needs to share the characteristics of individuals or groups involved in research – their gender, for example, or their ethnicity – in order to produce valid knowledge. In the context of much youth research, this is further complicated by the almost inevitable age difference between researchers and the young people involved in their research. The first part of the chapter, then, considers some of the practical and analytical challenges which may arise when researching 'across difference' (Nairn et al., 2005).

   Following on from this discussion, the second part of the chapter considers the challenges of conducting research among groups of young people who are effectively 'hidden' or difficult to access, research which often includes a focus on potentially sensitive topics. After a brief consideration of the general problem of accessing hard to reach groups, we focus on some specific examples to illustrate these broader points, including the challenges of conducting research with gay, lesbian and bisexual young people, care leavers, and young refugees and asylum seekers. Our argument in this chapter is that difference undoubtedly *matters*, and that individual researchers need to respond to the challenges of difference in order to conduct research which is sensitive to the impact of individual identity.

Negotiating sameness and difference

The significance of sameness and difference within the research process is an important issue to be considered when conducting research with young people. In other words, does it matter whether researchers share similar or different characteristics to the young people involved in their research? This is a question which relates in part to broader philosophical discussions within the social sciences concerning what is known as 'standpoint epistemology'. Standpoint approaches are based on the assumption that those with insider status have a privileged role in the creation of knowledge about that group and, by virtue of their insider positioning, have a more complete and less distorted knowledge of the social world. Fay (1996) captures this position in terms of the 'you have to be one to know one' thesis. Approaches based on a feminist standpoint, for example, privilege the voices of women over those of men, and stress the importance of women conducting research on women (Stanley and Wise, 1993). Standpoint approaches are also concerned with giving voice to the less powerful and the marginalised. The current emphasis on participatory research among young people – which we discuss in the next chapter – reflects all of these concerns, leading some to conclude that peer research – research *by* young people *on* young people – is critical to the production of valid knowledge about young people's lives. This suggests that shared age might be a particularly critical dimension in the process of youth research, an assertion which we discuss later in this chapter.

Alongside the epistemological concerns raised by sameness and difference, however, there is a range of more practical issues, concerned with the extent to which young people will feel comfortable working with a researcher perceived to be different from them in some way. This difference might relate to key characteristics such as age, gender, social class, ethnicity, sexuality, (dis)ability or other characteristics that might impact upon the dynamics of a research encounter. Padfield and Proctor (1996), for example, in considering the significance of a researcher's gender in their study of young women in transition to adulthood, concluded that in general terms a shared gender identity appeared to be irrelevant, but that it might make a difference in relation to certain gender-sensitive topics. In this particular instance, the researchers found that some young women were less forthcoming in discussing their experiences of abortions when interviewed by a male rather than a female researcher. Their findings suggest that where a research topic is salient to the particular dimension of difference, youth researchers should ensure that fieldworkers share similar characteristics to those of their research participants – particularly in cases where the characteristics of a researcher would otherwise place them in a majority group and therefore in a position of power relative to the research participant. White researchers might therefore find it difficult to conduct research on racism with people from ethnic minority groups, for example, while by the same logic it might be inappropriate for able-bodied researchers to carry out fieldwork with disabled young people which focused specifically on their experiences of disability, or for heterosexual researchers to conduct research with young lesbians and gay men which focused specifically on their experiences of homophobia or of 'coming out'. Not only might researchers find it difficult to establish a rapport with those they were researching under such circumstances, but their 'outsider' status might make it impossible for them to appreciate the realities of the lives of those involved in their research.

Others, however, reject the idea that 'sameness' necessarily makes for better data. Hollands, for example, argues that a desire to eliminate potential difference is based on an unhelpful 'unitary' notion of the theoretical underpinnings of the researcher–researched identity, one which implies that 'women studying girls via feminism equals a "shared femininity"; working class men studying working class boys via Marxism equates to "male class resistance"' (2003: 159). Nairn et al. also argue that attempts to match researchers and research participants by prioritising certain characteristics over others represents a simplistic and essentialist solution to researching 'across difference'. They are concerned that this approach not only ignores the potentially equal importance of other social characteristics, but also that 'this strategy might be used as an excuse by researchers from dominant groups … to absent themselves from interviewing "the other"' (2005: 336). Carter has also argued that the deliberate *mis*matching of researchers and research participants might actually be a good strategy to adopt in order to avoid taking things for granted: 'it is the gap in experience between interviewer and interviewee that creates a space for respondents to describe and tease out meanings and assumptions that may otherwise remain unspoken' (2004: 348).

Taft (2007) concurs that a researcher does not need to share the same characteristics as those they are researching in order to gain valuable insights into their social worlds. Nonetheless, she advocates a reflexive approach to the impact that difference and similarity might have on a research encounter. Taft's interest in the 'political selves' of teenage girls led her to conduct observation, interviews and focus groups in two sites: the Teen Women's Action Program in Washington, DC, an organisation primarily involving young black and Latina women, and a Girl Scout camp, attended predominantly by young white women. These contrasting sites allowed her to reflect on the impact of her own status as a white researcher. She asserts that 'research is a racialised process whether it is conducted by racial insiders or racial outsiders … being White and talking to White girls and asking them things that include racial politics requires as much consideration as being White and talking to Black and Latina girls' (2007: 213). She argues further that the research encounter, like any other social interaction, is itself an important site for the production and negotiation of race.

Mac an Ghaill's (1993) methodological reflections on his ethnographic research with young people drawn from a variety of different ethnic minority backgrounds lend weight to Taft's view that sameness is not a prerequisite for gaining valuable insights into the social worlds of others.

In addition to involving two different groups of anti-school young men in his research (the self-styled Afro-Caribbean 'Rasta Heads' and the 'Asian Warriors'), he gained research access to a group of young Black women of Afro-Caribbean and Asian parentage at a sixth form college where he had a part-time post. It becomes clear from Mac an Ghaill's account, however, that not just any researcher would have gained access to these young women, whom he referred to as 'the Black Sisters':

> The Black Sisters informed me that my anti-racist stance within the college was of primary significance in their deciding to participate in the study. My visiting their homes and accompanying them to such places as the cinema, theatre, Asian restaurants, and anti-racist meetings enabled us to break down the normal hierarchically-structured relationship between teacher and students. (Mac an Ghaill, 1993: 153)

He argues further that his own outsider status as an Irish man enabled him to develop a shared political consciousness with the Black Sisters. In Mac an Ghaill's case, then, his political reputation went before him and facilitated access to his research participants. Nonetheless, he was aware that his status as a white male researcher was not unproblematic. In particular, he notes that his interactions with young Black women were likely to have been informed – however unconsciously – by both racism and sexism. He concludes that

> I hope that by adopting a theoretical position that sees racism and sexism as the major barriers to the schooling of black youth, I have become more sensitive to the question of how social location, in a stratified society including differential power relations, influences one's perspective and that this, in turn, influences the present study. (Mac an Ghaill, 1993: 153–4)

Race and gender were, then, in a process of continual negotiation within Mac an Ghaill's research encounters. Pascoe (2007) has made a similar point concerning the impact of gender within the research process. In conducting ethnographic research on the construction of masculinities amongst American high school students, she notes that

> Sexuality is not just a set of behaviours studied by researchers but is part of the very research process itself in that it mediates, complicates, and illuminates researcher–respondent interactions. Masculinising processes in adolescence take place not only between peers but also between a female researcher and male respondents . . . As a female researcher I was drawn into a set of objectifying and sexualising rituals through which boys constructed their identities and certain school spaces as masculine. In the end I was not just studying their sexual identities, but I also became part of the very process through which they constructed these identities. (Pascoe, 2007: 176)

This demonstrates that a researcher's personal characteristics are by no means irrelevant to the conduct of research. In Pascoe's case, she writes of trying to adopt a 'least-gendered identity', and of trying to present herself as an individual in possession of certain forms of 'masculine cultural capital' of her own in order to minimise the sense of difference between herself and the young men she was researching. For example, she notes that she dressed and carried herself very differently from the other young women in the school, and often made reference to her hobby of mountain biking. The fact that she lived in a notoriously dangerous area of the city also seemed to mark her out as different. Nonetheless, the young men in her study clearly continued to position her as 'other', and as someone against whom they were able to define themselves. (We consider this example further in Chapter 6.)

A researcher's sexuality may also have a significant bearing on the research process and, as we hinted above and discuss in more detail later in the chapter, could be particularly critical in determining whether gay, lesbian and bisexual young people decide to participate in research. In much youth research, as in the social world more generally, heterosexuality is often implicitly or explicitly assumed unless explicitly stated otherwise. Accordingly, researchers will in all probability be assumed to be straight by most (straight) young people, whilst all too often youth researchers might themselves assume that the young people they are working with are heterosexual. In all cases such assumptions serve to mask an important dimension of difference, even if the issue of sexuality may appear to be largely irrelevant to the topic under investigation. In certain cases, assumptions of heterosexuality can further translate into the reinforcement of heterosexuality as normative and the effective silencing of difference (Allen, 2006; Driver, 2007). Harrison (2000), for example, has noted how the language used in interview-based interactions on the topic of sexual health between male researchers and young male participants often assumed heterosexuality on the part of respondents ('how do you meet girls?', for example, or 'say your girlfriend or someone else's girlfriend got pregnant ... what would you say?'). She also notes how the language used by some male researchers to refer to specific sexual behaviours was underpinned by a form of hegemonic masculinity which not only denied the active desire of young women but also privileged penetrative heterosexual sex. Such practices led Harrison to question the assumption underpinning the project's research design that the use of male researchers with young men would necessarily produce better quality data: 'as the data suggest, the techniques for gaining rapport can see facilitators using hyper-masculine patterns of communication which produce attitudes and behaviours that many sex educators are trying to challenge' (Harrison, 2000: 28).

This is by no means a problem unique to male researchers, as Best's methodological reflections on her US-based ethnography of school proms makes clear (Best, 2000). Writing of the difficulties she encountered when interviewing a bisexual young woman about her participation in proms, she notes her realisation that the types of questions which she asked of most of her interviewees reflected particular assumptions about hetero-sexuality and gender that made it 'exceedingly difficult for her (respon-dent), as a bisexual, to find a space to speak about the prom' (2000: 175). Realising her error, and trying to move away from what had become an uncomfortable and stilted encounter, Best instead asked the young woman 'to speak to her experiences as a bisexual student' (2000: 175). Whilst the dynamic of the interview improved as a consequence, she notes that 'silences persisted': 'The interview was plagued by the silences that heterosexual schooling enforces and that I may have even inadver-tently reinforced with my questions' (2000: 175).

Whilst in general young people might assume heterosexuality on the part of a researcher, a focus on certain topics might lead them to assume otherwise, rightly or wrongly, and with consequences for the conduct of research. Mac an Ghaill (1994) has highlighted how a research interest in 'sexuality' is often interpreted as an interest in *homo*sexuality by potential research participants, and is in turn regarded as indicative of a homosex-ual identity on the part of the researcher. This was certainly the case in Proweller's (1998) research into the construction of gendered and classed identities in an elite fee-paying US girls' school. Proweller notes her sur-prise at discovering that some of the young women involved in her study had erroneously assumed that she must be a lesbian because of her inter-est in feminism and the construction of gendered identity, despite Proweller having spoken to some of the girls of her own relationships with men. She argues that her participants were unable to decouple fem-inism and lesbianism, concluding that this conflation represented 'a sig-nificant gender dynamic that is telling of the ways that female informants position female researchers in uneasy sisterhood with them, on one hand, as their ally, and on the other, a perceived threat to normative forms of sexuality' (Proweller, 1998: 220). We do not know from her account whether any of these young women were themselves lesbians; unwit-tingly, Proweller may be equally culpable of making assumptions about normative sexualities among her research participants.

Similarly, in Pascoe's (2007) ethnographic study of high school mas-culinities and sexualities, her specific research focus led some of the young women in the school (but none of the young men) to assume – correctly, as it turned out – that she was a lesbian. She notes that two groups in particular – the 'Basketball Girls' and female members of the school's Gay/Straight Alliance – both wanted to lay claim to her, 'see-ing me as someone who echoed their non-normative gender practices' (Pascoe, 2007: 187). She notes that she felt obliged to 'delicately patrol boundaries of and information about my own identity because of the rampant homophobia at River High, even amongst these girls' (2007: 188).

Pascoe made the conscious decision not to reveal her sexuality to any of the young women – even in response to direct questioning – until after the study had ended. She notes, though, her discomfort at adopting this position, as 'I found myself wanting to be "out" to these girls as a role model and an ally because there were no other gay adults at River High' (2007: 191; see also Morris-Roberts, 2004).

These examples illustrate the complexity of trying to tease out the significance of sameness and difference in the context of youth research, a process made more complicated, according to Pascoe (2007), by young people's engagement in the active negotiation of their *own* identities during this stage of their lives. As such, the researcher's own identity becomes 'one of the resources they mobilize(d) to create identity and meaning' (2007: 192). Having considered the significance of difference in relation to characteristics such as gender, ethnicity and sexuality, we turn now to focus specifically on a consideration of age differences in youth research, arguably a particularly critical dimension of difference.

Researching across the age divide

Despite the increasingly widespread use of peer-led youth research strategies (see Chapter 4), it remains the case that the vast majority of youth research is conducted by researchers who tend to be older than those they are researching. Sometimes this may be only by a matter of a few years, but in many instances youth researchers are old enough to be the parents of the young people involved in their research, or even old enough to be their *grand*parents: an insistence on shared age would rule out most youth researchers from ever conducting empirical research in their chosen field again! In Chapter 1, we considered the political implications of adults conducting research on young people, and noted that it is possible to argue that youth researchers are just as complicit in the regulation of young people's lives as other youth 'experts'. Nairn et al. argue, however, that 'given that we do not have a culture of adults listening to young people, then adults listening to children and young people is a political act, and one that we need to continually improve' (2005: 237). In our view, improvement lies in giving greater consideration to the significance of age within the research encounter, rather than taking it for granted, or even ignoring its potential impact. Accordingly, our focus in this section is on the practical implications of the age differences that exist in much youth research. This is an issue that is treated particularly well in Best's recent edited collection (Best, 2007), and several of the examples in this section are drawn from that source.

Raby (2007: 39) has argued that adult researchers must cross a 'great gulf of development, culture and inequality' when engaging in research with young people. Some older researchers might convince themselves that a shared experience of 'youth' is sufficient to bridge that gulf, however long ago that experience might have been. Raby maintains, however, that given the temporal specificity of the experience of youth, relying on memories of one's own experience of youth is of little use in attempting to cross this gulf. Indeed, even if adult researchers were to work only with young people from very similar backgrounds to their own, a reliance on memory would be a relatively useless strategy, given the pace of change within society and the rapidly shifting nature of youth culture and experience. Merely by virtue of having once been young themselves, adult researchers cannot claim any privileged insight into the nature of what it is to be young today. And the older a researcher gets, the greater the gulf becomes, not least because of the likelihood that advancing age also increases the degree of material inequality between researchers and young people. As Richman notes, 'as adults, "youth" is the only category of oppression that we have all experienced and then left behind to become members of the more powerful, non-target category of "adult"' (2007: 194). Consequently, adult researchers inevitably operate from a position of privilege and distance relative to those whom they involve in their research, regardless of how well they might feel they are capable of empathising with young people.

Hey (1997) discusses this tension between distance and empathy in her ethnographic study of girls' friendships. During her research, she became particularly close to a young woman called Carol, a working class young woman who took it upon herself to become Hey's personal 'minder' and 'key sponsor' during the fieldwork. In attempting to make analytical sense of Carol's life, Hey talks of finding herself powerfully reminded of her own childhood, in particular of being 'a different sort of working-class schoolgirl' and of 'growing up with and *against* girls like Carol'. She notes that

> My intention in claiming resonances between an ethnographic text and aspects of my biography is not to stake a privileged claim on truth. Rather it is to recognize the significant (if immeasurable) effects of personal history ... In getting to know Carol and other schoolgirls I have been continually reminded of resonances from my own girlhood. At a deeper level it is, however, 'difference' that constructs our relation and relationship and my rendition of it. (Hey, 1997: 89)

As this example illustrates, a sense of shared experience and the spectre of one's own past can prove to be a potent brew. Hey acknowledges the impact this had on the analytical process, and in particular is acutely aware both of the power dynamic which operated between her and Carol and of the 'distance travelled' from her own working class girlhood, best captured by the fact that it is *she* who is telling Carol's story and not the other way round.

Other older researchers have also engaged in memory work as a means of trying to establish 'semi-insider status' based on their experience of having once been young. As Biklen (2007) notes, and as the example of Hey's research demonstrates, it is common practice for youth researchers – particularly ethnographers – to describe and reflect upon their own experiences of growing up relative to those of the young people they are studying. Typically, it is argued that such memories increase a researcher's access to young people, enhance their knowledge of their culture, and help them to relate to their informants. Gordon et al. (2000), for example, describe how, before beginning their school-based fieldwork in Helsinki and London, all researchers on their project engaged in memory work in relation to their own schooling experiences. As a team, they then subjected these memories to sociological analysis, examining them in terms of categories such as class, gender and nationality. They then returned to their memories later on in the study, to help analyse the feelings, behaviour and responses generated by their research.

Another strategy adopted by some older youth researchers in order to bridge the age divide is to emphasise their 'youthfulness'. By virtue of their interest in young people's lives, many youth researchers do indeed remain strongly orientated towards youth cultures and may have a relatively 'youthful' outlook in comparison with other adults of the same age. They may also dress in clothing associated with young people, and might even look younger than they actually are. However, as Taft (2007) wryly observes, 'The fact that I look young does not mean that I am young' (p. 207), a point which will not be lost on most young people, who are unlikely to have much time for someone who plays on their apparent youthfulness. She notes further, in the context of her research on young women's 'political selves', that it is quite stressful trying to remain 'cool' at all times, and is much less stressful to admit one's ignorance of youth culture. Indeed, being an obvious outsider in relation to youth culture and experience may well allow one to get away with naive questioning which would be considered strange if coming from someone of a shared age.

Notwithstanding this last comment, such an obvious element of difference as age can be difficult to negotiate for those who clearly cannot make strong claims to insider status on the basis of either a genuinely young age or a youthful appearance. Commenting on their comparative ethnographic study of Finnish and English secondary schools, Gordon et al. (2000: 59) note that

> One of the most concrete points of vulnerability can be seen as embedded in our embodiment. When women in their 30s, 40s and 50s position themselves in classrooms full of 13–14 year olds to observe and to participate, there is no ready-made position available for them. Finding their own space, physically and metaphorically, can be a daunting process. (Gordon et al., 2000: 59)

They go on describe themselves as 'ambivalent borderliners' in a space where the only two readily available positions were 'pupils' or 'teachers'. Nonetheless, Raby (2007) has outlined a number of alternative roles that might also be available to youth researchers, including friend, adult interviewer and fellow worker. These roles, she argues, should be more widely embraced as they can help to disrupt hierarchical divisions between adults and teenagers, be at least as productive as other roles, and avoid the power dynamics associated with young people's subcultures.

One response to concerns regarding the significance of age is, then, to focus on the quality of the research encounter. Pattman and Kehily (2004), for example, argue that the key to good interview-based research with young people is not necessarily linked to the age of the researcher, but to the art of listening, and that young people will respond well to older researchers if they perceive their desire to listen to be genuine. Similarly, Frosh et al. (2002: 24) have noted in the context of their research on young masculinities that 'most boys were eager to accept the offer of a non-judgemental, open interview which gave them a chance to think creatively about their experiences in the presence of a supportive (male) adult'. In the context of interview-based research, then, young people may appreciate the chance to talk to a genuinely interested adult in a non-judgemental and confidential setting. Indeed, researchers often find that in the interview setting young people are willing to discuss topics which are usually out of bounds in discussions with family members and friends, and that they may also find the experience helpful in some way.

Older researchers must be careful, however, not to view their role as surrogate parent or therapist. Thomson and Holland, commenting on the 'therapeutic potential' of narrative interviewing in particular (see Chapter 5), note that this must be 'treated with caution, recognising the costs of self-exposure for the participant's privacy and integrity' (2003: 239). Moreover, researchers are (not usually) trained therapists; and even if they are, and despite some similarities, research interviews should not be viewed as quasi-counselling sessions, even though the language and etiquette of the therapeutic encounter have become commonplace terms of reference within 'the interview society' (Atkinson and Silverman, 1997).

Of course, not all youth researchers are much, if at all, older than those involved in their research. Morris-Roberts (2001) was in her mid-twenties when she conducted her research on girls' friendships, and found that many people assumed that she was even younger than this on the basis of her youthful appearance, not helped by the fact that the school where she conducted her ethnographic fieldwork did not impose a uniform on its pupils. As a consequence of not being able to distance herself from pupils by her choice of clothing, teachers often mistook her for a pupil, and she notes that others were surprised to discover that she was in fact a researcher. She comments on being introduced to the head of geography, with whom she had only previously spoken by telephone:

> The first thing she says to me is, 'You know when you build up a picture in your mind about someone, well I was completely wrong' ... my instinct is that she is referring to my age, and subsequent discussions confirm this. Even when I have been in lessons for months, it sometimes takes teachers a while to acknowledge my presence ... I walk the corridors at break time and I am often subject to the same treatment as the teenage girls I work with. At times I am trampled on and knocked against the wall, albeit by accident. (Morris-Roberts, 2001: 149)

Frustrating as it may have been to be taken for someone younger than she actually was, the ambiguous space occupied by Morris-Roberts within the school was nonetheless invaluable in gaining an insight into the lives of the young women whose friendships she was studying. Others have also spoken of the advantages that they believe followed on from their relatively young age. Proweller (1998), for example, argues that being of the same gender and only in her twenties helped to facilitate close relationships in her ethnography of an elite girls' school, while Moore (2003) notes how her youthful looks helped to get her into clubs (the site of her research) and gain acceptance by those she was observing. Pascoe was also in her twenties when she conducted her research on young masculinities. After giving considerable thought to how she should present herself to the young men in her study, Pascoe (2007) decided on what she calls a 'least-adult' identity, to suggest that she was 'simultaneously like and not like the teens I was researching' (2007: 233). She attempted to position herself as a mediator between the adult world and the world of the young men; an adult, but not much older than they were.

In common, then, with other areas of potential difference between researchers and their participants, age differences *matter*. By this we do not imply that age differences are necessarily a good or a bad thing, merely that their likely impact needs to be taken into account in the conduct of youth research, and not simply ignored. This should be part of a broader reflexivity on the part of youth researchers, based on a consideration to how other aspects of our individual identities might impact upon the research process. So far we have focused on the potential significance to the research relationship of difference and similarity between youth researchers and research participants. In the remaining sections, we focus on a closely related issue, that of the challenge of gaining access to groups of young people who are either effectively hidden or difficult to access and/or potentially vulnerable within the research process. After a discussion of some general issues, we consider a number of examples relating to the conduct of research with hidden or hard to reach young people, with specific examples drawn from research with gay, lesbian and bisexual youth, with care leavers and with young refugees and asylum seekers.

Researching hidden or difficult to access groups

Gaining access to young people via youth-oriented institutions is often viewed as the easiest route for accessing large and representative research samples. It is usually much easier to facilitate access to a group of young people through a school or a youth club, for example, than through other methods, even when the topics that are subsequently explored are sometimes of no relevance to the institutional setting in which the research is conducted. However, whilst institutional access is commonly regarded as an expedient way of accessing a broadly representative sample of young people, it is by no means an efficient – or even legitimate – way to explore topics requiring very specific groups of young people. This is particularly the case where the characteristics of their identity which are of interest to researchers are effectively hidden, where those characteristics might render them particularly vulnerable, or where the topic of research is a particularly sensitive one. Certain topics are, then, inherently harder to research than others, due to the greater likelihood of experiencing difficulties in gaining access to potential participants. These difficulties may arise as a result of sampling limitations, with certain groups of young people being less accessible than others in the first place, particularly in the absence of clearly definable sampling frames, and/or because the research is concerned with a topic which, for various reasons, might deter individuals and groups from readily agreeing to involvement.

In general terms, there are a number of tried and tested methods for establishing contact with hidden populations and/or when conducting research on sensitive topics (see, for example, Lee, 1996; Feldman et al., 2003). It is not uncommon for researchers to place advertisements in relevant specialist magazines, newsletters or newspapers, for example, or to publicise their research through specialist organisations or support groups. Having established a small number of initial contacts, many researchers then adopt networking or 'snowballing' sampling methods, asking their initial contacts to put them in touch with friends or acquaintances who also meet their sampling criteria. Increasingly, as we describe in Chapter 10, researchers also make use of the opportunities afforded by the internet to establish contact with otherwise hidden sub-populations, via specialist chat rooms and websites, for example. All of these are potentially useful methods, although researchers need to be mindful of the potential sources of bias which might creep into their sample depending on the methods they choose to adopt. In practice, it is not uncommon for researchers to use a combination of different methods, which might have the effect of cancelling out some, if not all, sources of bias. A research team might also seek to recruit field workers who are 'insiders' in relation to the groups of interest, in an attempt to facilitate access and put potential participants at ease. Nonetheless, hard to reach groups tend to remain, by definition, hard to reach, and those who are the *hardest* to reach are likely to remain under-represented in most youth research.

It is important to note, of course, that not all hard to reach groups are necessarily vulnerable: they are merely hard to locate because of the absence of obvious sampling frames. In research on young people living in shared households, for example, Heath and Cleaver (2003) resorted to a wide variety of strategies for locating their target sample. The most successful strategies included mail-outs to tenants on behalf of the project by local letting agencies, telephone calls to shared households advertising rooms to let in the local newspaper, personal contacts, and snowballing from initial contacts gained through these various methods. Each of these methods introduced particular forms of bias to the sample; the letting agency contacts were confined to sharers in the private rented sector, for example, while the contacts gained through the 'room to let' adverts were by definition households in a state of flux, while *all* the households who were prepared to participate were a self-selecting group who in all probability were rather more unified and socially cohesive than households who were not interested in participating in the research. The achieved sample was by no means representative of *all* shared households, but nonetheless represented a certain segment of the shared housing population.

By way of illustrating some of the broader challenges associated with researching hidden populations, in the rest of the chapter we focus on examples of research conducted with groups of young people who are either effectively hidden or, for various reasons, hard to reach. Other relevant examples appear throughout the book in relation to the use of specific methods, sometimes in relation to the same groups which we highlight in this chapter, but in other cases in relation to other equally marginalised and hard to reach groups. In focusing on the groups that we do, we note that it is not our intention to problematise their lives and experiences, as is often the case in research involving hard to reach young people. Rather, we are using these examples to illustrate broader points concerning access. We also argue that good youth research on *any* topic should seek to include a broad representation of both easy *and* hard to reach groups, as an important step in seeking to normalise rather than problematise the lives of young people outside of the mainstream, and to better represent the experiences of young people from a wide range of backgrounds. There are, then, important lessons to be learnt about the diversity of approaches that might need to be adopted in any given study if researchers are to achieve such representation.

Our first set of examples is drawn from research involving gay, lesbian and bisexual young people, whose experiences still remain marginal to much mainstream youth research. This is partly because of the way in which non-heterosexual identities are rendered marginal within society more generally, but also because of the likelihood that many young people are, for good reasons, reluctant to 'out' themselves to researchers – if indeed they are out to anybody other than their closest friends. Valentine et al. (2001) describe some of the dilemmas encountered in conducting research on the transitional experiences of young lesbians and gay men. In particular, they highlight their respondents' potential vulnerability within the research process, given that lesbian and gay sexualities remain largely stigmatised identities. As a consequence, some of the usual locations for conducting youth research, such as the home or the school, tended to be out of bounds in their research as 'potentially difficult spaces' (2001: 120). Many of the young people they spoke to were not 'out' to their parents, for example, whilst most headteachers were fearful of allowing research specifically on homosexuality to be conducted in their schools. Even where headteachers might have been comfortable with this, Valentine et al. felt that it was unlikely that many lesbian and gay young people would have volunteered to participate in a school context, given the homophobia which provides the backdrop to the schooling of many young people in this group. In order to conduct their research, then, the research team sought out alternative spaces such as women's centres, health centres and young people's drop-in facilities, as well as gay and lesbian venues. In contrast to places such as schools or the home, these spaces offered 'safe and private environments for sensitive conversations' (2001: 22).

Valentine et al. (2001) sought to conduct their research among a broad cross-section of gay, lesbian and bisexual young people, and faced various dilemmas in doing so. Dunne et al. (2002) were faced with an even greater challenge in researching an even more specific sub-group: gay, lesbian and bisexual young people who had experienced homelessness, and who were therefore even harder to reach. Their research revealed a strong association between homelessness and non-heterosexual identity, yet they note that homelessness organisations 'rarely collect information on sexual identity and if they (do) so it is likely to be questionable – young people may be unwilling to disclose this information or be unsure about their sexuality' (Dunne et al., 2002: 108). In the context of homelessness organisations, they argued that heterosexuality only tended to be assumed on the part of a young person if they conformed to certain gay stereotypes, but that even under such circumstances workers (and researchers) were reluctant to raise the issue, in case they 'got it wrong'. They conclude that many organisations working with young people – in this instance, homelessness charities, but the point is equally applicable to other organisations – are likely to underestimate the incidence of service use by non-heterosexual young people. Despite these practical concerns, Dunne et al. were able to gain access to members of their target group through a number of specialist organisations, including an organisation providing supportive lodgings with lesbian and gay adults in two locations, and a mainstream gay-friendly hostel providing short-term accommodation in London.

Even where access to gay, lesbian and bisexual young people is secured, a researcher's own sexuality may prove to be critical to the quality of the data subsequently generated, as participants may feel extremely wary about talking about many aspects of their lives to a researcher whom they might perceive (rightly or wrongly) as having little understanding or empathy. Perry et al. (2004), for example, were commissioned by a support agency for lesbian, gay and bisexual young people to conduct interview-based research into the experiences of potential service users, and so had direct access to a sample of young people in the target group. The senior researcher on the project was herself a lesbian, and debate ensued with the other (heterosexual) team members as to whether or not this should be disclosed to interviewees. It was eventually decided that it would be good practice to do so, for both ethical and practical methodological reasons: ethically, as knowledge of the researcher's own sexuality could arguably impact upon the process of obtaining informed consent, and methodologically in terms of the richness of the data that might be generated by the interview encounter. This decision did indeed reap benefits, particularly in terms of establishing a rapport and encouraging openness. As one young person noted

> It's like when you're talking to a straight person, you could talk to them 'til you're blue in the face and they're just thinking, 'Well you're a dirty old cow.' But they're not saying that to you ... they don't even know what you're talking about because they don't go there. We know that because *we've been there*. (Perry et al., 2004: 141, emphasis in original)

This particular comment lends support to the idea discussed earlier in the chapter that insider status facilitates privileged knowledge and insight. However, Perry et al. note that there were also some disadvantages to a shared non-heterosexual identity between the researcher and her respondents, as there were a number of occasions when the young people being interviewed wrongly made assumptions of shared knowledge about their lives between them and the researcher.

Care leavers are, effectively, another hidden population. However, there is increasing interest, not least amongst policy makers, in the experiences of this group as they move from the care of the state towards independence. Much of this concern focuses on the very poor educational outcomes of young people who have experienced care, and which renders them a particularly vulnerable group in the post-16 transitional period. Access to care leavers in existing research studies has tended to be mediated by social workers based within local authority leaving care teams and after-care support teams (e.g., Biehal et al., 1995; Jackson et al., 2005), often supplemented by contacts made via organisations working with vulnerable young people. Ward et al. (2003), for example, accessed some of the research participants involved in their study of drug use and care leavers via foyer projects, YMCA centres and night shelters for homeless young people (these sites being indicative of the vulnerability of care leavers). Given the poor educational outcomes of many young people who have passed through the care system, Ward et al. ensured that they used research methods which did not assume literacy on the part of their potential respondents. The study was based on a face-to-face interview survey with 200 care leavers, followed by in-depth interviews with a sub-sample of 30 survey respondents with experience of drug use. In deciding whom to invite to take part in this second stage, the researchers took into account the emotional robustness of the young people, as they did not feel that all their initial contacts would be equally capable of coping with the demands of an interview which would be focused on a range of sensitive issues.

In a related paper reflecting on the project's methodology, Ward and Henderson (2003) noted the specific difficulties they experienced in tracking care leavers even over just a six month period. One problem related to the sheer number of accommodation moves which had been experienced during that period, partly reflecting the high degree of residential transience amongst young people generally, but also reflecting the lack of support which many care leavers experienced in the process of leaving care to live independently. The rapid turnover of social services staff also resulted in little or no institutional memory of either the earlier stage of the research or where these young people might now be located. An additional problem related to the fast turnover of mobile telephone contact details amongst this group of young people, as well as the frequent lack of credit on their telephones. All of these difficulties presented enormous challenges for effective follow-up amongst this group.

Jackson et al. were responsible for conducting research among 'by far the largest group of educationally successful young people in care that has ever been studied' (2005: 6). Their focus was on the experiences of the small minority of care leavers who, against the odds, continue on into higher education. Their study was conducted over a three year period and, in common with Ward and Henderson (2003), the researchers noted that maintaining contact was a major challenge. Again, initial recruitment was mainly via local authority contacts, including lead officers with responsibility for the education of looked after children, but it was noted that the contact details held by local authorities were often inaccurate or out of date. This is an interesting finding in its own right, but clearly was problematic for the research team in relation to locating their potential sample and maintaining contact with them. Despite this, 129 young people were eventually involved in total. It was observed that the young people were generally very keen to tell their stories, with many noting that they had never previously had the opportunity to do so without interruption, despite the number of encounters that they had had with social workers over the years. Jackson et al. also note that a few young people disclosed abuse in their interviews, 'perhaps feeling enough distance but also sufficient trust in the researchers to speak openly about painful experiences' (2005: 6). It was important, then, that the research team were aware that issues of this kind were likely to arise, and that they knew how to respond to them when they did.

Finally, we consider some of the challenges of gaining access in research involving young refugees and asylum seekers, especially those who are unaccompanied by adults. Hopkins (2008) notes that around 12,400 unaccompanied asylum-seeking children arrived in the United Kingdom between 2001 and 2003, two-thirds of whom were male and three-fifths of whom were aged 16 to 17. A large proportion of these young people arrived in the UK from Iran, Eritrea and Afghanistan. In common with care leavers, the experiences of young people from these groups are becoming of increasing interest, yet they are an extremely vulnerable group within the research process, especially when one considers their reasons for coming to the UK: some of the most common reasons for seeking asylum include the death of family members, forced migration, persecution, trafficking, rape and sexual violence (Hopkins, 2008).

Perhaps not surprisingly, research by Franks (2006) suggests that most young refugees and asylum seekers do not wish to draw attention to their situation, and are often extremely reluctant to talk about their experiences. To a large degree this is due to the often traumatic nature of what they may have witnessed. However, Thomas and Byford (2003) also suggest that young people may fear stigma or reprisals if they take part in research, whilst a research interview may be perceived as too closely resembling the long interviews they would have experienced as part of the asylum application process. Conversely, they note that this perceived similarity may make some young people feel pressured to participate if invited to do so, as they may believe that taking part in a research interview will help their case. Hopkins (2008), in his evaluation for the Scottish Refugee Council of service provision for unaccompanied young asylum seekers, for example, noted that he was aware that the young people involved in his research 'may well have felt compelled to maintain their participation, because of a broad range of assumptions and expectations around adult power and control, gender, race and other markers, and determinants of power and privilege based on their pre-flight experiences as well as their circumstances in Scotland', despite constant reminders to his participants that they were free to drop out of the research at any time (2008: 40).

The choice of research methods would appear to be particularly critical in research on young refugees and asylum seekers. Hopkins' research was largely based on interview methods, but he took care to structure the interview schedule so that the present was discussed first, the immediate past second, and only if he judged that the young person felt comfortable did he go on to discuss their experiences prior to arriving in Scotland. He also made provision for the use of a more participatory research exercise which allowed the young people to respond to his questions in a diagrammatic, non-verbal manner should they prefer to do so, a strategy also adopted by Finney and Rishbeth (2006) in their use of photographic methods in their study of refugees' perceptions and experiences of urban public open space in the UK. Franks (2006) similarly chose to adopt participatory methods in his study of young refugees' experiences of the education system. A large element of the fieldwork was conducted via the use of peer research methods, with seven young refugees being trained in interview skills. Whilst this might have made the research process less daunting, some of the difficulties noted in the previous paragraph might still have applied, but all of these examples nonetheless demonstrate the potential for using participatory research methods with young people, a theme which is explored in detail in the next chapter.

Summary

This chapter has explored a range of issues in relation to the conduct of youth research 'across difference'. In the first part of the chapter we considered the impact on the research process of a researcher's individual identity, noting that researchers are divided on whether or not the sharing of certain key characteristics – such as gender, ethnicity or sexuality – are essential to the generation of valid knowledge about and insights into young people's lives. We then explored the added complication in youth research of the almost inevitable age difference between researchers and research participants. In the second part of the chapter we considered some of the challenges associated with conducting research among groups of young people who are effectively 'hidden' or difficult to access, and included a number of illustrative examples. Critically, it is clear that *difference matters*. Regardless of whether or not youth researchers take up a standpoint position on these issues, it is evident that youth researchers need to have an acute awareness of sameness and difference and of the implications that these similarities or differences might have for the research process. These are considerations which are central to some of the claims made by the exponents of participatory research methods, which we now go on to consider.

Suggestions for further reading

Fay, B. (1996) *Contemporary Philosophy of Social Science: A Multicultural Approach*, Oxford: WileyBlackwell. With chapter titles including 'Do you have to be one to know one?' and 'Do people in different cultures live in different worlds?', this book provides a useful introduction to some of the epistemological issues underpinning some of the themes discussed in this chapter.

Feldman, M., Bell, J., and Berger, M. (2003) *Gaining Access: A Practical and Theoretical Guide for Qualitative Researchers*, Walnut Creek, AltaMira Press. This is a very accessible book (no pun intended) on the challenges of gaining access in qualitative research, but with broader lessons for gaining access in all forms of research.

Lee, R. (1993) *Doing Research on Sensitive Topics*, London: Sage. This is a classic text on some of the challenges of researching hidden populations and conducting research on sensitive topics.

4 Involving Young People in Research

Introduction

This chapter takes as its focus the active role that young people can play in the research process. In Chapter 1 we noted a growing emphasis on the facilitation of young people's participation in various aspects of civic society. From active involvement in school councils and youth parliaments through to the control of designated local authority budgets and direct engagement in policy and service evaluations, the promotion of active participation amongst young Britons is firmly on the agenda, as indeed it is in other countries such as Australia and the USA. In parallel with these shifts in the realm of youth policy, we have also witnessed a growing emphasis on involving young people in the design and conduct of social research. This chapter starts by highlighting some of the key events, policies and debates which relate to this rise in interest in involving young people in research. It then turns its attention to a consideration of the ways that young people can be involved in various stages of the research process – from research design to data generation, to analysis and dissemination. The penultimate section of the chapter then considers some of the potential tensions which surround the active involvement of young people in research. The chapter concludes by revisiting an important central question: what is the purpose of undertaking participatory research with young people?

The participatory agenda

As we have suggested in earlier chapters, it is now widely acknowledged that young people are social actors in their own right, who have the potential to play a significant role in social research: not just as 'research subjects', but as active partners in the process of research itself. This recognition has emerged from a range of theoretical, methodological and policy advances over the last four decades which have refocused our understanding of young people in society and the roles that they can meaningfully play. Before discussing young people's potential research roles, it is useful briefly to outline these broader developments.

Participation as a research tool

We noted in Chapter 1 that the new sociology of childhood (Solberg, 1996; James et al., 1998) mounted a challenge to two prevailing trends in the social scientific study of children and, by extension, young people, both of which tended to view younger people primarily as passive, future members of society: 'human becomings' rather than 'human beings'. First, it questioned the viability of developmental models of childhood and adolescence which viewed children and young people as progressing from a simple, irrational and biologically immature state to full human status (Harden et al., 2000). Rather, the new sociology of childhood argued that the biological was mediated through a series of historical, social, geographical and cultural contexts (Holloway and Valentine, 2000). Second, it posed a challenge to the well established sociological notion of socialisation, which viewed both children and young people as blank slates who, through a complex process by which dominant societal values and expectations are inculcated, became rational and competent adults. Derived particularly from ethnographic and qualitative traditions, the new sociology of childhood allowed children and young people to be seen as competent agents, active within a range of complex social worlds. Whilst this approach did not deny the powerful status of adults in the lives of young people, it recognised that adults alone do not control or steer the full range of social experiences of children and young people (including friend, student, daughter/son, sister/brother, employee, carer, girlfriend/boyfriend to name but a few), and that young people themselves are active in making sense of the world around them.

Those working within this new paradigm recognised early on that there was a need to develop different methods for working with younger people that reflected their agency as social actors. In the UK, this recognition was consolidated in the late 1990s by the Economic and Social Research Council's 'Children 5–16: Growing into the Twenty-First Century' research programme, which aimed to advance theoretically the study of children as social actors and to develop innovative methodological approaches in relation to this theoretical focus. It is important to note that many critical youth researchers had been grappling with similar issues, including the particularly thorny issue of how their own research endeavours might have the unintended consequence of further objectifying young people's lives, well before the emergence of the new sociology of childhood (see the earlier discussion of this in Chapter 1). Nonetheless, it is hard to deny that the 'Children 5–16' programme and the subsequent ESRC programme on 'Youth, Citizenship and Social

Change' (focusing on 16–25 year olds) led to a much broader awareness of these issues and an increasing acceptance of young people as researchers in their own right. There are now a number of publications dedicated to involving children and young people in research (for example, British Youth Council, 2000; Fielding and Bragg, 2003; Alderson and Morrow, 2004; Kirby, 2004; Browning, 2005; Delgado, 2005; Kellet, 2005; Brownlie et al., 2006), whilst in the sphere of education the development of participatory approaches in the action research tradition has been used to improve educative encounters (see, for example, Fielding, 2007). However, these developments within the research community cannot be viewed in isolation from a series of parallel developments within the policy arena. The discussion now moves to chart these changes.

Participation as a policy tool

The seeds of the children's rights movement were, like those of many other marginalised groups, sown in the 1960s and 1970s. More recent policy interest in the rights of young people has stemmed from the publication, two decades ago, of the United Nations Convention on the Rights of the Child (1989) and, in the UK, the Children Act 1989. The UN Convention on the Rights of the Child is the first international instrument to set out the full range of human rights for children including civil, cultural, economic, political and social rights. In particular the well known Article 12, which states that children and young people have the right to have their views heard in matters affecting them, has been a key driver in the policy developments which we outline below. The Children Act 1989 was similarly influential in the UK in prioritising children's welfare over parental rights in court cases which were seeking to make decisions about children. This represented a fundamental shift in power between children and their parents specifically within the court system, but with broader repercussions in other spheres in terms of facilitating a re-conceptualisation of the nature of adult–child relationships.

More recently, the Every Child Matters: Change for Children (HM Government, 2004) programme has set out to change the way the state supports and cares for children and young people, with the aim of achieving five key outcomes for all children and young people. One of the five outcomes, that children and young people should be empowered to make a positive contribution to society, has been applied in a series of papers and guidance documents. These outline the ways in which young people can be helped to exercise their right to have an impact on issues that affect them. For example, Working Together (Department for Education and Skills, 2004) provides guidance for schools in England on the ways in which students can be involved in, and consulted about, many school issues. Changes to the inspection of public sector services provided for young people have sought to review the quality of provision at a local level by actively involving service users in the inspection process, and have encouraged all services for young people – including schools – to consult regularly with their users as part of a system of reflection and self-evaluation (Office for Standards in Education, 2005). Similarly, the *Youth Matters* Green Paper (Department for Education and Skills, 2005) included proposals for the introduction of a Youth Opportunity Fund in each local authority, which would involve young people in deciding for themselves how these monies should be spent in their area. The introduction of the fund has been seen as a way of encouraging young people to consider local needs and circumstances and of providing opportunities for young people to gain experience of decision-making. The ten year youth strategy published by the Department for Children, Schools and Families in summer 2007 has committed itself to an extension of this scheme, and the development of other schemes designed to 'empower' young people (Department for Children, Schools and Families, 2007).

These trends cannot simply be attributed to the growing recognition of young people's rights per se. They are also linked to the growing trend for politicians, public service providers and commercial organisations more generally to ask their 'consumers' what they think about the services they provide. As Flutter and Ruddock state, the value of consultation is that it 'not only makes consumers feel that they matter, but also provides valuable information for tailoring services (or manifestos) to suit consumers (or voters) at large' (2004: xi). Young people's 'voice' is therefore increasingly sought on the one hand in recognition of the right of young people to have a say and, on the other, as a useful tool for targeting services and products more directly to the needs of young people.

These various developments have clearly positioned young people as active citizens with both rights *and* responsibilities (Hall et al., 1998; Clarke, 2005). One of the most widespread manifestations of this development arrived in the form of the statutory requirement to teach Citizenship Education in secondary schools in England from 2002. Notwithstanding some more critical evaluations of citizenship education (e.g, Biesta and Lawy, 2006; Faulks, 2006) Ireland et al's (2006) longitudinal study of the first cohort of students entitled to citizenship as a national curriculum subject concluded that citizenship education can provide a useful platform from which to develop processes of interaction, participation and active citizenship due to the nature of its subject content and the possibility for schools to teach it less formally than traditional curriculum subjects. Following on from the introduction of Citizenship Education, the government also commissioned an enquiry into how best to engage young people in their communities through full- and part-time volunteering. The Russell Commission report, *A National Framework for Youth Action and Engagement*, was published in March 2005 (Russell, 2005), and its recommendations are being implemented by the charity 'v'. v has an advisory board consisting of 20 young people and, according to v's website, 'we've put young people at the heart of our organisation, working alongside staff and trustees in all aspects of decision-making' (www.wearev.com).

An understanding of the changing policy environment with regard to young people's participation is crucial on two counts. First it shows how the wider participatory research agenda has been mirrored and paralleled in the policy realm and how young people's voice in social research can complement and feed into current policy initiatives and developments. Second, it reveals how the changing policy context in which young people live can, in turn, feed into the research process. As we explore later in this chapter, such developments are open to the accusation of tokenism. Nonetheless, the implications of these changes may well be that, in addition to the demands of academics, policy makers and practitioners to develop new ways of accessing young people's perspectives, successive cohorts of young people may no longer be prepared just to sit back and be 'researched'. Instead they may increasingly expect to feed into the research process at a range of levels, with implications for those undertaking research with young people.

From the beginning to the end: involving young people in the research process

Having discussed the background to the rise of participatory research with young people, we now turn to a consideration of the ways in which young people can be involved to varying degrees at every stage of the research process. Before doing so, it is helpful to consider the usefulness of existing typologies of participation. Hart's oft-cited (1992) Ladder of Participation (Figure 4.1) is perhaps the most widely used model within the context of youth participation, and is itself a modification of an earlier model by Arnstein (1969). The first three rungs on the ladder, Hart argues, do not actually constitute real participation but rather manipulation, 'decoration' and tokenism. The five higher rungs of the ladder relate to varying degrees of participation and range from the lowest rung where young people are assigned a role in the project by adults but are fully informed about the project, to the highest rung where the project is initiated and run by young people who invite adults to share in the key decision making (Hart, 1992).

But does this model tell the whole story? Hart's Ladder of Participation has been criticised by some for its hierarchical nature, and the assumption that the lower degrees of participation ('young people assigned and informed', 'young people consulted and informed', and 'adult-initiated, shared decisions with young people') are less valuable than the higher rungs of the ladder ('young people initiate and lead' and 'young people and adults share decision-making') (Barber, 2007). In response to such criticisms, Kirby et al. (2003) created a simplified model of participation (see Figure 4.2), which is perhaps more useful for participatory research, not least because it does not promote any degree of participation as preferable or superior to others.

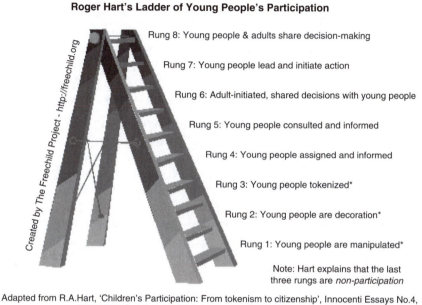

Roger Hart's Ladder of Young People's Participation

Created by The Freechild Project - http://freechild.org

Rung 8: Young people & adults share decision-making

Rung 7: Young people lead and initiate action

Rung 6: Adult-initiated, shared decisions with young people

Rung 5: Young people consulted and informed

Rung 4: Young people assigned and informed

Rung 3: Young people tokenized*

Rung 2: Young people are decoration*

Rung 1: Young people are manipulated*

Note: Hart explains that the last three rungs are *non-participation*

Adapted from R.A.Hart, 'Children's Participation: From tokenism to citizenship', Innocenti Essays No.4, UNICEF International Child Development Centre, Florence,1992.

Figure 4.1   Hart's Ladder of Participation (www.freechild.org/ladder.htm)

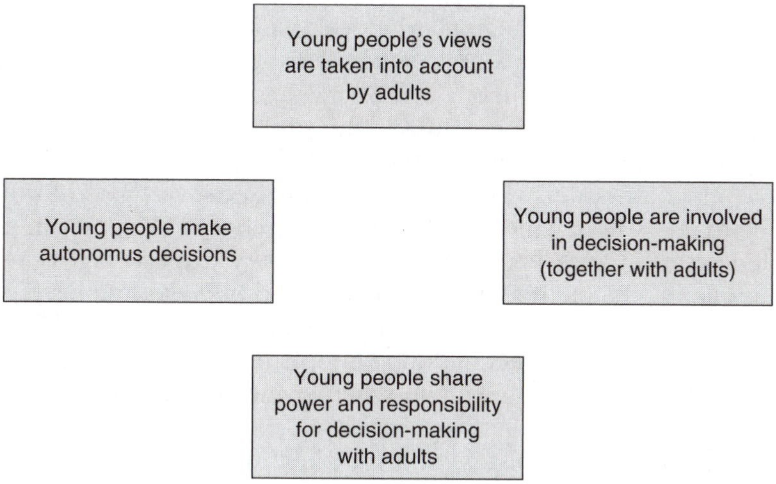

Young people's views are taken into account by adults

Young people make autonomus decisions

Young people are involved in decision-making (together with adults)

Young people share power and responsibility for decision-making with adults

Figure 4.2   Kirby et al's Model of the Level of Participation

Adapted from Kirby et al., 2003

Kirby's et al's model better reflects the reality of involving young people in participatory research. The roles of young people and researchers in such projects are dependent on a whole range of issues, from the time line of the project, the resources available for training and supporting young people, the purpose of the research and the interest, motivation and availability of the young people. Different levels of involvement will be appropriate for different types of projects and/or young people and there can be no one correct or 'best fit' model for such research. We turn now to some specific examples to illustrate different levels of involvement at different stages of the research process.

Involving young people in research design

Kirby (2004) and Alderson (2001) both advocate the involvement of young people in the initial design of youth research studies, even if young people are not subsequently involved in data generation or other stages of the research process. Involving young people at an early stage can raise research questions that adult researchers may not have themselves considered and gives young people an opportunity to have input into the focus of the research. Stafford et al. found that young people value the input of their peers into the design of research in which they participate, as they are deemed to 'know what questions to ask' (2003: 367). Holland et al. (2001), for example, worked with a group of young consultants, recruited from a secondary school, who made recommendations about the language, methods and instruments to be used in the *Inventing Adulthoods* project, a longitudinal study of the transitional experiences of 120 young people from five contrasting communities in England and Northern Ireland. Similarly, Thomson and Gunter (2007) involved a group of students in developing a survey designed to explore the impact of a major programme for change instigated in their school. Although the school's senior management team had already identified certain topics for inclusion, the students added a set of issues of their own, and on the basis of the survey findings subsequently identified a range of issues which they wished to see investigated further.

Due to the way in which funding for research is secured, it can often be difficult to involve young people at the very earliest stages of project design. As the methodology, timetable and budget often need to be planned in detail before funding can be secured, it can prove difficult – but not impossible – to recruit young people to a project when no budget is available and it is uncertain whether the project will actually go ahead (Pole et al., 1999). As a consequence, most participatory research projects tend not to involve young people at the earliest stages but, as in the two examples above, only once the broad design of the project has already been decided upon. As we have seen, though, at this stage young people can still have meaningful input into the research design, for example by helping to refine research questions and make recommendations about language and specific methods.

Involving young people in data generation

Peer-led data generation involves young people in playing a lead role in fieldwork: undertaking interviews, for example, or administering questionnaires with their peers, even if they have not been involved in the specific design of fieldwork. In her research on youth offending, for example, Murray (2006) recruited young people to carry out focus groups with their peers. The 'peer leaders' were given training and had cards to guide the topics of discussion. The focus groups were recorded and then analysed and written up by an adult researcher. This project worked well and the peer researchers were able to recruit participants and carry out the data generation with reasonable success. In addition, many of the peer researchers found it an interesting and enjoyable experience.

One of the drawbacks of involving young people *only* at this stage of the research is that they are likely to feel limited ownership over the project as a whole and, as Robson (2001) found, this can have a real impact on the success of their involvement. She reports on the recruitment of disadvantaged young people to carry out interviews with young people from similar backgrounds for the government-funded Youth Cohort Study. The adult researchers encountered considerable difficulties in recruiting, training and retaining young researchers, partly due to the complicated lives that the young people were leading, but also due to the fact that the young researchers could have no impact on the questions they were asking or the topics the research was exploring as they were working on a well-established longitudinal, standardised survey which could not be changed (see Chapter 9 for more information on the Youth Cohort Study). It seems that in order for young people to be successfully involved in data generation, they either need a real interest in the research topic, or some ownership of the project through involvement in other stages of the research process.

Task centred activities during data generation

Task centred activities can be used to give young people involved in research as participants (rather than as researchers) more control over the research process. Instead of using traditional methods such as surveys, one-to-one or group interviews, young people can be given, or are able to choose, different tasks or activities to carry out on the topic of the research. Such tasks might include visual activities such as taking photographs, doing drawings, making posters and producing videos (discussed further in Chapter 7), or alternative text based tasks such as writing stories, keeping diaries, word ranking exercises, and discussion based activities such as group debates, role-playing and brainstorming. Some tasks (such as taking photographs) can be carried out when young people are away from researchers or other adults in authority, giving them the freedom to collect the data which they feel are important to them (Barker and Weller, 2003). Task based activities also give young people more control over the pace and intensity of data generation, and can be used alongside more conventional methods as a useful 'time out' device when researching topics which young people may otherwise find difficult to discuss (Harden et al., 2000). These methods also give young people who may have low levels of literacy or who do not enjoy communicating through discussion a way to express their views in a form of communication with which they feel more comfortable (Thomas and O'Kane, 1998). Having a group task or activity can also decentre a group interview situation and take the focus of the interview away from the researcher and on to the participants or the specific task (Holland et al., 2001). Finally, practitioners of task based research often recommend allowing young people to choose which research task or activity they would like to do, as this can go some way towards redressing the power imbalances between adults and young people in the traditional research situation (Goodenough et al., 2003).

Involving young people in the interpretation of findings

Holland et al. (2001) argue that of all the different stages of the research process, the analysis and interpretation of findings is the most important stage at which to involve young people. At this stage the power differential between researchers and participants is potentially at its greatest, because this is when data about the participants are turned into knowledge that is disseminated to others. In addition, involving young people in the interpretation of findings can ensure that changes that are made on the basis of research evidence are genuinely beneficial to young people. Jones (2004) provides a powerful illustration of this point in reporting on the way in which the International Labour Organisation has worked with children and young people in the interpretation of research on child labour, and the significant differences in the conclusions reached by adults and young people. In response to research on dangerous work carried out by child labourers, adults were keen to push for the abolition of all child labour. The implication of the research for young workers, however, was that workplace regulation was needed to ensure that children and young people did not have to carry out dangerous work. They disagreed with the conclusions of the adults that child labour in *all* forms should be abolished, as they felt children and young people should have a right to work and earn money to support themselves and their families. Jones concluded that 'research findings increase the knowledge about the scale and complexity of the problem, however children can identify what the findings mean to them and their perceptions are important in planning corrective measures' (2004: 127).

The extent to which research participants should be involved in the analysis and interpretation of data in this way has long been a point of debate amongst researchers from across the social sciences. On the one hand, and as the example above demonstrates well, it is argued that involvement in making sense of the data helps to reduce the power imbalances between the various partners to the research process, and contributes to a more valid interpretation. On the other hand, the analysis and interpretation of data involves specific research skills, knowledge and experience that most young people simply will not have, including sufficient understanding of the academic and policy contexts within which the research is located. Skeggs (1995), for example, outlines her dilemma about how to respond when her own analysis was directly challenged by her respondents. When writing up in book form her longitudinal ethnographic study of class and gender in the making of young women's lives, she intended to use the title 'An Ethnography of Working-Class Women'. However, in sharing her analysis and her proposed title with the young women who had been involved in her research over several years, they explained that they were very resistant to being labelled 'working class' and thought her title offensive. Skeggs duly changed her title, whilst recognising that this reaction provided interesting insights into the complex negotiation of gendered class identities.

Peer-led research: involving young people in the whole research process

Perhaps the most comprehensive involvement of young people is found in examples of peer-led research where young people are involved in *all* aspects of the research process. Projects which take on peer-led methodologies aim to give young people an experience of the entire research process, and to raise their voices in relation to a particular issue affecting them. In this type of participatory research young people take a lead in several aspects of the research process from deciding on the research topic and questions, designing the instruments and generating data, through to analysing and disseminating the findings.

The HAYS project (Kirby et al., 2001) provides an interesting example of peer-led research. This project, funded and set up by the charity Save the Children, had the aim of giving young refugees and asylum seekers an opportunity to carry out research with their peers. Seven young researchers aged between 16 and 21 years of age took part in the project, which took place over 13 months. They worked with a researcher who provided them with 35 hours of research training, a development worker who helped to administer the project budget and liaised with external organisations, and a youth worker who provided individual and group support. With some guidance from the support workers, the young people decided upon a research topic which was important for their community: the educational support needs of young refugees. They planned to carry out one-to-one and group interviews with young refugees, and one of the young researchers worked with a research worker to design the interview schedule. A total of 33 interviews were carried out by the young researchers, and interviews were also conducted by the support workers with adult education and community professionals. The young researchers played a small role in the analysis of the data, were involved in writing some sections of the report, but critically played a large role in planning and giving presentations at a launch of the research (Kirby et al., 2001).

Calenda et al. (2005) provide a second example of the value of participatory research methods, in this case in relation to conducting research on the needs of socio-economically disadvantaged young people living in San Francisco. All three of the report's authors were members of the Youth Empowerment Team of the San Francisco Lesbian Gay Bisexual Transgender Community Centre, and they conducted the research with a view to improving the opportunities available to this group. Interestingly, whilst the major focus was on gay, lesbian, bisexual and transgender young people, the scope of their research extended to include the experiences of heterosexual young people, on the grounds that 'we wanted to include all people so they're not excluded like we've been, based on the way they identify' (2005: 9). In reflecting on the lessons they had learned from the process of conducting their own research, they rather pithily noted that 'we learned and hope to show others to never underestimate the power of intelligent, informed and pissed off youth' (2005: 23).

Peer-led research such as this can, then, be very empowering to those involved, giving young people an opportunity to have a major influence over the direction of research about aspects relating to their own lives, and to feed into the improvement and development of services targeted at their communities. Peer-led research can also have real benefits for those involved in terms of the development of skills and self-confidence through the provision of opportunities to experience new things and by being able to bring about change. This kind of research is, however, very resource intensive, requiring training and ongoing support for the young people involved. Questions may also be raised about the quality of the research carried out by young people and the extent to which it will be taken seriously by academic and policy audiences, an issue which we revisit in the conclusion to this chapter.

Dissemination to and by young people

Considering the large amount of research carried out on and with young people, dissemination targeted specifically at young people as the primary audience is surprisingly uncommon. What is also interesting is that where dissemination targeted at young people does take place, it is not necessarily viewed as an end in itself. For instance, in longitudinal studies (whether quantitative or qualitative) the provision of feedback to young people is an accepted way of engaging with them to reduce respondent attrition. For example, the evaluation of Citizenship Education in secondary schools in England, the Citizenship Education Longitudinal Survey (CELS), produces broadsheets about latest findings, which are available to download from the websites of both the Department for Children, Schools and Families (the funders of the evaluation) and the National Foundation for Educational Research (the organisation commissioned to conduct the evaluation). While these are targeted at young people in general, they also provide a useful strategy for keeping longitudinal sample schools 'on board' and for maintaining contact between periods of data collection with the young people who take part in research. Many other surveys produce similar newsletters and information sheets targeted at their participants (see Chapter 8), as indeed do many more qualitatively-orientated research projects. More radical forms of youth-friendly dissemination include the representation of research findings in the form of 'ethnodrama' or 'performance ethnography' (Denzin, 2003; Saldana, 2005), whereby qualitative research data are used to generate dramatic representations of key research themes and findings, produced by and targeted primarily at young people rather than other audiences.

And what of dissemination *by* young people? Almost a decade ago, Pole et al. (1999) argued that many policy and academic audiences do not view papers, reports and presentations produced *by* young researchers as acceptable outputs of research. However, as the policy community becomes more attuned to the rights of young people, this may be becoming less the case. One of the positive aspects of dissemination *by* young people is the fact that it resonates with a range of policy initiatives about young people's participation. Thus, whilst having the opportunity to contribute to reports and presentations of research findings can be a valuable learning experience for young people themselves, their involvement can also generate greater interest from both adults and young people than if adults alone carried out the dissemination. This was certainly the case for the HAYS project which we outlined above and which consequently attracted more media attention than a research project in this area would have normally (Kirby et al., 2001). In another example, Tyler et al's peer-led research on bullying, the young people involved in the process produced a series of six posters based on the findings of their research, which were sent to service providers as well as being distributed more widely. The young people also presented the findings in a number of other settings, including presentations to service managers, to delegates at a conference of the charity Barnado's, and at a local school (Tyler et al., 2006). These were effective strategies and also provided the young people involved with opportunities to acquire a range of new skills as a result of their participation.

Key questions about participatory research with young people

So far we have considered a variety of ways in which young people can be actively involved in the research process. Giving research participants the opportunity to play a more active role raises key questions that are important for all types of research where the dividing line between the researcher and the researched is more fluid than in traditional approaches. However, the specific participation of *young people* in research of this kind also brings to the fore considerations relating to their particular position in society and the contexts within which they live their lives. The discussion below therefore highlights three further issues that should be considered when undertaking or evaluating projects which involve young people in the research process. These questions problematise certain aspects of the participatory research agenda and are designed to raise difficult questions about whose agenda is really being served by the use of participatory approaches in any given research project, an issue we also return to in the final section of the chapter.

Whose voice is being heard?

There is a danger that where a group of specially selected young people are actively involved in research it will be assumed that this research is therefore a more valid representation of the views and experiences of *all* young people. In this context, Harden et al. (2000) point out that, like any other social group, young people are by no means a homogeneous group and that other factors such as socio-economic class, ethnicity and gender play as important a role in their life experiences as their age. Ultimately, young people who are less able and/or more excluded from society are, with notable exceptions, just as unlikely to be represented in participatory research as in any other form of inquiry (Matthews, 2001; Brownlie et al., 2006). Indeed, young people themselves have raised concerns about events which are presented as participatory exercises (such as youth forums), suggesting that such activities only represent the views of a minority of young people, whilst the voice of the majority remains silent (Stafford et al., 2003).

To address this issue, France (2000) argues that researchers working with young people need to be careful to aim for representativeness in their sample. But is this possible, or even desirable? At a practical level the reality is that participatory research is more often than not qualitative in nature. Often only a very small number of young people have the opportunity to get involved, whilst an even smaller number of young people *remain* involved throughout the process, and it is debatable as to what extent fair representation is possible with these small numbers. Moreover, there can be advantages in involving a non-representative group of young people who already know each other and can work well together from a position of trust and rapport. Such groups might include members of established youth forums or young people linked to existing support groups of various kinds.

The involvement of young people at the data generation stage may also facilitate the participation of groups of young people who would otherwise be unwilling to take part in adult-led projects, or who might be difficult for adult researchers to access. We noted earlier, for example, that Murray (2006) involved young people in running focus groups in her research on youth offending. She asked peer researchers not only to conduct the focus groups, but also to take responsibility for recruiting focus group participants. The peer researchers invited their friends to take part, with the outcome that focus group participants all had very similar levels of offending (or of *non*-offending), something that would have been much harder for an adult researcher to arrange. So while representativeness is clearly not one of the selling points of participatory research, it is not necessarily a reason to rule out the involvement of young people. Giving some young people a voice whilst being aware of and reflecting on whose voice is, and is not, heard will often be preferable to conducting research with no input from young people whatsoever. As Murray (2006) found in relation to the characteristics of her achieved sample, this may also lead to unexpected benefits for a research project.

Are young people being 'used'?

Hart (1992) defines tokenism as asking young people for input into a topic, but giving them 'little or no choice about the subject or the style of communicating it, and little or no opportunity to formulate their own opinions' (1992: 9). Research that is promoted as being participatory whilst young people's voices are in practice restricted may indeed fall into this trap. Given the increasing popularity of participatory research with young people in both academic and social policy arenas, there is a growing probability of such tokenistic gestures, as more researchers and funders of research jump on the participatory bandwagon as a means of securing funding, or of raising interest in their work with little understanding of the wider issues at stake. One outcome of such tokenism is that young people can develop a lack of trust in and a cynicism towards research and researchers who appear only to be paying lip service to their views. Stafford et al. (2003) highlight this point well. In their research on the views of young people who had been involved in consultation exercises, those who felt that adults had used these as an opportunity for self-promotion and had not really listened to their opinions became cynical about future consultation attempts. In such circumstances young people can become highly attuned to the possibility that adults are not as interested in their points of view as they are led to believe.

In recognition of these issues, a number of researchers and organisations have attempted to collate measures that can be taken to guard against tokenism and manipulation in participatory research. These include ensuring that participation is voluntary and that young people can choose *how* to get involved, that they are fully informed about all aspects of the project, that their involvement will have real influence, and that there will be personal benefits for those involved (Kirby, 2004). In a similar vein, and in this case with reference to research involving disabled young people, Badham (2004) reasons that in order to avoid tokenism, participatory projects need to be based on issues which concern and interest young people and actually lead to a change or improvement in young people's lives or the services they use. In order to help organisations to achieve this, the National Youth Agency (NYA) in England has developed the 'What's Changed?' tool (NYA, 2007b). This tool can be used to map the impact of participatory activity and to record evidence of the listening, planning and change resulting from young people's involvement. The NYA suggest that the tool should be used both to plan participatory activity, as well as to record successful outcomes. The tool has been developed to help organisations to involve young people in a broad range of participatory activities and events, and to develop structures through which young people can participate in meaningful ways, yet it also provides a useful reference tool for those specifically undertaking participatory research.

Armed with such awareness and information, participatory research projects have the potential to avoid tokenism and to empower those directly involved, whilst bringing both short and longer term benefits to other young people. In relation to educational research, for example, 'students as researchers' projects have led to personal benefits for the students involved, such as improved skills of enquiry, increased self confidence and greater agency, and have also led to changes in the teaching and learning methods used in lessons, potentially of benefit to all students in the school (Fielding and Bragg, 2003). Other examples include a participatory research project involving disabled young people in the West Midlands which led to action by a local authority to improve access to parks and playgrounds (Badham, 2004), and the HAYS project with young asylum seekers and refugees referred to earlier that gave a voice to members of a marginalised group and allowed them to play an active role in the development of practices affecting them (Kirby et al., 2001).

Who holds the power?

Participatory research with young people is often used as a way of trying to lessen the power imbalance between researchers and the young people involved in research. Some projects, in an attempt to move away from mirroring the power dynamics between adults and young people in society, have 'matched' peer researchers to respondents with similar backgrounds and experiences (Alderson, 1995). This method has the advantage that young interviewers may have more insight and understanding of the situations faced by their interviewees and that, in turn, their interviewees may be more likely to be willing to take part in the research and to converse with someone they view as unthreatening (Jones, 2004). As we have seen, other ways in which young people can be empowered within the research process can include asking young people to carry out data collection themselves, free from the presence and influence of adult researchers, and allowing them more freedom to choose the method(s) by which they would like to participate in a research project.

However, it cannot be assumed that using participatory research will necessarily lead to more equal relations between researchers and research participants. Indeed, when done without due attention to the interests and needs of the young people involved, such research can further exacerbate the inequalities between adults and young people. The following comment by Harden et al. in relation to research with children is equally true of research involving young people: 'The child researcher thus becomes a conduit through which adult researchers (who remain at the top of the hierarchy) gain access to children's views of the world' (2000: 6). Moreover, what appears empowering to adults may not prove to be so in practice, as Barker and Weller (2003) found in their use of visual methods with young people. Photographic methods were chosen in order to reduce the influence that the researchers had over data collection and to give the young people they worked with more freedom to collect the data, yet in some cases they found that *parents* took the photographs and then tried to pass them off as their children's work.

Despite negative examples such as this, youth researchers can and should actively work towards empowering young participants in research by undertaking a continual process of reflection on the power relations implicit within a research project and thereby rendering them more visible. Ultimately, though, the research process sits within the wider legal and social frameworks of society and at some point in the proceedings adult researchers will almost inevitably be required to exercise authority. This is borne out in the experiences of Pole et al. (1999), who aimed to treat participants as equal partners in their research on the employment of young people but found that, despite the researchers' best intentions, the extent to which young people could play an equal role in the project was constrained by structural limitations related to their subordinate position in society. What is important, then, is to make sure that the power of older researchers, as adults, is not exercised unnecessarily or manipulatively in such circumstances.

Practitioners of all forms of participatory research emphasise that one of the main reasons for giving those researched a greater voice is that the people with the most knowledge and expertise about the research topic are of course the 'subjects' of research themselves. Put simply, involving young people in youth research can improve the quality of the data that are generated, by accessing understandings and meanings not available to adult researchers. In some subject areas and for some young people, both the reliability and validity of research can be improved by the use of methodologies that allow young people an active role in defining how to approach a research topic, in participating in the generation of the data and in taking part in the interpretation of the findings (Thomas and O'Kane, 1998). Perhaps, then, a useful way of conceptualising participatory research is as a partnership to which young people bring subject expertise and researchers bring academic and methodological expertise.

One final question

In the preceding discussion we have sought to demonstrate that there are a variety of ways in which young people can become involved in research and that this can be achieved at all stages of the research process. Moreover, participation at each different stage and level of involvement can be effective if consideration of, and reflection on, a range of cross-cutting issues take place. With this discussion in mind, we now take a step back from the detail of the research process to ask a simple but important overarching question: what is the purpose of undertaking participatory research with young people? It is this question which should be asked before any project involving young people is begun. If the purpose of involving young people is to empower them, then participatory research can provide real opportunities for young people to improve their skills, knowledge and confidence and have the potential to effect real change. If the purpose of involving young people is to improve our understanding of and knowledge about their lives, then there are clearly advantages to participatory research over other methodologies. Each is a laudable objective, but is it possible for a piece of research to meet both objectives equally? And if not, which should take priority?

The answers to these questions remain open to debate amongst the youth research community. Many researchers, for example, feel that they have to choose between *either* maintaining the rigour and quality of their research *or* facilitating young people's participation in a project. In reporting on a peer-led research project on bullying, for example, Tyler et al. (2006) acknowledged a tension between the conduct of 'rigorous research' and maintaining the active participation of those involved in the process. In this particular case, the adult facilitators concluded that 'it was felt that it was more important to view the project as an opportunity for young people and to test the difference it makes to have young people carrying out the project instead of professional researchers, rather than insist upon the quality of the research study taking precedence' (2006: 17). In turn, Dyson and Meagher (2001) turn this line of argument on its head by questioning the standards by which such 'quality' research is being judged. They argue that whilst participatory research may not be as robust as research conducted using more traditional approaches, it can still have high 'catalytic validity': the capacity to allow marginalised voices to be heard and to challenge dominant discourses. As participatory research does not always have the same main purpose as mainstream research (i.e., the advancement of knowledge), they argue, it should not be judged by the same values. Where participatory research may fail on robustness and reliability, it can excel by championing the views of young people and bringing about change.

For certain forms of research, then, the prioritisation of young people's own involvement throughout the process may well be more important than adherence to notions of 'research quality' based on the professional standards of experienced adult researchers. Whilst Tyler et al. (2006) acknowledged that their research was not as high quality or as cost-effective as it might have been if carried out by adult researchers, the involvement of young people in the project raised the interest of influential groups. In short, the project had greater impact on those that mattered than if the young people had not been involved. In a world increasingly full of competing information and knowledge about society and different social groups, many would argue that the objectives of research with young people should not simply be to create further understandings of, and knowledge about, their lives, but to have an impact and to effect change.

Suggestions for further reading

Browning, S. (2005) *Engaging Young People in Evaluation and Consultation*, Big Lottery Fund Research: Issue 10, London: Big Lottery Fund: www.renewal.net/Documents/RNET/Research/Engagingyoungpeople.pdf This is a short and very practical introduction to participatory approaches to service evaluation.

Delgado, M. (2005) *Design and Methods for Youth-Led Research*, London: Sage. This is a thorough overview of a range of practical and more conceptual issues relating to peer-led research.

Kirby, P. (2004) *A Guide to Actively Involving Young People in Research: For Researchers, Research Commissioners and Managers*, Eastleigh: INVOLVE: www.invo.org.uk/pdfs/Involving_Young_People_in_Research_151104_FINAL.pdf This is another very accessible introduction to some of the key issues to consider when involving young people in research.

PART TWO

METHODS FOR YOUTH RESEARCH

5 Qualitative Interviewing

Introduction

The qualitative interview is probably the most widely used research method in youth research. It is generally regarded as a young person-friendly strategy, providing opportunities for young people to talk about their lives on their own terms. Given the frequent marginalisation of young people's voices within society, the interview can be a powerful tool for – quite literally – giving voice to their experiences and concerns. This is important in a world where the meanings of young people's attitudes and actions are all too often either assumed or based on adult interpretations. The interview is also a method which has a certain iconic status in contemporary society. In what has been referred to as 'the interview society' (Atkinson and Silverman, 1997), interviews have become a familiar social encounter, whether in the form of the celebrity interview on television chat shows, the radio phone-in, the market research interview in the high street, the job interview, or the therapeutic interview. Young people may be familiar with some or all of these forms, and may therefore have preconceptions about the research interview which may not always bring a positive gloss to their expectations of what this method might entail.

This chapter provides an introduction to the use of qualitative interviewing in youth research. The first part of the chapter considers some of the different interviewing strategies available to youth researchers, starting with semi-structured interviews, moving on to consider the use of unstructured interviewing techniques and the status of interview data, and then focussing on the use of group interviews and focus groups. The second part of the chapter then considers the importance of interview location, and the potential value of repeat interviewing within a longitudinal framework.

Different approaches to qualitative interviewing

Qualitative interviewing is a research method which is grounded within interpretivist epistemology. As noted in Chapter 1, interpretivism is an approach which emphasises the subjective meaning of social action, and therefore gives priority to seeing the world through the eyes of those who are being researched (Bryman, 1988). In accordance with this epistemological stance, qualitative interviews are designed to allow research participants to tell their stories on their own terms and in their own words. They are characterised by their flexibility and relative lack of structure, ranging from semi-structured interviewing, where the interviewer will typically have several themes which he or she hopes to explore across each interview, through to unstructured forms of interviewing, where the person being interviewed is more or less able to set the agenda following a broad opening question. Of these two types, semi-structured interviews are most commonly used within youth research, although unstructured interviews – particularly in the form of narrative interviews – are becoming increasingly common.

Using semi-structured interviews in youth research

Semi-structured interviews tend to be used in cases where the researcher has identified a relatively clear focus to their research, as well as where they may wish to draw comparisons across a sample of research participants; by exploring similar themes with each participant, patterns and trends are more readily identifiable. To facilitate this, semi-structured interviewing is usually based on the use of an interview guide which maps out the broad areas which a researcher wishes to address within an interview encounter. These areas are identified through the sifting of what Lofland and Lofland (1994) refer to as the 'puzzlements' of a research question: in other words, what is it that puzzles a researcher about a particular research topic? Each of these puzzlements may point to an important sub-theme in relation to that topic. By way of illustration, Figure 5.1 provides an excerpt from an interview guide that was used in Heath and Cleaver's study of young people living in shared households (Heath and Cleaver, 2003). Having decided upon our key themes, we then considered a sensible order in which to raise each of the sub-themes if they had not already arisen within each interview, ensuring that there was a good 'flow' between each theme, and also considered various prompts and examples which might generate further discussion if required.

Importantly, an interview guide is just that – a *guide*. Within the semi-structured interview format, not only is there no requirement to tackle themes in a set order (as in the structured interview format used in survey interviewing), but the person being interviewed is free to explore other issues which may be equally relevant to the topic being explored,

---

Household history

- Time together?
- Formation/history?
- Why here?
- New members – how, when and why?

Organisation of the household

- Ground rules: what, when, how and who?
- Negotiating time and space:

    – kitchen
    – bathroom
    – communal living rooms (NB guests/objects, e.g., TV/video)
    – private living spaces.

- Social interaction:

    – in the house
    – outside the house
    – 'extended household': family, previous housemates etc.

Household division of labour

- Division of household tasks (explore relevance of skills, gender, equality, availability …)
- Informal pressures (jokes, hints) or formal (rota/contract)?
- Avoidance? Tactics? Responses to this?
- Assistance from friends, partners and families?

Care and support

- Knowledge of everyone's whereabouts
- Advice and support
- Illness
- Friendship with families of other members

Figure 5.1   Excerpt from interview guide for Heath and Cleaver's shared households research

even if the connections are not always straightforwardly transparent to the researcher. This is one of the major strengths of the semi-structured interview format, as it allows research participants to explore themes on their own terms, and by so doing they will invariably introduce themes and make connections which simply had not occurred to the researcher. When this occurs, the semi-structured format provides the flexibility to enable the researcher to pursue these unanticipated themes and connections in detail.

The topics outlined in any given interview guide are not necessarily explored through the use of a direct question on the topic. Rather, a respondent might be asked simply to reflect on their experiences of a particular phenomenon, for example 'I would be interested to hear about your experiences of student debt' or 'Tell me about your experience of leaving home for the first time'. This accords with Eder and Fingerson's view that 'in studies of youth, it is especially important for interviewers to emphasise non-directed, open and inclusive questions. If the questions are open-ended, children [sic] will have more opportunity to bring in the topics and modes of discourse that are familiar to them' (2003: 36). Researchers should nonetheless be prepared for a young person to ask for clarification; for instance, 'What exactly do you want to know about my student debt?' might be a common response to the invitation above, for example.

Non-directive questioning in the context of youth research is also important in avoiding the type of question–answer dialogue with which young people are all too familiar from their dealings with adults in authority, whether in the context of schooling or in other encounters with 'officialdom'. In such contexts, there is often an expectation of a 'right' and a 'wrong' answer, with negative consequences often attached to giving the 'wrong' answer. Faced with what they may consider to be a similar style of questioning in a research interview, young people may attempt to second-guess the 'right' answer, or may find it difficult to formulate any answer at all. Frosh et al. (2002), for example, argue that young people interviewed in educational settings may often equate the interview experience with a 'difficult and frustrating lesson'. One of the young men interviewed in their study of young masculinities was relatively inarticulate in his first one-to-one interview, in contrast to a second interview where he was 'open, fluent and relaxed'. When asked about this difference, the young man explained that 'he did not know what to expect in the first interview and did not realise that he was free to say what he wanted' (Frosh et al., 2002: 27).

On the occasions where a topic *is* approached in the form of a direct question, it is critical that it is phrased in such a way that simple yes/no answers are avoided. A necessary skill of qualitative interviewing is the ability to encourage people to elaborate on their answers when this does occur, whilst also recognising that a short answer may sometimes indicate a reluctance to discuss a particular topic. Becker (1998) recommends the use of 'how' rather than 'why' questions within the context of qualitative interviewing, as the former encourage an emphasis on process or the telling of a story, whilst the latter might be interpreted as a request to justify a course of action or an attitude, which might put research participants, particularly young people, on the defensive. A young person might, for example, interpret a question such as 'Why didn't you vote in the 2005 election?' as an implicit criticism of their course of action. In contrast, a question such as 'How did you arrive at a decision not to vote at the last election?' is likely to come across as rather less threatening. As Becker notes from his own experience

'How' questions, when I asked them, gave people more leeway, were less constraining, invited them to answer in any way that suited them, to tell a story that included whatever they thought the story ought to include in order to make sense. They didn't demand a 'right' answer, didn't seem to be trying to place responsibility for bad actions or outcomes anywhere ... As a result, they invited people to include what they thought was important to the story, whether I had thought of it or not. (Becker, 1998: 59)

Using unstructured interviewing approaches: the narrative turn

Although the semi-structured format is perhaps the most widely used form of qualitative interviewing within youth research, less structured formats where the researcher intervenes in the interview as little as possible are increasingly used. Whether or not one can legitimately refer to these approaches as genuinely unstructured is questionable, as it is arguable that any interview requires at least *some* residual structure in the form of an opening question at the very least in order to provide it with a meaningful focus. Nonetheless, it is becoming increasingly common for youth researchers to use approaches which foreground young people's own stories, particularly through the use of narrative interviewing techniques (Chamberlayne et al., 2000; Wengraf, 2001), whereby participants are invited to reflect upon specific events in their lives through telling stories about them, or through being invited to reflect upon a particular period in their lives, sometimes in relation to an identified theme or themes. In addition to group interviews involving all household members, for example, Heath and Cleaver (2003) conducted one-to-one narrative interviews with individual housemates. They were asked to respond to the following opening question: 'Starting where you like, and in your own words, I'd like you to tell me about the places you've lived and the people you've lived with, and your experiences and memories of living in each of these places'. In most cases, interviewees responded extremely enthusiastically, and at great length, to this opening question, generating a range of idiosyncratic narrative accounts relating to their housing histories.

According to Polkinghorne, the term 'narrative' 'refers to a discourse form in which events and happenings are configured into a temporal unity by means of a plot' (Polkinghorne, 1995: 5), whilst Czarniawska notes that: 'in order to understand their own lives people put them into narrative form – and they do the same when they try to understand the lives of others' (Czarniawska, 2004: 5). Youth researchers who are drawn to narrative are concerned, then, with the ways in which young people make sense of their lives through the stories they tell about themselves, and what these same stories reveal about their identities:

the underlying assumption ... is that the stories one tells of oneself are probably the best possible approximation to who one is ... in telling stories about themselves people simultaneously describe and construct who they are and how their various experiences accumulate to form a sensible, intelligible and communicable story of identity/biography. (Noy, 2004: 83)

The narrative form is particularly well suited to youth research given that so much research in this area is concerned with *process* and *transition*. Within this context, it makes a lot of sense to explore young people's lives through the stories that they construct about themselves. It is also a method which sits comfortably with recent engagement by youth researchers with Beck's individualisation thesis (see, for example, Furlong and Cartmel, 2007; Dwyer and Wyn, 2001; Henderson et al., 2006a). Beck (1992) has written extensively about the emergence of 'choice biographies' as a key feature of 'late modernity', and narrative approaches have allowed researchers the opportunity to reflect upon the nature of the biographical accounts which are proffered by young people in the interview context. Du Bois-Raymond (1998), for example, used narrative approaches to highlight the extent to which young people's accounts remain highly structured by factors such as social class and educational attainment, allowing her to distinguish between the 'choice biographies' of middle class and highly educated young people and the 'standardised biographies' of working class and less well educated middle class young people.

Narrative accounts are marked by a number of common features. They are stories told from the perspective of the teller, who surrounds her- or himself with a cast of significant others who are woven in and out of the story; they tend to have a clear trajectory, with a beginning, a middle and an end, or some sense of a resolution, even when the story is not yet complete; they have a distinct plot; and they are often marked by discernible 'genres', such as the morality tale, the horror story, or the fairy tale. Interviews based upon the narrative form can lead to two distinct types of analysis: on the one hand, holistic or narrative analysis, and on the other hand categorical analysis or the analysis of narratives (Polkinghorne, 1995; Lieblich et al., 1998). Holistic or narrative analysis focuses on the form of each individual narrative in its own right, highlighting the dominant narrative genre for example, or the key themes which run through an individual narrative. In contrast, categorical analysis or the analysis of narratives is an approach whereby certain themes are compared cross-sectionally across an entire set of narratives, enabling the researcher to identity common themes as well as significant differences across the data set, differences which may for example be related to factors such as gender, locality, or social class. In practice, it is not at all unusual for narrative researchers to draw upon both styles of analysis within the same study, as together the two approaches can present a more rounded interpretation.

Noy's research on the 'travel narratives' of young Israeli backpackers provides a good example of the complementary use of these two approaches to analysis (Noy, 2004). Noy conducted narrative interviews with 40 secular Jewish Israelis in their early twenties who had all backpacked on completion of their period of compulsory military service, a practice which has become something of a collective rite-of-passage from youth to adulthood amongst young Israelis from middle class and upper middle class backgrounds. He describes backpackers as 'an ad hoc community of storytellers' and, given this, notes that backpacking as a practice is 'highly conducive to narrative identity work' (2004: 81). In developing a categorical analysis of his data, in which he compared similar themes across the narratives, Noy points to the dominant genre of conversion and self-change which emerged in most of the backpackers' accounts in response to a single general question about their experiences throughout their trip. Categorical analysis also revealed some interesting differences across the narratives, including a tendency for young men to make an explicit connection between self-change and their involvement in specific risky activities, in contrast to the young women, who often expressed disapproval of the macho attitudes of their male counterparts on the backpacker trail and accounted for change by referring to the experience of the trip as a whole. Noy's holistic analysis of the data, in which he focused on the form of each narrative in turn, highlighted that these themes were invariably located towards the end of the narratives and functioned as a 'commonsensical' conclusion. Holistic analysis also revealed two pervasive sub-genres in many of the narratives, one inspired by romanticism and the other by the imagery of religious pilgrimage.

'Critical moments'

A major advantage of the narrative approach is that it tends to foreground the most significant events and moments in young people's biographical accounts *by default*. There is a danger inherent within more structured approaches to qualitative interviewing that the topics identified in an interview guide may not be as significant to the young person as they are to the interviewer, yet by their inclusion these topics may be privileged over the issues which matter more to young people. The narrative approach tends to avoid this pitfall, as young people are able to flag up the issues which are central to their own stories without being given too much of a 'steer' by the researcher. In particular, this allows for the possibility of identifying key pivotal moments in young people's lives above and beyond some of the moments which are all too often *assumed* to be of significance. Experiences such as leaving school and starting work may well be of importance in young people's lives, but there are many other landmark events which we fail to pick up on by over-emphasising the significance of these traditional 'transitional' markers.

The narrative approach is particularly good, then, at facilitating the unprompted uncovering of what have variously been referred to as 'epiphanies' (Denzin, 1989), 'turning points' (Hodkinson and Sparkes, 1997) and 'critical moments' (Thomson et al., 2002). This strength has been capitalised upon in the *Inventing Adulthoods* research project, a longitudinal study of the transitional experiences of 120 young people from five contrasting communities in England and Northern Ireland. Thomson et al. have described their research in terms of 'a life story approach to understanding key moments of biographical change in young people's lives' (2002: 336). Through the use of narrative accounts they have developed the concept of the 'critical moment', defined as 'an event described in an interview that either the researcher or the interviewees see as having important consequences for their lives and identities' (2002: 339). Their use of this term as a descriptive concept for considering significant events within young people's narratives builds upon Anthony Giddens's concept of 'fateful moments', 'times when events come together in such a way that an individual stands at a crossroads in their existence or where a person learns of information with fateful consequences' (Giddens, 1991: 113).

In their analysis, Thomson et al. (2002) were not only able to identify a wide range of critical moments in young people's accounts, but were also able to identify the undertaking or otherwise of subsequent 'identity work', allowing them to consider the differential responses of young people to the critical moments in their lives. These critical moments included some which appeared to have universal application, such as family, education and relationship-related events, as well as others which appeared to be location- and class-specific, such as instances of chronic illness in the accounts of young people living in deprived estates compared with accounts of passing the driving test in the narratives of young people from middle class suburbs. Their work allowed them to explore the differential resources which young people were able to draw upon in dealing with these critical moments. The narrative approach, then, is a particularly useful method for research which focuses on processes of change and transition, and hence is potentially of great value to youth researchers.

Weaknesses of the narrative approach

One of the potential weaknesses of the narrative approach is an over-emphasis on individual agency as an artefact of the research method. In other words, if young people are asked to tell a story in which they are invited to place themselves centre stage, then the stories they tell will inevitably tend to downplay the influence of external structures and constraints as well as the impact upon their lives of the prior actions and decisions of significant others. In considering the differential nature of young people's responses to the critical moments in their lives, for example, Thomson et al. concluded that

> While most young people may speak the language of individual choice, control and agency, it is only for some that the rhetoric is accompanied by the requisite resources and constraints ... A 'can do' approach to life

> may be a necessary condition for progressive personal change, yet it is
> unlikely to be sufficient in the face of structural constraints. (Thomson
> et al., 2002: 352)

It is also the case that some young people are simply better able to tell
stories about their lives than others. For example, whilst Heath and
Cleaver (2003) found that most of their interviewees spoke with ease
and at length in response to the invitation to narrate their housing
histories in an unstructured format, a small number dried up after a relatively short period of time and demanded more direction. This
suggests that any emergent differences may sometimes have more to
do with the extent to which individuals are able to articulate their
views, rather than any more fundamental reason.

Roberts (2002) notes further that this potential over-emphasis on individual agency may not only have consequences for the validity of one's
analysis, but that it may also place limitations on possibilities for
change. From a feminist perspective, for example, a series of highly
individualised accounts of young women's experiences of discrimination and harassment within the youth labour market might appear to
give young women a voice, but it might be at the expense of down-
playing or even denying the impact upon their lives of patriarchal structures. This is not to argue against the use of narrative approaches
per se, but to point to the need to consider young people's accounts
within a broader structural context: a need which is by no means
unique to narrative analysis.

Youth researchers who use narrative approaches also need to be aware
that the task of securing informed consent can be rendered more difficult
by the use of a method which can be considered to have a relatively
open-ended and possibly under-defined agenda. It is often impossible to
predict in advance what topics might emerge within a narrative interview,
in contrast to more structured approaches where topics for discussion are
largely pre-defined in advance (Jossellson, 1996). As such, it is sometimes difficult to communicate to young people exactly what they are
consenting to do when agreeing to be interviewed using this method.
One possible way round this is to make this clear at the outset and to
then seek a reconfirmation of consent *after* the completion of the interview, once it is clear what has been covered in the interview. What this
does not avoid is the possibility that a young person may end up talking
about sensitive or potentially upsetting issues which they might not otherwise have agreed to discuss if they knew in advance that they might
arise. Reeves, for example, in her narrative research on youth fathers from
disadvantaged backgrounds, notes that 'in some instances during the
research process I found myself having to choose between pursuing a
story about an intimate issue and protecting participants from the upsetting memories or emotions the incident raised for them' (2007: 258).
However, whilst this might be more likely to occur when working within

the narrative format, this problem could equally arise in any form of inter-viewing. Researchers using any interview format need to be prepared to cope with this possibility.

The epistemological status of interview data

A focus on narrative interviewing and on different narrative forms high-lights an important issue concerning the epistemological status of interview data. As noted in Chapter 1, epistemology is a branch of philosophy which is specifically concerned with the nature of evi-dence and of what counts as valid knowledge within the social world, and researchers have long argued about the degree to which interview data can be said to correspond with objective reality, or whether they are merely the product of an artificial social encounter. Despite the oft-quoted reference to research interviews as 'conversations with a pur-pose' (Burgess, 1984: 102), interview data are undeniably the products of a very specific and 'manufactured' interaction. By no means 'naturally occurring', a research interview is a joint process consisting of the con-struction or reconstruction of people's experiences and understandings. It is for this reason that many qualitative researchers prefer to use the term 'data generation' rather than 'data collection' when referring to their fieldwork endeavours (a convention we have followed in this book). This in turn raises a question concerning the relationship between inter-view data and observed behaviour and experience. While observation captures an event as it happens, interviewing captures an *account* of an event, and the two sources of data might provide very different per-spectives on the same phenomenon. For example, some young people might talk about their disregard for the law, yet through observation of their behaviour it might transpire that this is only so much bravado. Atkinson et al. (2003) have reframed this question as 'How do you know if your informant is telling the truth?' (2003: 119) and, depending on a researcher's stance, the answer to this question will be more or less con-sequential. For some purposes, truth claims are important; for others, the telling of the account itself is equally valid, as it sheds light on the sense that is made of events by individuals after the event.

This highlights two very distinct approaches to the analytical treatment of interview data, captured in a debate as to whether interview data should be treated as a *resource* or a *topic* (see, for example, May, 2001). In relation to the former, a researcher may be interested in using interview data to (re)construct certain events, such as a young person's experiences of a death in the family, and of their emotions and responses to these events. A researcher might believe that an interview focusing on this event will provide a relatively accurate and factual account of what had occurred. Nonetheless, it is important to acknowledge that 'accuracy' in this sense seems to be a more appropriate criterion for measuring the quality of *quantitative* rather than qualitative research, the former being governed by well defined concepts of validity and reliability (Bryman, 2004). Qualitative research eschews notions of one single knowable account of social reality, and instead emphasises notions of situated knowledge and subjective understanding. All interview-based accounts are, then, *representations*: there may be other equally credible representations of the same phenomena. As such, many qualitative researchers argue for the application of criteria other than validity and reliability. Lincoln and Guba (1985), for example, prefer to talk in terms of 'trustworthiness' and 'authenticity', while Hammersley (1998) looks for an account that is 'plausible' and 'credible'. Interviews may not, then, be 'factual' accounts, but can nonetheless provide us with important insights into a particular issue. Using interviews to generate accounts of this kind is of course very common, but it is important to address these kinds of concerns rather than assume that interview data automatically bear a direct resemblance to experiences and behaviour outside of the interview situation.

In contrast, a researcher may be more interested in using interview data as a topic, where the focus shifts from the accuracy or otherwise of the account to the way in which that account is presented. The narrative approach to interviewing reflects this conceptualisation of interview data as topic, highlighting the way in which the language and the specific storytelling techniques used by an interviewee become a focus of attention in their own right. As discussed above, in asking someone to talk about their life, or an aspect of it, individuals tend to *tell a story*. Indeed, one often gets a sense that the stories told in interviews have been told – or at least have been rehearsed in an individual's mind – on many occasions. This emphasis on form rather than on 'facts' can provide invaluable insights into the sense which people make of their social worlds. Marks (1996, cited in Alldred and Gillies, 2002), for example, conducted interviews with young people who had been excluded from school. She found that the stories that were told to her were characterised by a discourse of repentance and of responsibility for their bad behaviour: 'Reluctantly, she recognised that the interviews functioned as yet another site for these pupils to reproduce themselves as reformed characters, as reflexive, self-regulating (and therefore now trustworthy) individuals' (Alldred and Gillies, 2002: 150). Focusing on interview data as topic can, then, provide an alternative and possibly more nuanced understanding of a research topic.

Group interviews and focus groups

This chapter has so far discussed the use of one-to-one interviews. Whilst most interviews are indeed conducted on this basis, there are occasions when it is preferable to interview young people in pairs or in larger groups. Eder and Fingerson (2003) even suggest that group interviewing should be the default option when interviewing young people. They offer a number of reasons for this. First, they argue that group interviewing reduces the power and influence of the interviewer and thus creates a less threatening environment in which to be interviewed. Many young people may indeed find the individual interview to be an intimidating experience and might prefer to be interviewed with a friend if at all possible. A researcher interviewed as part of the study conducted by Rose Wiles and colleagues on informed consent procedures (see Chapter 2) noted, for example, that the number of young people willing to be interviewed in a school-based study increased dramatically when they were given the option of being interviewed with a friend if they so wished. Fine and Weiss (1998) have also noted that the group interview format is more empowering and emotionally supportive for young people. Commenting on their interviews with working class young Americans living in poverty, they found that

> group interviews tended to be far more hopeful than individual interviews as we sat with interviewees through many a tearful individual session. While certainly tears flowed in the groups, other members of the group supported and jumped in to tell the tearful person how they had handled particular situations. The individual is not left so emotionally spent in a group interview as participants share their experiences, faith and hope. (Fine and Weiss, 1998: 297)

Second, Eder and Fingerson argue that the group interview is a more 'natural' context for exploring young people's lives, given that young people 'acquire social knowledge through interaction with others as they construct meanings through a shared process' (Eder and Fingerson, 2003: 35). Group interviews, then, 'grow directly out of peer culture' (2003: 35) and allow researchers to explore the processes whereby young people create shared meanings and understandings. In Heath and Cleaver's (2003) research on young people's experiences of living in shared households, for example, it made sense to conduct semi-structured interviews with housemates *as a group,* alongside individual narrative interviews. In most cases, the full membership of each household met with us as an entity to discuss their experiences of living together. In this particular case, we were interested in the collective, publicly-presentable accounts of shared living that were thus generated, and which were then contrasted with the individual accounts generated in the subsequent one-to-one interviews with each housemate.

This emphasis on group interaction is strongly connected to the rationale for using *focus groups* in social research, where the analytical focus is as much on the interplay between group members as it is on a particular topic. Focus groups have grown in popularity in recent years. Much loved by market researchers and political spin doctors, they are an economical way of collecting a large amount of data in a relatively short space of time from groups of people usually brought together by virtue of sharing a characteristic of particular relevance to the research in question. Lindsey (2004), for example, brought together groups of under-25 year old hairdressers in an Australian study of young people and risk-taking behaviours; hairdressers having been identified in an earlier survey as a group of workers who were more likely than other occupational groups to take risks in their personal lives. Smalley et al. (2004) also drew upon groups of young people with a clearly defined shared characteristic in their study of services for suicidal young people, by conducting focus groups with groups of young people considered to be at high risk of suicide – including care leavers, former drug users and young lesbians and gay men. In other cases, focus groups often consist of fairly heterogeneous sets of individuals whose only point of commonality is their ability to express a view on the topic in question. Nonetheless, such groups may still be stratified by factors such as gender, age or ethnicity, in order to allow researchers to draw comparisons between the collective views of different social groups.

Although members of a focus group do not need to know each other in advance, and in research with adults they often do not, the use of focus groups within recently published youth research suggests that more often than not youth researchers do indeed endeavour to bring together people who already know each other. In the case of the two studies mentioned above, for example, Lindsey (2004) recruited the membership of most of the focus groups in her study through the various salons in which the hairdressers worked, whilst Smalley et al. (2004) recruited the members of each of their respective focus groups from the existing memberships of support groups for young people within the various at-risk categories. The advantage of prior association is that interaction might be eased and initial nervousness circumvented. However, it might equally be the case that some young people will be reluctant to talk in detail about their own experiences and attitudes in front of people who know them. Whilst Lindsey (2004), for example, felt that overall it was advantageous to bring together people who knew each other, she has speculated as to whether the relative silence of a young gay man in one of the focus groups was because he did not wish to disclose too much personal information to his co-workers.

This example highlights a potential weakness of focus groups, namely that a focus on the processes whereby young people create shared meanings and understandings may reveal just as much about peer pressure and the influence of dominant individuals in shaping those 'shared' meanings. This is also illustrated well in the case of Fingerson's exploration of young women's interpretations of family television programmes (Fingerson, 1999, cited in Eder and Fingerson, 2003). In Fingerson's study, a group of young women were initially interviewed individually, many stating strong opinions and beliefs which were then modified in subsequent group interviews in line with the group consensus – a consensus which very much reflected the views of one of the more popular members of the youth club at which the interviews were conducted. This example demonstrates the value of the complementary use of group and individual interviews, in this case allowing the researcher to reflect on the construction of both individual and collective understandings in relation to the topic in question.

Allen (2005) has considered the construction of normative attitudes and approaches in focus groups in a slightly different light. In asking groups of 17-19 year olds to discuss the gap between sex education and the reality of young people's sexual practices, she found that the young men involved in the research engaged in displays of hegemonic masculinity, by such means asserting their heterosexuality both to each other and to the researcher. Rather than regarding this as a problem and as a source of data 'contamination', Allen chose to focus on what these displays implied about the making of male sexuality within the focus group setting, an environment which she viewed 'as constitutive of male sexual subjectivities in the way that it provides a public forum for young men's presentation of self' (Allen, 2005: 35). Allen began to regard their talk as a form of 'performance' in relation to their sexual identities and, as such, valuable data in their own right. She concluded that

> The nature of focus group interaction offers young men opportunities to fashion their masculinity through what they choose to reveal and conceal about their sexuality to other participants. This type of engagement can be conceptualised as 'identity work' and enables us to study masculinities in the making. From this perspective lewd remarks or boasting about sexual conquests are not behaviours which hinder the collection of 'good' data, but offer insights into how male sexuality is constituted. (Allen, 2005: 53)

Following on from our earlier discussion, then, Allen's analysis provides a further example of how interview data might be treated as a topic in their own right, rather than viewing the data as a resource providing an 'objective' account of young people's lives.

Having outlined some of the different approaches which come under the umbrella of qualitative interviewing, the rest of the chapter considers two further issues which arise in interview-based research. We start by considering the importance of location when conducting interviews, before turning to a consideration of the value of a longitudinal approach to qualitative interviewing. It should also be noted that many of the points raised in the discussion in Chapter 3 concerning the impact of sameness and difference in the conduct of youth research are of particular relevance to qualitative interviewing and should be borne in mind when planning interview-based research.

Location, location, location

A particularly important issue when conducting interview-based research with young people is the question of where to hold interviews. This is important for two key reasons. First, physical space is rarely neutral, but instead has the potential to confer advantage on one or other party to the interview to the disadvantage of the other; and second, certain locations may place both the researcher and/or the participant at risk. Bearing these points in mind, the ideal is often for interviews to be held in a public space of a young person's choosing in order to minimise any potential discomfort and to minimise the power differential between researchers and interviewees. Cafes and bars are popular locations for holding interviews with older teenagers and young people, for example, not least because they are also public spaces which minimise the potential for risk both to young people *and* to researchers. Notwithstanding earlier discussions concerning the use of incentives in youth research, the use of cafes and bars also allows the researcher to extend some limited hospitality to the young person being interviewed, by buying them a drink, for example. The drawback of such locations is that they tend to be rather noisy, which may cause problems if an interview is being recorded, whilst in many cases it would be considered culturally insensitive to suggest meeting in a bar. Other popular locations might include youth clubs, shopping centres, or other public leisure spaces, such as skating rinks or skateboard parks. More expediently, it is not unknown for interviews with young people to be conducted in rather less comfortable spaces, such as on street corners, on park benches, in bus shelters, or in cars. In his research on rural young people, for example, Leyshon (2002) resorted to conducting interviews under the porch light of the village hall, in skittle alleys, in the men's changing room at a cricket pavilion, and on occasions quite literally 'in the field'.

The young person's home is another popular location for conducting interviews in youth research. Under such circumstances, the researcher is very much the guest within the interview setting, which in principle should maximise the young person's control of the situation. This is not always the case, however. Many youth researchers will have shared the experience of conducting interviews in young people's homes during the course of which parents, siblings or other housemates have either drifted in and out of the interview space, or have been in the space for the entire duration of the interview, on occasions even chipping into discussions. Not surprisingly, this will tend to have an impact on the willingness of the young person to discuss certain topics within that setting. Valentine et al. (2001), for example, note that the parental home is rarely an appropriate setting for conducting research with gay and lesbian young people where their sexuality forms the focus of the interview. Researchers also need to be sensitive to appearances; it would rarely be advisable, for example, to conduct an interview in a younger teenager's bedroom without parental consent or without a parent being in the home at the same time. Lincoln's (2005) research on teenage bedroom culture necessitated her conducting interviews with young people in their bedroom spaces in order to gain a full appreciation of the significance of these personal spaces, but she wisely chose to conduct these interviews with friendship groups of three or four young people together, rather than as one-to-one interviews.

There are a few examples in the youth studies literature of researchers interviewing young people in their *own* homes. In research on working class masculinities, for example, McDowell (2001) gave young men the option of being interviewed in her own home, arguing that this provided 'an informal and non-intimidating environment'. Before allowing the young men into her home, she ensured that they were over the age of 16, that they had sought parental permission to meet with her at a specific time, and that someone else was in the house at the same time. She also notes that she conducted the interviews in the front room of her house, which was directly opposite Cambridge's police station! Mac an Ghaill (1993) also talks of providing access to his home to the young people involved in his study of black students and their schooling, a practice which he claims 'undoubtedly contributed to the quality of the data collected' (1993: 156), whilst Hey (1997) talks of getting to know sufficiently well some of the young women involved in her study of girls' friendships to have been invited to their homes and in return inviting them to her home, although it is not clear whether this was primarily in order to conduct interviews. It is significant that all of these examples are of studies which were conducted over a long time period, allowing for a level of trust to have first developed between those involved. In general terms, though, this is not a practice which we would encourage, given the potential risks involved for both researchers and participants.

Youth researchers do not always have the luxury of presenting young people with a choice of location, particularly if their research is being conducted within an institutional context. Researchers working in schools, for example, are likely to be allocated to the nearest available classroom or office, which might not always prove to be the most suitable location for research purposes. This is starkly illustrated in Martino and Pallotta-Chiarolli's (2003) account of conducting interviews with young men in Australian schools as part of a study of bullying. In one school, the interviewer had been allocated a glass-walled room in the school library, which gave rise to two particularly difficult interview encounters. In one, a very distracted young man entered the room and sat himself in a chair directly facing the window into the library (not the one that the researcher had ushered him towards) and, until the researcher's intervention, spent the interview peering anxiously into the library. It eventually became clear to the researcher that the young man was being stared at by a large boy in the library:

> 'You're being bullied right now aren't you?' I ask. He nods and flushes, his eyes filling with tears, and averting them from my gaze as well as from the window. 'They're watching me, they're hassling me and they'll get me more later'. I end the interview at that point and tell the student I'm going to request another room. (Martino and Pallotta-Chiarolli, 2003: 32)

This interview was then followed by an interview with a self-defined bully who, again against the researcher's wishes, positioned himself in full view of the 'audience' in the library and proceeded to put on a display of bravado for their benefit, including various obscene hand gestures. Providing a powerful commentary on the importance of location, Martino and Chiarolli note that subsequent interviews on the same topic held in a 'safe and private' space produced very different responses.

In what might be seen as a radical departure from the usual practice of interviewing young people in fixed locations, some youth researchers have begun to experiment with the use of interviews 'on the move'. In other words, an interview will be conducted whilst walking through a particular locale, often a young person's own neighbourhood. Such techniques are often used in conjunction with visual methods such as photography and video, and as such are described in greater detail in Chapter 9. For many purposes it makes a great deal of sense to conduct an interview in this manner. Writing about their research on young people's responses to urban regeneration in South Wales, Hall et al. for example, note that

> The conversations we are engaged in with young people in South Wales have linked place and biography through movement; they have been conducted on the move, out and about, with respondents invited to walk us through their changing locales as they talk us through their changing lives ... At their best we have felt these walks to be three-way conversations, with interviewee, interviewer and locality engaged in an exchange of ideas; place has been under discussion but, more than this, and crucially, underfoot and all around, and as such much more of an active, present participant in the conversation, able to prompt and interject. (2006: 3)

Hall et al. also note that there is a certain logic to using physical movement as a research strategy in youth research given the predominance of metaphors of space and movement within the literature, including metaphors such as 'transitions', 'pathways' and 'trajectories'. This is a fascinating innovation and one which we imagine will be adopted more widely, particularly by youth researchers interested in spatiality.

In some cases, youth researchers might need to conduct interviews over the telephone. Telephone interviews are generally regarded as inferior to those conducted in person. First, the non-verbal cues that form such an important part of a face-to-face interview are absent, which might make establishing rapport particularly challenging. Second, an interviewer cannot guarantee that an interviewee is in a setting which respects their privacy; the household telephone might, for example, be in the family's main living room, with others listening in. Third, access to a landline, although widespread, is by no means universal, which might exclude some young people from participation. However, the near ubiquity of mobile telephone use amongst young people suggests that mobile technologies might prove to be an increasingly effective way of establishing contact with research participants and facilitating the conduct of interviews in settings which are within their control: in any location where they are able to establish a signal.

Longitudinal strategies

The final issue we discuss in this chapter is the use of longitudinal strategies for interview-based research. Given the major preoccupation with various aspects of transition amongst youth researchers, many have long seen the value of introducing some element of 'follow up' into their research. Williamson's research on 'the Milltown Boys', a group of teenage lads growing up on a Cardiff council estate in the 1970s, provides a particularly impressive example. In the late 1990s, he began to consider the possibility of a follow-up study, and against the odds managed to trace 47 of the original 67 young men involved in his research, all now in their forties (Williamson, 2004). Examples such as this, where the follow-up occurs at such a long period of time after the original fieldwork, are particularly unusual. Nonetheless, many youth researchers come to revisit their original research participants, albeit often on an ad hoc basis and as a result of serendipity, rather than as a deliberate element of a study's original research design. The *Inventing Adulthoods* project, which we discussed earlier in this chapter, is a case in point. It started life as a one-off cross-sectional study, but by default became a longitudinal study as successive waves of funding were granted to the project team, allowing for contact with some young people up to six times following initial contact in 1998 (Henderson et al., 2006a). Another example of a longitudinal study which has included a strong qualitative component includes the *Life Patterns* research project based at the Australian Youth Research Centre at the University of Melbourne (Dwyer and Wyn, 2001). The research team has been following a cohort of young people who left school in 1991. Now in their early thirties, the plan is to continue to follow up this cohort for the foreseeable future, alongside a new longitudinal project focusing on young people who left school in 2005.

McLeod (2000) points to the advantages of conducting interviews within a longitudinal context. She argues that such an approach is a powerful tool for shedding light on the ongoing process of the formation of identity. Writing of her research on young Australians, gender identity and schooling, she notes that

> Analysing interviews conducted over time can illuminate, confirm or unsettle initial and tentative interpretations, alert us to recurring motifs and tropes in participants' narratives as well as to shifts and changes, suggest continuities or disruptions in emotional investments, in desires and in dispositions, and provide a strong sense of how particular identities are taking shape and developing. This allows identity to be analysed as a process and not simply as a repository of one-off opinions or quotations. (McLeod, 2000: 49)

A one-off narrative interview can also provide a sense of change over time, but it can only do this through a retrospective account, and as such will inevitably be tinged by a perspective based on hindsight. In contrast, repeat interviews allow for an engagement with change as it unfolds over time, and also allow research participants to reflect back on what they might have said in a previous interview. Once again, this is an approach which sits well with the current engagement by many youth researchers with Beck's (1992) view that young people are increasingly engaged in the construction of their own biographies.

Nonetheless, some young people might be deterred from participating in a longitudinal study precisely because of the expectation of involvement over a considerable amount of time. Young people whose lives do not appear to follow a relatively clearly defined trajectory may find the experience of repeat interviewing to be a potentially distressing and alienating experience. Drawing again on the *Inventing Adulthoods* project, Thomson and Holland have noted that

> the interviewers were aware that the structure of the research encouraged young people to present themselves as being involved in a progressive and developmental process of change. Some of those young people who did drop out of the study were certainly those experiencing difficult circumstances. (2003: 241)

For some young people, then, a longitudinal approach might be experienced rather negatively, effectively reflecting back to them a sense of internalised 'failure' or 'stagnation'. It may be, then, that young people who are prepared to commit to a long term study might have a very different outlook on their lives than those who decline to take part or who are lost along the way. They may certainly be more long-suffering of researchers: McDowell writes wryly about a young man involved in her own longitudinal research taking a call on his mobile telephone during an interview, commenting to his friend 'Can't talk now, mate. It's that Linda again, interviewing me' (2001: 88).

Summary

This chapter has introduced readers to some of the different approaches which come under the umbrella of qualitative interviewing and which are particularly well suited to youth research. We have considered the strengths and weaknesses of semi-structured and unstructured interviewing strategies, including both one-to-one, group and focus group interviews. We have highlighted debates concerning the epistemological status of interview data and the implications this has for analysis. Finally, we considered the importance of location and a number of issues relevant to the conduct of longitudinal interview-based research. In the next chapter we turn to a consideration of the use of ethnographic approaches in youth research. Ethnography often includes an element of qualitative interviewing, but at its heart lies the use of sustained observation, and it is this aspect of the ethnographic approach which forms the focus of Chapter 6.

Suggestions for further reading

Gubrium, J. and Holsten, J. (eds) (2001) *Handbook of Interview Research: Context and Method*, London: Sage. This edited collection provides an excellent introduction to a very wide range of issues germane to the use of (mainly qualitative) interviewing in social research.

Henderson, S., Holland, J., McGrellis, S., Sharpe, S. and Thomson, R. (2006) *Inventing Adulthoods: A Biographical Approach to Youth Transitions*, London: Sage/Open University Press. This is the book of the project, and provides a very good illustration of the effective use of a narrative approach and within a longitudinal context.

Mason, J. (2002) *Qualitative Researching*, London: Sage. This best selling introduction to qualitative methods touches upon more than just interview-based approaches, but nonetheless is an essential read for anyone interested in qualitative interviewing as a research strategy.

6 Ethnographic Approaches

Introduction

Ethnography has long held a special place within youth research. Some of the classic ethnographies conducted by pioneers from the Chicago School from the 1920s onwards, such as Thrasher's *The Gang* (1927) and Foote Whyte's *Street Corner Society* (1943), had a central focus on young people's experiences. Even today, 30 years on since its publication in 1977, Willis's *Learning to Labour* remains one of the most well-known ethnographies not just within youth studies but within British sociology more generally. The term 'ethnography' is sometimes used to refer to a broad range of different qualitative methods, yet in many people's minds it is synonymous with some form of sustained observation, and that is the sense in which it is used in this chapter. This chapter will focus then on the use of participant and non-participant observation as a research tool in researching young people's lives. In doing so, it will discuss some of the key concerns of ethnographers, such as the gaining and maintaining of access to research sites, the pros and cons associated with either insider or outsider status, and relationships between researchers and the researched.

What is ethnography?

Ethnography is typically understood as the study of people in naturally occurring settings by methods of data collection that capture their ordinary activities and the social meanings that are attached to these. Often, the researcher participates directly in the activities he or she is observing, with the aim of understanding the situation from the perspective of the research subjects (Brewer, 2000). Hammersley (1998) also notes that, in addition to studying people in natural contexts and primarily through observation, ethnographic data collection is typically flexible and unstructured, aims to minimise the extent to which the researcher imposes his or her own meanings on the data collected, and is usually small scale, focussing on a single setting or group. There are, however, important variations between the theoretical perspectives that inform different types of ethnographic study (Gordon et al., 2001). For example, many distinguish between conventional ethnography and its 'critical' counterpart. While the former seeks to explore and explain behaviours and meanings within a particular social setting, critical ethnographers take a more radical political stance, typically aiming to theorise social structural constraints and human agency in order to consider how those being researched can be empowered (Jordan and Yeomans, 1995; Hollands, 2003). More recently, postmodern and post-structuralist ethnographies have been conducted (Lather, 1991; Denzin, 1997). These commonly reject the claims of conventional ethnographers that, through an ethnographic approach, one can gain a special understanding of people's world-views. Instead, they emphasise that all data, regardless of method, are produced by researchers, and that there is no single, fixed reality to capture 'accurately'. While relatively few of the studies discussed in this chapter locate themselves within a postmodern perspective, the post-structural challenge has had a more noticeable impact on the presentation of ethnographic data, an issue which we discuss later in this chapter.

Choosing to conduct an ethnographic study offers various advantages. First, it can – its proponents claim – allow researchers to delve below the 'official' version of events to explore the actual lived experiences of young people. This is illustrated well by O'Neill's (2003) study of young carpet weavers in Nepal. On the basis of two periods of ethnographic fieldwork in the Nepalese carpet industry, he contrasts the anti-child labour rhetoric common in Europe and North America with the more positive experiences of those actually working in the carpet weaving industry. Similarly, Aune's (2006) work contrasts the official rhetoric about women's position within the evangelical church (that husbands should lead and wives should submit) with the actual, and more egalitarian, behaviour of the young men and women she observed during her fieldwork at 'Westside', a British evangelical church.

Ethnography can also alert the researcher to disparities between accounts of behaviour provided in interviews, and actual behaviour observed within particular contexts. In his study of goths, Hodkinson (2004: 143) notes that although participants sometimes preferred to talk about their 'individuality' rather than the features they shared with other group members, 'critical participant observation emphasised that internal differences usually took the form of creative, yet subtle variations' rather than any more significant forms of diversity. Reflecting on her work on young men's sexual identities, Pascoe (2007) makes a similar point, emphasising the difference, to a researcher, of listening to young men talk about gendered norms and behaviours within interviews and engaging with them in practice.

A further strength of ethnography is the way in which it facilitates an exploration of context. Mac an Ghaill (1994) describes how seeing young people interact within the context of the 'Parnell School' and at the same time participating in this context himself were key to helping him infer meanings and explore the cultural production of different versions of masculinity. Kehily's more recent (2002) work on gender and sexuality in schools also emphasises the importance of context. She argues that if the symbolic boundaries shaping sexuality in school are to be understood fully, an ethnographic approach is required: 'Researching sexuality in schools calls for an approach which renders visible the social relations of schooling, which recognises the context in which sexuality is at once present and absent, the forms it takes and the responses it generates' (2002: 5). The flexibility of the ethnographic approach is also highlighted by many researchers, who claim that it provides them with sufficient time and opportunity to explore themes that are not initially anticipated (Mac an Ghaill, 1994; Gordon et al., 2000) and to be sensitive to changes in the lives of research participants over both time and space (Nayak, 2003).

Some researchers suggest that ethnography offers particular advantages over other methods when working with specific groups of young people. In her study of Scottish young people in care, for example, Emond (2003) argues that participant observation offered several benefits over an interview-dominated approach. In particular, she contends that many young men and women in care tend to associate being asked questions with a subsequent change in circumstances (for example, a change in placement or levels of family contact). Moreover, by being sensitive to her own reaction when she entered the care home where she lived and conducted her research on a full-time basis for six months, she argues that she was able to appreciate more fully the anxieties felt by young people when they too had made this transition into the institution. Emond's initial plan had been to base her research on qualitative interviews, but she was challenged by the residents to gain first hand experience of life in a children's home: 'If you want tae ken [know] what it's like to bide [live] here I mean really ken then you'd have to come and bide', as one young man put it (2003: 105).

Many youth researchers emphasise the importance of combining observation with other research methods within an ethnographic study. Allen (2001), for example, combined his observations of interactions between staff and residents within foyers (a form of supported housing for young people which also provides employment and training opportunities) with non-directive interviews with both groups. Similarly, Lincoln's (2004) study of the use of space within young women's bedrooms was conducted through visual and written diaries and interviews, as well as observations of the way in which bedrooms were used. More innovatively, as noted in Chapter 2, Hey (1997) supplemented her participant observation with an analysis of the notes (or 'bits of silliness' as her respondents called them) passed between young women during school lessons. Some researchers have gone further, arguing that combining methods in this way helps to overcome some of the limitations of a purely observation-based study. In a reflexive account of the strengths and weaknesses of her research as a 'lurker' (a non-participant observer) in internet chat rooms, Richman (2007) acknowledges that the main limitation of the role she took on was her inability to ask those who posted messages for a clarification or elaboration about their behaviour. In cases such as these, she argues, supplementing 'lurker data' with interviews and focus groups becomes extremely important. Alexander (2000), for example, reflects that, despite longstanding friendships with the young men involved in her study of 'the Asian gang' – developed through several months of participant observation – interviews with them nonetheless provided new insights: 'Although much of the interviews covered areas, events and attitudes I already knew well by this time, I also learned a surprising amount about the young men themselves, their histories and their more private thoughts' (2000: 36).

Within ethnographic research, observational methods have often been used to facilitate or enhance the use of other methods, particularly interviews. In the case of Moore's (2003) research on clubbing, participant observation provided a key means of identifying and recruiting potential respondents for interviews. Similarly, both MacDonald and Marsh (2005) and Proweller (1998) describe how a sustained period of observation with the young people they were researching (on the streets of 'East Kelby' in the UK and in an upper middle class school in the north east of the USA, respectively) enabled them to secure more acceptance by those involved in the research. This in turn had a positive impact on the interviews they later conducted as part of their projects. As McDonald and Marsh point out, it was their visibility within the local area that helped them recruit respondents to their study of 'disconnected youth':

> Dropping into these places on a regular basis, over a year, chatting informally with those present and spending time travelling around East Kelby by bus proved to be an effective way of getting recognised by, and to recognise, some of its young residents. It helped develop at least a degree of acceptance of us by young people. (2005: 41)

Similarly, Proweller describes how the four months she spent observing the young women in her study prior to embarking on her interviews with them helped to establish 'open lines of communication and beginning ties of friendship' which proved 'central for access and the willing participation of my informants in open-ended, in-depth interviewing' (1998: 222). While Proweller claims that her developing relationships with the young women facilitated a greater openness in interviews than would otherwise have been possible, Alexander (2000) suggests that the strength of her close relationships with her interviewees also gave them the confidence to signal when they did not want to discuss a particular topic within the interview.

Ethnographers can adopt a number of different roles whilst 'in the field'. Gold (1958) famously distinguished between four roles, each relating to different levels of participation: complete participant (participating as a normal group member, conducting research in a covert manner); participant-as-observer (researching the field while participating fully in it); observer-as-participant (here, participation is limited, and the role of researcher more obvious); and complete observer (where there is no participation in the field). However, as Brewer (2000) notes, these distinctions are best seen as ideal types; in practice, the distinction between overt and covert research is a continuum, encompassing different degrees of openness. A close reading of various youth ethnographies also demonstrates how, even in the course of a single study, researchers often move between these roles. For example, Alexander (2000) describes how she started to develop better relationships with the young Asian men in her research when she took on a more participatory role – as a volunteer youth worker, rather than just an observer. Similarly, Proweller notes that 'at times, I adopted the stance of "fly on the wall" as a removed, non participatory observer, and at other points found myself actively involved in class discussions and group exchanges outside of class' (1998: 222). The roles available to and taken up by researchers are in turn influenced by their status as either an insider or outsider and also have an important bearing on the relationships forged between researcher and researched, themes which are discussed further in later parts of this chapter.

The changing focus of youth ethnography

As noted in Chapter 1, there are a number of broad traditions within youth research. Several of these traditions are concerned to a lesser or greater extent with aspects of young people's transitions to adulthood, focusing in particular on their engagement with education, employment, housing and household formation. In contrast, the youth cultural studies tradition has been more concerned to explore subcultural styles and acts of resistance amongst the young, typically drawing on ethnographic approaches in doing so. In recent years ethnographic approaches have also been used very effectively to explore aspects of transition and some of the structural factors that impact upon young people's lives (MacDonald et al., 2001). There are also examples within the literature of attempts to investigate both aspects of young people's lives in a single study. MacDonald and Marsh's (2005) study of young people in deprived areas of the north-east of England is a particularly good example of this. They argue that there is value for both traditions of youth research in attempting to conceptualise and research (through both observation and interviews) the way that issues of youth culture impact on youth transition, and vice versa. Similarly, Nayak's (2003) research into the impact of economic restructuring in a youth community in the north-east of England also explicitly aimed to 'knit together historical, "structural" and cultural approaches' to reveal what he believes to be their interwoven patterning within contemporary youth lifestyles (2003: 306). Cieslik (2001) has argued that this hybrid approach is essential for gaining a more nuanced understanding of contemporary youth.

Historically, youth ethnography has also tended to focus on marginalised groups of young people or those considered outside of the mainstream. This was particularly evident in the youth-focussed studies of the Centre for Contemporary Cultural Studies at the University of Birmingham, but has also characterised many other studies of youth. More recently, however, ethnographic approaches have been deployed to research more conformist groups of young people, and those in more privileged social positions. For example, both Roker (1993) and Proweller (1998) have conducted ethnographies of schools catering for the (upper) middle classes in the UK and the USA, respectively; Saldanha (2002) has engaged in participant observation with affluent young people in Bangalore in India; and Prieto (2000) has spent time amongst the youthful congregation of 'Urban Mosaic', a regular Christian worship event held in a US nightclub. The focus of youth ethnography has also been widened by the increasing use of this approach within cross-cultural research. Madsen's (2006) study of schooling in Nepal, Denmark and Eritrea, for example, uses ethnographic cross-cultural comparisons to explore understandings of similarities and differences in the way in which young people construct meaning and identity in relation to schooling and how these constructions relate to globalising pressures within national education systems, whilst Gordon et al. (2000) conducted a similar exercise in relation to secondary schools in London and Helsinki.

As these examples suggest, schools and other educational institutions are frequent research sites for ethnographic studies. However, the range of alternative sites explored by youth ethnographers is diverse. Many of these relate to the age-specific contexts and institutions which so often shape young people's lives, such as youth clubs (Alexander, 2000); care homes (Emond, 2003); clubs and pubs (Bloustein, 2004); and public spaces frequented by young people (Chatterton and Hollands, 2003). More unusual sites have included: young women's bedrooms (Lincoln, 2004); tattoo parlours (Jacobson and Luzatto, 2004); 'rave churches' and other alternative places of worship (Flory and Miller, 2000); high school prom nights (Best, 2000); young people's cars (Best, 2006); the backpacker trail (Binder, 2004); peace-building projects (Gillard, 2001); and sports shops frequented by young people (Miles, 1996). Despite the increasing diversity of sites which have come under the ethnographer's gaze, some sites remain difficult to access. For example, while Lincoln (2004) succeeded in pursuing an ethnographic study of the uses of space within young women's bedrooms, in her work on the partnership practices of young evangelical Christians Aune (2006) acknowledges the difficulty of finding out about family practices through an ethnographic approach: although she got to know her respondents well through the time she spent with them in their church, the continued importance placed on the family as a private space prevented her from observing how gender roles were played out within their homes.

Gaining access

The wider research methods literature contains a number of recommendations about the ways in which researchers should go about choosing ethnographic sites, particularly if they are keen to further the generalisability of their research. Hammersley (1992), for example, suggests that researchers pursuing the development and testing of theory need to coordinate their studies in a systematic manner. By way of illustration he cites the work of Hargreaves (1967), Lacey (1970) and Ball (1981), all of whom used participant observation to explore the impact of the differentiation of pupils in the form of streaming or banding on their attitudes to school. However, the accounts of numerous youth researchers testify that it is not always possible to adopt such a strategic approach to site selection. Difficulties in securing access from relevant gatekeepers are emphasised particularly by those who have sought to conduct ethnographic research within educational establishments (see Chapter 2). Kehily (2002), for example, provides a detailed account of her struggle to secure access to schools for her research on young people's sexuality and their experiences of sex education. To some extent, the problems she faced were related to her research topic which, in several cases, prompted anxiety and suspicion on the part of headteachers and other staff members. However, she also identifies a number of more general problems frequently encountered by educational researchers, including the impact of the wider political context in which schools operate, particularly the fear of 'bad publicity' which could, for the schools concerned, have serious and deleterious consequences within competitive education markets. Frequent legislative change also made some of the schools Kehily approached reluctant to allow access, fearing that the research would place more pressure on already overworked teachers. These obstacles are echoed in many other school-based ethnographies, and not only in the UK. Indeed, reflecting on processes of gaining access to both Finnish and English schools, Gordon et al. comment that 'access to schools was no easy matter. Schools were under pressure to perform, teachers suspected surveillance, school management expected surveillance. The process of negotiation to gain access was lengthy and often unsuccessful' (2000: 58).

The role of the gatekeeper can, then, have an important influence on the nature, quality and focus of ethnographic research. Alexander describes in some detail how one of the key gatekeepers in her study of 'the Asian gang' was important in suggesting a more productive and participatory role for her within the group she was observing: she 'persuaded me, encouraged me and often bludgeoned me into a more active role ... as a volunteer youth worker' (2000: 33). Other accounts are less positive. Proweller (1998), for example, was allocated a 'mentor' by the headteacher of the school she was studying, ostensibly to facilitate smoother access to students, but also as a means of attempting to control the research through close monitoring.

It is also worth noting that in many ethnographies conducted within institutional sites such as schools, youth clubs and care homes, young people themselves are rarely involved in initial decisions about whether or not to allow formal access (see Chapter 2). Whilst gatekeepers may consult with other staff members, few studies provide evidence of wider consultation with young people in the negotiation of initial access. This is not to say, however, that young people do not exert any power or influence in relation to what a researcher is or is not able to study. As Emond notes with respect to her work in care homes, 'young people are active social agents who, despite being formally "controlled" by adult practices and structures, create strategies to create a sense of control over their own environments' (2003: 107). She goes on to conclude that it is the job of the ethnographer to negotiate access to these social spaces. Similarly, reflecting on his research on young people's drug-related behaviour, Curtis (2002) argues that the selection of respondents or key informants within an ethnographic study is not always at the researcher's discretion. He describes how, as a researcher, he was often sought out 'by people who had a variety of motives for befriending me, that were not always helpful to my study' (2002: 303).

The process of negotiating access does not necessarily end once immersion in the field has begun, and many ethnographic studies have documented the ongoing negotiations which often ensue. Some suggest that this is a result of the ambiguities of the researcher's relationship with the young people he or she is observing, an issue which will be discussed further later in this chapter. Others point to the capacity of young people (indeed, their right) to withdraw their consent at any time in the study. This is illustrated well by Hey's painful (1997) account of an incident early on in her school-based fieldwork. Despite a prior agreement that she would spend some time shadowing Sandra (a 14–15 year old student) around the school

> I was met by Sandra behaving as if I was a known social outlaw. 'It's that woman!' she yelled, running to the back of the classroom, seeking protection from her teacher. I retreated, mortified by embarrassment, and muttered something incoherent to the bemused teacher and her class and disappeared into the sanctuary of the girls' toilet. (1997: 46)

While such ongoing negotiations are not restricted to youth-orientated sites, some access-related issues are nonetheless more age-specific. In the study cited above, for example, Hey was concerned to explore the friendships of young women, as played out within a secondary school. Peer networks have also been the main or subsidiary focus of several other ethnographic studies (Aggleton, 1987; Mac an Ghaill, 1994; Kehily, 2002), some of which suggest that negotiating access to peer groups can be particularly problematic because of the exclusionary nature of the friendship networks of many young people. As Proweller (1998: 222) notes: 'adolescent girls are staunch defenders of the bonds of loyalty that unite them as friends, and the intrusion of a peripheral observer is threatening to the identity of the group'.

Discussions about gaining access are often predicated on the assumption that the researcher will adopt an overt role within his or her chosen setting, yet this is not always the case. There is a large literature relating to the numerous ethical issues involved in deciding whether to take on an overt or covert role within a group, and these issues are addressed within various codes of practice. The British Sociological Association's (2002) *Statement of Ethical Practice*, for example, states that while 'there are serious ethical and legal issues in the use of covert research', such an approach 'may be justified in certain circumstances' (point 31). A number of youth researchers have advanced this type of argument to support their decision to adopt covert roles in their research. Allen (2001), for example, provides a particularly full account of his decision to be less than candid about his role, arguing that his decision to employ a covert observation role alongside his overt interviewing role in his study of the 'foyer industry' was made after assessing the moral consequences that could result from not using one:

> I ... felt my use of covert methods to be justifiable on the 'consequential' ethical grounds that they could uncover issues that were being concealed by foyer managers and, in doing so, generate knowledge that could be used to argue for necessary changes in youth policy and practice. The consequences of not using a covert strategy would have been to risk not uncovering these issues and so perpetuating the status quo. (2001: 473)

Similarly, Richman (2007) defends her decision to adopt a covert role in her work on internet chat rooms on the basis that her research sites were public spaces, and that young people post to bulletin boards largely in order to publicise what they write. For Richman, researching postings in chat rooms was analogous to analysing newspaper cuttings. This specific example and the broader issues it raises about the ethics of certain forms of internet-based research are discussed more fully in Chapter 10.

Other youth researchers are not always as reflexive about the ethical issues raised by their practice. For example, in exploring the relationship between young people's consumption and their lifestyles, Miles (1996) spent ten weeks working as a shop assistant in a sports shop, collecting data covertly. He notes that, as the chain of shops concerned placed particular emphasis on their assistants actively conversing with customers, the chosen location proved to be especially appropriate. He then outlines some of the advantages of assuming this covert role:

> ... it was possible to gain access to the sorts of meanings that were applied to these types of consumer goods. The researcher's role was unknown to customers, and as such it was possible to observe the shop as a site of consumption. In addition, customers were asked various questions, the intent of which was to address the significance of consumption in their lives, most particularly in relation to the training shoes they were considering purchasing ... pre-prepared questions were used as a means of stimulating discussions with customers. (1996: 46)

In some research locations there may also be significant practical limitations on the extent to which a researcher can assume an overt role. For example, as part of their research on tattooing and bodily adornments, Jacobson and Luzatto (2004) spent time 'hanging around' various public spaces frequented by young people, such as beaches, pubs and clubs, to observe how tattoos and piercings were displayed. Similarly, in researching punk lifestyles, Andes (1998) spent nine months as a part-time participant observer primarily in public spaces such as punk concerts and on the streets. From a practical perspective it would clearly be very difficult, if not impossible, to inform all young people frequenting these areas of the presence of a researcher.

Insider versus outsider status

Many youth ethnographers, particularly those who have focussed on young people's cultural groupings, have used their own familiarity with the setting as a 'way in'; a basis on which to secure relatively straight-forward access and establish easy rapport with respondents. Within such studies, the advantages of being an 'insider' are commonly emphasised. This status, it is argued, can facilitate access to particular groups of young people, and enhance the level of trust between researcher and researched. However, in his thoughtful account of the use of 'insider' knowledge in youth cultural studies research, Bennett (2002) engages critically with some of these assumptions. First, he questions whether 'an apparent "knowingness" of particular musical genres and attendant "subcultural" sensibilities' (2002: 190) is sufficient to secure a researcher's acceptance into a particular youth cultural group. As he argues, anyone who has made the transition from group member to academic researcher is likely to have undergone some personal trans-formation as a result. Second, with respect to youth and music research in particular, Bennett suggests that those who identify themselves as both researchers and 'youth cultural practitioners' often assume an authority to speak on behalf of those at the centre of the research; the descriptive authority of the researcher thus becomes 'a one-dimensional voice which echoes the self-assumed "rightness" of the movement which each study seeks to describe' (2002: 457). As others have noted, a particular challenge for the 'insider' is to 'make the familiar strange' (Delamont and Atkinson, 1995). A shared insider status may generate false perceptions of a common outlook, which can affect interactions between researcher and researched, as well as the interpretation of data. Finally, Bennett highlights some of the ethical issues that an insider needs to consider. Despite the ease that the researcher may feel in gaining access to and acceptance within the field, he or she must ensure that the purpose of the study is nonetheless fully explained to those involved.

These warnings about some of the potential problems of an 'insider' identity should not, however, overshadow some of the concomitant advantages. As a consequence of his 'insider' role as an international vol-unteer for a youth reconciliation project in the city of Mostar in Bosnia and Herzegovina, Gillard (2001) initially speculated that responses to him from his co-volunteers would be 'reconciliation-friendly'. However, he argues that the friendships he established with many of the partici-pants over the course of the ethnography made this potential bias less likely. Indeed, he claims that in cases where the interviewee identified him more as a friend than a co-worker, there appeared to be less desire to express 'reconciliation-friendly' opinions:

> Some expressed attitudes that were inimical to the multi-national ethos of the project – which I never heard them express openly in front of oth-ers within the project – stating that they were telling me things they would not tell others, even though they were aware that I was conduct-ing research that might be published. (2001: 79)

Those who enter the research site as outsiders face a different set of chal-lenges, related to perceptions about the difference between their own sta-tus and that of those they are observing. Aune (2006), for example, despite being of a similar age to many of those involved in her study of couples attending an evangelical church, appeared to be defined as an outsider, not necessarily as a result of her 'researcher' role, but by virtue of her single, childless status. This, she claims, hindered her ability to communicate on a shared basis with her (partnered) respondents. In Curtis's (2002) research, his status as an outsider to a group of young drug users had an obvious impact on their behaviour. He notes that many of them would not allow him to observe them injecting drugs, 'often turning their backs with a shameful look' (2002: 304). When he asked them why they acted in this way, they replied that they believed it would be 'disrespectful' to use drugs in front of someone who was carrying out research to try to help drug addicts. Nevertheless, outsiders bring with them a number of important advantages as a result of their status: they are more likely to question taken-for-granted practices and are less likely to become embroiled within community relations and tensions (Raby, 2007). Of course, a very important determinant of 'insider' status in the context of all forms of youth research, not just ethnographic research, is the age (or at least the perceived age) of the researcher, an issue which we discussed at length in Chapter 3.

Relationships with young people

As noted above, an important strength of an ethnographic approach is its ability to track changes over time. Associated with this is the opportunity it offers the researcher to develop relationships with respondents and, often, to establish a greater mutual trust, rapport and understanding than are possible in a one-off interview. Several ethnographers have reflected on the ways in which their relationships with the young people in their study changed over the course of the fieldwork. Alexander (2000), for example, established very close personal ties with many of the young men in her study such that she continued her involvement in the youth club long after her research had ended. Despite this, her initial relationships with them had been difficult. Commenting on those early days, she notes that 'an occasional smile and an even more occasional greeting was the only interaction I had with the members … and I despaired of ever establishing more meaningful contact or coming closer to understanding anything' (2000: 33).

While most youth researchers are generally positive about the capacity of ethnography to facilitate close relationships with young people, it is important not to forget the power imbalances which do remain, even when researchers and participants are close in age and share similar social characteristics. As Stacey (1988) has cogently argued, it is possible that the appearance of greater respect for, and equality with, research subjects in ethnographic research masks deeper and more dangerous forms of exploitation. Moreover, Hollands has noted that while youth ethnographers are often acutely aware of some of the structural inequalities faced by their respondents in the 'real world', 'they have sometimes remained quite blinkered when it comes down to analysing their own position of power and how this might influence both fieldwork relations and their final (re)presentations of their subjects' (2003: 159). Whatever the nature of the relationships established within the field, it remains the case that the researcher is far freer to leave the relationship than the researched, and the research 'product' (however collaborative the research design) is ultimately that of the researcher. Furthermore, within institutional settings, it may be particularly difficult for young people to remove themselves from the ethnographer's gaze – a classroom teacher might grant access, for example, without ensuring that students are happy with this arrangement. Nevertheless, there are many examples of youth researchers who have, on the whole, been sensitive to such power inequalities and who, in some cases, have adopted specific strategies to try to increase the influence of those they are researching, within both the research project and society more generally. Mac an Ghaill (1994), for example, reports how he worked closely with some groups of students in deciding the particular focus of his study, while Hollands (2003) aimed to make the voices of his respondents (working class young men on vocational training schemes) as visible as possible to people within the trade union and labour movements. Chapter 4 considered other ways in which the influence of young people can be increased in youth research.

It is also important to recognise that ethnographic research is a two-way process, and that young people should not be seen as the entirely passive objects of an ethnographer's gaze. Hey, for example, describes what she calls the 'implicit microeconomy of exchange and barter' that developed during her research on girls' friendships, in which 'the young women provided access to their social lives in return for certain tangible goods: my attention; advice; sweet money; access to a warm room; or absence from lessons' (1997: 48). Other researchers have reflected on the ways in which they themselves were observed by the young people in their studies and how, in some respects, they became a particular source of interest. Both Aune (2006) and Alexander (2000) describe, for example, how their own marital status became of great interest to their respondents. In Aune's case, this interest was not unrelated to the topic of her research (attitudes to gender amongst young couples in an evangelical church), and was played out through various matchmaking attempts by church members over the course of her fieldwork. For Alexander, this interest was related more to her particular role and identity as a researcher, to her gender, and to the relatively narrow age gap between herself and her respondents:

> As a young(ish) woman in almost daily contact with a large proportion of the young men in a small and closely knit community, I was bound to be a focus of curiosity ... My marriage became the symbol of all these concerns; a means of analysing, locating and, to an extent, policing me and my relationships within the community. (2000: 37)

More problematic is Pascoe's (2007) account of her research exploring the sexual identities of teenage boys, conducted over the course of 18 months in a suburban high school in California. As we noted in Chapter 3, she claims that as a female researcher she was drawn 'into a set of objectifying and sexualising rituals through which boys constructed their identities and certain school spaces as masculine' (2007: 176), including through lewd comments and verbal insults. She goes on to argue that, as a result, she ended up not just studying the young men's sexual identities but becoming intimately caught up in the very processes through which they were constructed.

Many ethnographies, particularly those conducted in relatively large institutions such as schools, have revealed how perspectives can differ considerably between groups of young people. Mac an Ghaill (1994) distinguishes between five main groups of young men within the school he studied, each with their own distinctive relationship to schooling and masculine identity. Similarly, Nayak's (2003) typology of 'Real Geordies', 'Charver Kids' and 'White Wannabes' explores differences between groups of young men with respect to their class backgrounds, family histories, place, locality and, in particular, attitudes to 'whiteness'. There are important issues here about whose 'side' a researcher takes in conducting and writing up an ethnography, and whose voices are privileged (Devine and Heath, 1999). It is also important to be aware of some of the consequences of how the researcher positions him- or herself within the field. In particular, it is likely that if a researcher chooses to identify with a specific group of young people, and not another, this will have implications both for how he or she is seen by other potential respondents, and the access he or she is able to gain to other peer groups. Kehily (2002), for example, recalls how she developed particularly close relationships (at both the schools in which she conducted fieldwork) with young women between the ages of 14 and 15. Although this was productive with respect to the data collected from these respondents, she suggests that her known association with these groups may have impacted negatively on her ability to become accepted by members of male peer groups in both schools. Similarly, both Morris-Roberts (2004) and Glesne (1989) have described how, by making alliances with certain groups of young people, they automatically distanced themselves from others.

Whilst issues of 'getting on' in the field are critical to ethnographic practice, so are issues associated with 'exiting the field', in terms of both physical removal and emotional disengagement (Brewer, 2000). In relation to ethnographies of young people in particular, some writers have emphasised the increased responsibility of the researcher to think carefully about how they will manage their relationship with respondents once the period of fieldwork comes to an end, recognising the potential vulnerability of some young people in this process. Some ethnographers choose to maintain links, either in the form of friendships or as part of an ongoing research relationship. Gordon and Lahelma (2003), for example, describe how their solution to some of the difficulties of leaving the field was not to make a complete exit, resulting in a series of follow-up interviews with 63 of the 70 young people involved in their original ethnographic study between five and nine years later. In other cases, maintaining links with young people is driven not necessarily by a sense of responsibility for those involved in the research but by a genuine sense of friendship (Skeggs, 1994; Hollands, 2003). This is particularly well illustrated in Alexander's (2000) account of the period after her research with the Asian youth club had formally ended. She reflects that 'for me, largely because of the close personal ties which are woven through the research, there is no sense of completion, no moving away from the fieldwork site, no autonomous reflection. I still attend every club session, and the project office has become my second home' (2000: 51). Although many ethnographers describe the establishment of close bonds with one or more of their respondents – in some cases maintained for a significant period after the end of the research project – Alexander's account is unusually personal. Indeed, she describes the impossibility, as well as the undesirability, of distinguishing between the intellectual project and its more private, emotional dimension: 'the study is about people I care about deeply and with whom I have developed bonds that explode any simple discrete notion of the research relationship' (2000: 49).

(Re)presentation of findings

Reflexive accounts by youth ethnographers outline a number of important issues that influence the way in which ethnographies are written up. First, some researchers have reflected on the potentially vast amount of data that can be generated through an ethnographic approach, and the difficulty of doing justice to such a complex collection of material within a single written account. Gordon et al. also remark on the temptation to include only those accounts that startle and surprise, noting that ethnographies often provide sufficient material to render stories 'in a gripping style of semi-warfare' (2000: 57). However, they explain how, in both their analysis and writing up, they sought to focus on incidents of cooperation as well as on stories of conflict. Second, some researchers have highlighted the potential difficulty of writing up ethnographic research in a format suitable for sponsors (Allen, 2001). Finally, ensuring confidentiality in the writing up of ethnographic accounts can be more difficult than in other approaches (see Chapter 2). Researchers often face a difficult balancing act between the need to give enough information about the site of an ethnography to give contextual life to the data, and the danger of giving too much, which may identify the location of the research. Furthermore, as a result of the small-scale nature of much ethnographic research, considerable care needs to be given to protect the identities of respondents within particular sites.

Perhaps the most fundamental challenge to the way in which ethnographies are written up, however, derives from what has been referred to as the 'crisis of representation' within the cultural field (Brewer, 2000). This describes the disillusionment surrounding the ethnographer's claim to provide a special insight into the 'reality' of a research site by means of 'thick description'. This disillusionment emerged out of postmodern critiques of realist assumptions that an independent reality does exist and that it is possible to represent it accurately within an ethnographic text. However, as Hollands (2003) notes, ethnographic research methods often make it difficult to abandon a naturalistic style and the tendency to invoke a kind of authenticity when reporting findings. He does, nevertheless, outline two concrete ways in which youth ethnographers can both represent a social grouping like youth while also exploring the social relations of fieldwork, thus responding, to some extent, to the postmodern critique. First, he suggests that youth researchers develop forms of representation whereby they make themselves and their actions more visible in the text. Second, he advocates opening up the research project to participants, by having them define issues or placing their accounts alongside researchers' own ethnographic interpretations. As discussed in Chapter 4, some researchers have highlighted some of the practical and theoretical difficulties of implementing such strategies (e.g., Skeggs, 1995), yet others have made concerted efforts to ground their writing within a more dialogic foundation. The following account by Alexander (2000) clearly outlines such an ambition:

> Rather than privileging the myth of ethnographic experience as 'Truth', I have attempted to highlight the interaction of researchers and subjects in the production of a highly situated knowledge. The result is an explicitly partial and personal account of a set of encounters located within a particular space and time – what I have chosen to label 'fiction'. While resisting claims to 'Truth' or 'the real' in this portrait, the aim has not been to abdicate responsibility to the wider context of racialized representation, inequality and violence that frames 'the Asian Gang', but to insist on the implication of research and writing within this framing and the necessary contestation of the mono-dimensional caricatures and too easy solutions on offer. (2000: xv)

Summary

This chapter has outlined some of the main characteristics of an ethnographic approach and some of the advantages it can offer to youth researchers. It has explored some of the ways in which ethnographies have been more widely deployed over recent years – investigating processes of transition and associated structural influences, as well as the construction of particular youth cultural styles. It has also highlighted some key issues which need to be thought through before embarking on an ethnographic study and also at regular points throughout the research: gaining and maintaining access; establishing one's role (whether as an outsider or an insider); and developing relationships with the young people within the research site. Finally, it has discussed some of the issues that have to be considered when writing up ethnographic research and how these are also often bound up with relationships established within the field.

Suggestions for further reading

Best, A. (2000) *Prom Night: Youth, Schools and Popular Culture*, London: Routledge. One of the best ways to learn about ethnography is to read an exemplary study: this is a fascinating and detailed account of the US school prom phenomenon, with much insightful methodological reflection along the way.

Hammersley, M. and Atkinson, P. (1995) *Ethnography: Principles in Practice*, London: Routledge. This is a classic text on the ethnographic method.

Hobbs, D. and May, T. (1993) *Interpreting the Field: Accounts of Ethnography*, Oxford: Oxford University Press. This is a revealing collection of insider accounts of some classic ethnographic studies.

Lurie, A. (1967) *Imaginary Friends*, New York: Owl Publishing. This is a very amusing novel based on Festinger et al's classic (1956) ethnography, *When Prophecy Fails: A Social and Psychological Study of a Modern Group That Predicted the Destruction of the World*, itself almost beyond parody. How *not* to do ethnography!

7 Visual Methods

Introduction

It is hard to ignore the growing recognition of the importance of the visual within contemporary society and, also, the high degree of visual literacy increasingly demanded of young people, as well as of older adults. From the instant availability of images produced by mobile phones and digital cameras, and the ever-increasing array of digital TV channels, through to the ubiquity of webcams, Google Earth images and the placing of advertisements not just on hoardings but on virtually anything that moves, we are constantly bombarded with visual images. This has led to a focus on the visual as a substantive area of enquiry in its own right, as well as recognition of the visual skills of potential research respondents and how these might be tapped through particular research methods. Simultaneously, recent years have witnessed an increasing interest across the social sciences in the spatial analysis of society, and visual methods – particularly the use of photographs, video and mapping techniques – have offered researchers an effective means of exploring such spaces. As Valentine (2004) has argued, space is no longer seen as merely a backdrop for social relations, but has come to be understood as playing an active role in the constitution and reproduction of social identities, while social relations themselves often produce material, symbolic or metaphorical spaces. Visual methods are also thought to fit well with the growing emphasis on the use of participatory research methods in youth research (see Chapter 4), which emphasise young people's position as active social agents who play an important role in shaping the world around them. It is felt by many youth researchers that visual methods have a particular potential to give young people more control over the process of data generation, and to express themselves in a medium with which many appear to be particularly comfortable.

For all of these reasons, visual methods are becoming increasingly widely used within youth research, and this chapter will explore various ways in which they can be deployed effectively in youth studies. After first outlining the wide range of approaches available to youth researchers, the chapter will go on to explore some of the particular advantages offered by an engagement with the visual. It will then consider the extent to which visual methods can produce new knowledge, before discussing some salient practical and ethical issues.

The range of approaches

A wide range of different techniques can be included under the broad umbrella of visual research methods. These can be loosely grouped into three main families: first, those based on the analysis of naturally occurring visual material (such as illustrations in magazines, pictures on websites and advertisements on television); second, those which are produced by researchers (such as photographs of respondents or research settings); and, third, those generated for the purposes of a research project by research participants themselves.

Naturally occurring visual material

There is a vast array of naturally occurring visual imagery readily accessible to youth researchers. Photographs, films, artwork and other illustrations have all been drawn upon by those investigating young people's lives. Some have sought to explore how young men and women are depicted in materials which are aimed at young people but produced by older adults. Jewitt's (1997) research is a good example of this: she analysed a total of 74 images used in a sample of leaflets and posters drawn from sexual health material with the aim of identifying the ways in which masculinity and male sexuality are managed at a visual level. Photographs of young people on government websites have also come under critical analysis. Newman et al. (2006) contrasted the conflict-rich context of schools with the discourse of the student constructed through officially-sanctioned images on the UK's Department for Education and Skills website, in which young people are always happy and work hard, get on well with their peers and teachers, and where conflict is notably absent.

Others have focussed more specifically on images produced by young people themselves for consumption by others (often other young people). Harris (2004) and Leonard (1998) have both analysed the visual representations of young women in fanzines, particularly those produced by 'riot grrrls', members of a punk-inspired feminist network that developed in underground music communities in the USA in the early 1990s and which then spread to the UK and Australia. Harris (2004) argues that, in many of these publications, key ideas are often expressed through pictures rather than text. For example, she points to the juxtaposition of apparently opposing images (such as a collage of 'beautiful' women from the media alongside newspaper clippings about the horrors inflicted on not-so-glamorous women in society) and suggests that this is one way in which young women express the conflicting narratives and double standards to which they feel subject: 'a central issue that is tackled in these spaces is the notion that girls are content to purchase a can-do image primarily constructed around neo-liberal narratives of choice, self-invention and consumption' (2004: 166). Pursuing a similar argument, Leonard argues that the young women who produce the fanzines use images effectively to offer a 'visual critique of beauty standards and expected behaviour' (1998: 105) by juxtaposing material from comics, teen magazines and fashion photography. In this way, she contends, the images help both writers and readers to explore the ways in which femininity is constructed in contemporary society. Boundaries between textual and visual analysis do, however, become blurred in some work in this area. For example, Luzzatto and Jacobson's (2001) analysis of graffiti drawn by Israeli young people in the months following Yitzak Rabin's assassination in 1995 pays attention to both the words that were written and the visual presentation of the material (such as the way in which some of the writing became intertwined).

Youth researchers have also used visual artefacts (rather than images) in a creative way in their research. The fashion choices of young people have provided the focus for some studies, particularly those that have explored processes of consumption (Miles, 1996) and identity construction (Hodkinson, 2002; Nayak, 2003) among specific groups of young people. The visual appearance and layout of rooms has also been explored in several studies. In her research on young women's 'bedroom culture', for example, Lincoln investigated the 'physical and visible arrangement of furniture, technical equipment, beauty products, [and] school books' within bedroom spaces (2004: 97). Similarly, Heath and Cleaver (2004) investigated the layout and material content of communal living areas within households shared by young adults. On the basis of their data, they suggest that there are close links between various spatial and material aspects of shared household living (as evidenced through room layout, for example) and levels of social cohesion among household members.

Some researchers have focussed more specifically on young people's *responses* to visual material, rather than the material itself. Heath's (1999) study of the responses of young men and women to a documentary called 'Men Aren't Working' (shown in the UK in October 1995), for example, analyses both the dominant discourses relating to gender and academic achievement constructed in the documentary itself, and the differing ways in which the programme was interpreted by young viewers. Sparrman's (2006) research with young people in Sweden was motivated by similar concerns. In 2003, the Swedish government provided funding for all upper secondary school children to watch 'Lilya 4-ever', a film that aimed 'to promote a society without a sex trade and characterised by gender equality' (2006: 167). Sparrman took part in the showings of this film and then video-recorded the discussions that followed within the classrooms. On the basis of her data, she sought to explore how notions of exclusion and inclusion were constructed and mediated by the film, and the extent to which visual images can be part of normalising or marginalising ideas within education. Her conclusions strongly suggest that visual images play an important role in the normalisation of certain understandings of masculinity. Indeed, she claims that:

> When schools show this film, they tend to become educational institutions that promote a masculinity embedded in a rhetoric of blame and gender differences as 'normal'. After watching the film, not only does male sexuality seem unchangeable, but the differentiated gender orders of the pupils are further established. (2006: 181)

Visual material produced by the researcher

It is now commonplace for visual material to be produced by researchers as part of a research project. Video recording has offered researchers the opportunity to record actions visually, rather than having to rely on their fieldnotes or audio recordings in isolation. Similarly, photographs have enabled researchers to record a range of different visual material – from tattoos (Jacobson and Luzatto, 2004) through to sites of gap year expeditions (Simpson, 2007). Drawings or mappings have also been deployed quite frequently to record the layout of particular spaces. This is particularly common within educational research, where researchers may want to note the layout of classrooms, the position of different students, or patterns of interaction between students (e.g., Hargreaves, 1967). They have, however, also been used to record other spaces inhabited by young people. In their research on shared households, Heath and Cleaver (2004) produced sketches of the layout of the rooms shared by their respondents, noting aspects such as the position of furniture, details of posters and photographs and even the contents of the alcohol shelf. In all of these cases the analytical emphasis is usually on the speech, action or image which has been recorded rather than on the framing or production of visual images per se (although a researcher may obviously reflect on his or her decision to record certain actions, events and/or images rather than others, for example).

Visual techniques have also been used to stimulate discussion as part of an individual interview or, more commonly, a focus group or group interview. Within this context, the use in interviews of visual material previously produced for the purposes of the research by young people themselves has become increasingly common, and is discussed further in the next section. However, a number of youth researchers have also sought to produce their own images for discussion by respondents. In their research on young people's understandings of 'the political', Marsh et al. (2007) used 17 different photographic images (on very broad political themes) to encourage respondents to talk and to stimulate discussion of their own experiences. The images (of a hostel for the homeless, a protestor and a hospital scene, for example) were passed, one by one, round the group and the young people were asked to discuss what they thought about each one.

Moving images have also been used in similar ways in various research projects. Heath and Cleaver (2004) structured their interviews on shared household living around a series of video clips from popular TV shows that were based on groups of friends living together, such as *This Life* and *Friends*. Clips from recent television programmes were also used by Punch (2002) as part of a project on young people's perceptions of their problems and the coping strategies they used. In her interviews with the 13 to 14 year olds involved in the research, she used three short clips, each of which depicted a problem the young people were trying to deal with (such as an argument between a mother and daughter about a boyfriend, which was shown on the Australian soap opera *Home and Away*). Punch argues that this technique offered a number of advantages: it provided useful concrete examples of problems that could be used to explore other problem-solving strategies and it also helped to stimulate memories about when something similar had happened to respondents or their friends. However, Punch also alludes to various practical impediments to using this kind of technique, including the difficulty of finding appropriate video clips that could stand alone and be understood easily by respondents not familiar with the show, and the time-consuming nature of showing even short clips within an interview. Moreover, there is a danger that the specific content of a clip may close down certain discussion threads, by leading young people to respond in particular ways and not in others.

Visual material produced by young people

Partly as a result of the increasing emphasis on prioritising young people's perspectives and ensuring that their own voices are heard within research, a growing number of studies are making use of visual material produced by respondents themselves as part of a research project. Perhaps the most common technique used by youth researchers is that of photo elicitation, in which respondents are asked to record specific people, places or objects, either on a camera or mobile phone of their own or on a camera supplied by the researchers. Typically, the photographs are then discussed as part of an individual or group interview (e.g., Morrow, 2001; Thomson and Gunter, 2007) and/or used as the basis for some form of written work (e.g., Mizen, 2005), with the analytical emphasis put on the visual data relative to the non-visual data produced by such methods differing between research projects. For example, the photographs produced by the young people involved in Weller's (2007) study of the spaces in which citizenship activities are enacted are used primarily to illustrate the points made by respondents through other channels, such as in interviews. In contrast, Bagnoli (2004) places more emphasis on interrogating visual images in their own right. She describes how, in analysing photographs produced by young people in her study of the identities of young people in contemporary Europe, she explored 'who were the participants, where the photographs were set, and what topics or narratives were being told' (2004: section 6.12). The context of production and the kind of interaction going on between photographers and subjects were also taken into account, as well as the overall style of the photographs.

Less commonly, video diaries have been used as a way of recording individuals' experiences and reflections over a period of time (e.g., Noyes, 2004). They have also formed the basis of more collective enterprises with groups of young people. Back (2005), for example, used 'group video walkabouts' as a way of exploring his respondents' responses to particular spaces in their local area. As noted in Chapter 5, other researchers have also made use of similar types of videoed 'interview walks', in which young people are encouraged to talk about the places through which they are moving, including buildings, landscapes and other visual stimuli. Elsley (2004) led a group expedition in which the young people in her research on responses to public space photographed and then discussed the places they liked and disliked in their local area, whilst Hall et al. (2006) have made similar use of 'walking and talking' to explore young people's understandings of their local area and, in particular, the impact of regeneration projects on the spaces around them. In their project, a respondent would, typically, lead a researcher around the area in which he or she lived, talking about the places they saw and recounting associated life experiences.

Mapping is another method which has been used effectively to explore young people's understandings of space and place, a method which can be used as a stimulus in interviews as well as a data source in its own right. Mapping can take various forms. As part of their quest to uncover the 'spatial imaginings' which informed their respondents' relationship to local geography and mobility, Reay and Lucey (2000) used an 'emotional mapping' exercise. This was intended to help young people articulate how they perceived local spaces and to elicit their understandings of symbolic as well as geographical landscapes. This resulted in them producing various images of 'deprivation, dirt, crime and violence' which they believed characterised the housing estates on which many of them lived. The maps also suggested that those young people living on the estates tended to experience their locality as more restricting and dangerous than peers who lived in other forms of housing. Maps can also be used to explore movements over time. The young people involved in Leonard's (2006) study of mixed Catholic and Protestant areas of Northern Ireland produced maps which charted their movements across this 'shared territory' over a typical week, indicating the areas in which they felt safe and unsafe.

Mapping need not focus only on spatial representation in a geographical sense. Brooks (2005) used friendship maps in her research on the influence of friendship on the higher education choices of a group of A-level students in a sixth form college, whilst concept maps have been used within interviews to offer young people a non-verbal means of expressing themselves. Prosser (2007: 24) argues that this kind of exercise allows respondents to work at their own pace rather than the 'rapid mode expected in semi-structured interviews where pregnant silences are considered out of place'. Pursuing a similar argument, Punch (2002) contends that the spider diagrams she used largely as a brainstorming technique in her work on young people's coping strategies helped to avoid imposing her own categories on respondents. This was employed at both group and individual level:

> In the groups, on a large sheet of blank paper with 'coping strategies' circled in the middle, each young person wrote the different ways in which they dealt with their problems (each suggestion added a leg to the spider diagram). In the individual interview I asked them to create their own spider diagram which indicated all the people who were important to them which led to a discussion about who they were most and least likely to turn to. Thus, these diagrams were used as a visual aid on which to build more information and probe more in-depth. (2002: 53)

Although less commonly used than video diaries, photo elicitation and mapping, drawing-based methods of data generation are also increasingly used by youth researchers. Frost (2003) and Bagnoli (2004), for example, both asked their respondents to draw self-portraits as part of their research. Frost's study (which is discussed in more detail later in this chapter) focussed on young women's understandings of their body, and her choice of method was underpinned by a belief that for some of her respondents drawing their body would be easier than talking about it, at least initially. The self-portraits drawn by the young people in Bagnoli's research constituted part of a wider participatory project and complemented other methods such as diary-writing and interviews, which were intended to explore their identities and how they viewed their own lives. During the first interview, respondents were asked to draw a self-portrait and then to add pictures of important people in their lives. This was then used again in a second interview (several weeks or months later) and the young people were asked whether or not they would represent themselves in the same way. In reflecting on this technique, Bagnoli argues that it helped to break the ice during the initial interview and also made it easier for the young people to communicate sensitive feelings and aspirations.

Gauntlett and Holzwarth (2006) describe other examples of the use of creative methods in researching issues of identity with young people, including asking young people to draw a famous person whom they would like to be, asking young people to design a magazine cover which reflects their identity, and asking young people from different ethnic communities to make collages representing how they see themselves, and how they think others see them. They also describe the use of Lego in research on identities, whereby participants are asked to build models which serve as metaphors for different aspects of their identity: 'it's an alternative way of gathering sociological data, where the expressions are *worked through* (through the process of building in Lego, and then talking about it) rather than just being spontaneously generated (as in interviews or focus groups)' (2006: 86, emphasis in original).

Finally, Thomson and Holland (2005) provide a fascinating account of the use of 'memory books' in the *Inventing Adulthoods* project. Memory books – 'receptacles for memorabilia' – were based on a drawing together of a variety of the methods already outlined in this section, with young people invited to keep a record of their everyday lives through writings, drawings, photographs, newspaper and magazine cuttings, stickers, and other forms of memorabilia such as tickets, love letters, valentine cards, party invitations, song lyrics – even a hair extension! They were designed to explore young people's constructions of self over time via 'a more embodied and visual methodology' than that provided by interviews. These memory books served several functions at once. They were not only sources of documentation in their own right, but were also useful resources for elaboration in interviews, and critical tools for the understanding of changing identities. Thomson and Holland note that 'the memory books have proved to be a rich and provocative resource, which as researchers we feel privileged to access' (Thomson and Holland, 2005: 217).

'Age appropriate' methods?

Visual methods are generally argued by proponents to offer a number of advantages over other methods when researching the lives of young people. Morrow (2001), for example, has suggested that the use of participant-produced photographs can offer an effective alternative to participant observation, enabling young people to choose what *they* want to depict. Inviting young people to produce images via their mobile phones might be particularly effective in this regard, given that there seem to be few contexts in which the utilisation of a mobile phone is regarded as inappropriate by young people. Punch (2002) has also suggested that engaging young people in a range of visual activities (such as photo elicitation and mapping exercises) can be less intimidating than asking them to participate in one-to-one interviews, particularly if the interviewer is unfamiliar to them. Reflecting on her own research, she contends that providing visual activities for respondents to focus on created a relaxed atmosphere and seemed to increase their confidence at taking part in interviews at a later stage of the project. Similarly, Bagnoli's (2004) account of her research on British and Italian young people's identities suggests that the visual methods she used – particularly the self-portraits which respondents were asked to draw – helped most of them feel more comfortable during subsequent interviews. Several researchers have also suggested that offering respondents a variety of different visual methods with which to experiment can increase the flexibility of the research and cater for the differing interests and needs of young people (see, for example, Elsley, 2004). Back's (2005) work – on the ways in which young people negotiate the spaces of inner city London – was conducted through a multimedia ethnography; respondents were able to use a variety of representational strategies to construct their 'landscapes of safety and danger', including photography, art work, mapping activities and videos. Back argues that the multimedia nature of the project allowed participants to find the medium with which they were most comfortable.

Implicit within some of these accounts is an assumption that more conventional research methods, such as one-to-one interviews and questionnaires, are adult-orientated, relying on a high degree of oral or literacy skills and, sometimes, considerable social confidence. In this analysis, it follows that researchers should make more effort to find other ways in which to engage young people in their research projects – and visual methods are often seen as a particularly effective alternative. Nevertheless, as Valentine (1999) cautions, there is a danger that debates about the ethics of adopting different methodologies when working with young people (as well as with children) conceptualise them in opposition to adults, rather than recognising similarities across the age range. Valentine argues further that if (as many authors have suggested) young people are becoming less deferential towards adults, far from needing particular research methods of their own, they can be more questioning about the purpose and outcomes of research than many adults, and can come to 'challenge and invert the research process in complex ways' (1999: 150).

Visual techniques also offer a number of advantages over other methods that are not so intimately related to the age of respondents. First, in the context of her analysis of the images used in health promotion materials with young people, Jewitt (1997) has argued that as we constantly use visual images to interpret our lives, visual methods help to articulate the everyday realities that research based solely on written data may overlook. Second, some visual methods can allow the exploration of particularly sensitive issues that may be difficult for participants to talk about. This is illustrated well by Frost's (2003) work on teenage girls' understandings of their bodies. Frost was keen to compare the views of those for whom body issues (such as anorexia) had been diagnosed with those who had experienced no such diagnoses, and recruited one group of respondents from a school and another from an adolescent psychiatric unit. She describes how, given the potentially emotional nature of her research topic (i.e, body like or dislike), she sought a method that she hoped 'might start a process whereby private, unarticulated feelings which might remain concealed in an interview or group discussion can … find expression' (2003: 126). She eventually decided on the use of self-portraiture. In addition to giving respondents an opportunity to express feelings that may have been difficult to verbalise, she suggests that this method also had an important effect on young women's ability to 'distance' themselves from their bodies:

> The approach through art, and specifically through self-portraiture, also offered girls the potential to distance themselves – even objectify themselves – in a way which seemed to offer a place of retreat in what could be very personal interviews. Rather in the way that writing in the third person allows a more detached engagement, then talking about 'the young woman in the portrait' gave the girls a chance to discuss 'her' appearance, rather than directly their own. (2003: 126)

Third, some youth researchers have used visual methods to achieve a less directive line of questioning. For example, in their work on young people's understanding of and engagement in politics, Marsh et al. (2007) used a variety of visual vignettes to stimulate discussion in their focus groups. The researchers were anxious to avoid imposing their own view of what constitutes 'the political' on respondents and equating non-participation in formal politics with apathy. Thus, respondents were shown a series of photographic images and asked to free-associate, narrating their response to the image in light of their own experiences and priorities. This, the authors contend, minimised the researchers' influence on the young people's responses. They do, however, acknowledge that their choice of visual images for participants to discuss was not neutral. Although they strove to encompass a very broad range of political content (the images were related to one of four themes: socio-economic inequality; political inclusion and exclusion; identity; and citizenship and public services), some researcher-generated definitions of 'the political' were inevitably embedded within them.

Producing new knowledge?

As with many types of data, visual material can be analysed at a number of different levels. First, it is important to consider the distinction between realist and constructivist approaches to the visual. While researchers taking a realist approach will typically accept photographs, video recordings and some other types of visual data as evidence of real world events, places and objects, those whose work is grounded within a constructivist perspective will usually place more emphasis on the context in which the image was created and in which it is viewed, as well as the power relations involved in its production. Second, within a broadly constructivist approach, visual material can be analysed from the producer's perspective, from the reader's or viewer's perspective and/or in terms of the image itself (Jewitt, 1997). Within both realist and constructivist approaches, however, an important issue for researchers to consider is whether employing visual techniques can generate new forms of knowledge.

Visual images have often been used to illustrate issues raised primarily through other research methods, such as interviews. Photographs, in particular, are frequently deployed in this way. Over recent years, however, researchers have emphasised the new forms of knowledge that can be generated by such methods, and which can complement, extend or even challenge our understandings of young people's lives as gained through more conventional means. It is argued that visual methods can help to challenge researchers' assumptions and allow young people to have greater control over the research process. This is articulated well by Bolton et al. (2001) with respect to their project on young people's employment:

> The decision to photograph a jumble of chairs taken by a part-time glass collector and general dogsbody at a social club conveys very clearly the reality of the tasks to be carried out as part of the cleaning regime at the club ... [The pictures] are representations of their work culture, rather than an external researcher/photographer's representation about their culture. (2001: 512, italics in original)

Similarly, in his study of young Londoners' sense of belonging and place, Back (2005) describes how some of the images produced by respondents (through a variety of different technologies) were initially surprising to the research team but, as the young people narrated them, they revealed considerable subtleties within the everyday spatial maps they produced. For example, although the Isle of Dogs (one of the two research sites) showed evidence of significant levels of racism, Back argues that the young Bengalis in the study had developed a range of fairly sophisticated strategies to convert 'this ostensibly white racist place into a space that was both navigable and habitable' (2005: 39). This involved constructing a series of non-threatening places (such as libraries or youth clubs) across which safe passage could be negotiated.

Visual methods can also allow researchers to explore aspects of young people's lives that may remain uncovered by more conventional research methods. This can work at two levels. First, images can allow respondents to show parts of their lives that are hard to articulate in words (perhaps for reasons of discomfort, oversight, embarrassment, or assuming they will not be of interest to the researcher), and so are unlikely to be captured by an interview, focus group or questionnaire. This is illustrated well in Mizen's (2005) research on the employment practices of young people still in full-time education. He argues that the photographs his respondents took of their workplaces brought to the surface tensions in their relations with employers that had only been hinted at in the interviews. For example, he notes that some photographs 'showed employers made uncertain, surprised even, by the attention of their young employees … the tables turned momentarily as [the young person] took control, each looks back with a degree of obvious discomfort' (2005: 137). Second, certain visual methods can provide access to more private spaces that are usually off-limits to the researcher. As part of their research on young adults living in shared households, for example, Heath and Cleaver (2004) gave disposable cameras to a sub-sample of respondents and asked them to take photographs of what they believed to be the significant and meaningful aspects of living in a shared house. While some of the images merely confirmed what had already been said in the household and individual interviews, other photographs (such as those of an extensive row of shirts hanging up to dry in a bedroom, multiple cereal packets in a kitchen cupboard, and children's foam letters stuck on a bathroom mirror by way of a household message board) provided access to more private spaces within the household and, as a result, also provided glimpses of experiences of shared living that were not always articulated in interviews.

Visual methods can also enable researchers to identify differences between messages given verbally and those transmitted by images. Jewitt's (1997) study of the pictures used in sexual health promotion material aimed at young people provides a good example of this. Her analysis of official leaflets and posters suggests that they present a stereotyped image of male and female sexuality and are informed by conventional concepts of gender. For example, she argues that the physical aspects of sex are represented as male concerns while sexual safety and the emotional aspects of sex are depicted as female concerns. She goes on to contend that the images used in this material 'present male sexuality and masculinity in ways that would be unacceptable in words to young men and sexual health professionals' (section 5.6). In this way, she identifies an important mismatch between the messages conveyed to young people orally and through visual means.

Research has also highlighted the ways in which visual images can be interpreted very differently between individuals and groups. Marsh et al's (2007) use of visual vignettes to explore understandings of 'the political' highlights the impact of personal experience on how an image is viewed. For example, they describe how an image of Oldham (a town in the north west of England) was discussed by most of the focus groups as an image of a 'race riot'. However, there was significant disparity between the groups in the discussion that followed: while some white respondents then focused on the inadequate police response to the disturbances, South Asian group members were more likely to talk about underlying structural problems and to see the 'rioters' as merely taking action to protect their homes and communities.

Practical issues

Alongside these various insights offered by visual methods, it is important to recognise some of the potential limitations. These have been discussed most explicitly with reference to the use of photography. At a very practical level, Morrow (2001) recounts some of the problems encountered in her research when she asked young people to take photographs of places that were important to them. These included: photos that did not come out, respondents forgetting to take their camera on the designated group trips to take photographs, and friends 'borrowing' each other's cameras to take photos (as a result of this kind of activity, one young person ended up with a lot of photographs of the school roof!). Morrow also acknowledges that the time of year in which the research was conducted had a significant impact on the results: the places young people visited to take their photos in the winter term when the weather was bad were very different from those visited during the less inclement weather of the summer term.

Finney and Rishbeth (2006) also emphasise the importance, when analysing images produced by respondents, of recognising the cultural conventions of photography, such as taking photographs of friends, arranging photographs of oneself in prestigious locations, and taking photographs of panoramic views. They argue that while video or photographic diaries are becoming more commonly used across the social sciences, it is rare for participants to have the technical skills to 'move beyond the expression of simple subject matter to communicate their individual perspectives' (2006: 31). In their research, which investigated refugees' perceptions and experiences of urban public open spaces in the UK, they attempted to disrupt some of these cultural conventions and practical limitations by varying the types of photos they asked respondents to take and providing photographic training.

Ethical issues

In common with all the approaches discussed in this book, visual methods bring with them their own set of ethical issues. In particular, the use of photographic and video images of young people (whether generated by researchers or respondents) can often make it very difficult to ensure anonymity. While most youth researchers will give their respondents pseudonyms when writing or speaking about them, and will also often change details of locations or events in order to protect their identities further, these options are not available to those using photographs, videos, films or personal artefacts. Some researchers have responded to this problem by concealing the eyes or faces of young people in any output from a project (e.g., Weller, 2007), but such examples are relatively rare, and not unproblematic. Williams et al. (2006), for example, have argued that such a practice reduces the capacity of researchers to interpret what is going on in a given setting, not least because facial expressions may be central to analysis, while it also takes away the identity of research participants in a particularly profound and graphic way. In many texts based on photographic research, the identity of some respondents, despite the blurring of faces, may still be clear. It is also the case that it may be difficult to track down all those captured on film or in photographs to seek their consent – for example, when video footage of public spaces has been taken by respondents or researchers as part of a research project or when young people are showing a researcher old family photos.

A second set of ethical dilemmas relates to how visual material (again, particularly photographs, videos and film) is produced and displayed, and whether when respondents agree to be filmed at the beginning of a project they can really be sufficiently 'informed' about how they will be represented and how others will interpret this. Some researchers have tried to resolve this issue by showing respondents unedited video footage and photographic material and allowing them to become involved in the processes of editing and production. Whether or not this participatory approach is taken, Pink argues that all researchers employing visual methods should, at the very least, attempt to 'anticipate how one's representations will be interpreted by a range of other individual, institutional, political and moral subjectivities' (2001: 154).

In engaging with ethical debates and recognising some of the problems surrounding the protection of anonymity, many youth researchers have nonetheless emphasised some of the benefits that can accrue to the young people who are involved in visually-based research. Most commonly, these are voiced in terms of the shift in the control of the research agenda away from the researcher and towards the respondent. This is particularly evident in projects where young people have produced images themselves, through photographs, videos, artwork and mapping.

In his work on the employment of school-age young people in England and Wales, Mizen (2005: 126) notes that 'decisions about what and what not to record, of sampling and content, perspective and framing, all crucial considerations in the design and process of (visual) research' were left to the sensibilities of respondents. Similarly, Back (2005) describes how the dialogical approach that characterised the period of data collection in his study also informed subsequent stages of the research process:

> It was an attempt to redesign the relationship between the observer and the observed. We gave young people cameras, audio diaries and video cameras to grind their own lens to look at and speak about the world through which they moved … In the writing and analysis of this work there is both a commitment to hold — however unevenly — to the spirit of dialogue while at the same time offering critical insights and reflections on what was offered in the representations made by the young people themselves. (2005: 21)

Some researchers argue that visual vignettes – even when produced by the researcher rather than respondents – also have the power to shift the research agenda in a similar direction. Marsh et al. (2007), for example, suggest that the way in which they used photographic images in their research on political understandings allowed them to avoid imposing their own definition on their respondents. They also reflect on the way in which the images that were introduced to the young people subsequently affected how they were understood. They describe how, in a pilot stage of the project, they realised that when they held up the images to respondents, or projected them onto a screen, attention was focussed on the researchers, as if they were teachers or experts. As a result of this experience, they decided to use two identical sets of images and pass each photograph, one at a time, around the group. They conclude that being able to handle the photos was significant as they became a tool: 'by using the image as evidence to reinforce their argument or speculate about the image, the participant was freer to develop his or her interpretation using the image without being influenced by the researcher' (2007: 77).

It is also argued that visual methods can offer some groups of marginalised young people an opportunity for self-expression that would not otherwise be available. Finney and Rishbeth (2006) contend that as a result of multiple factors of mainstream disengagement – social, linguistic, spatial and educational – the young asylum seekers involved in their research were limited in their ability to speak English and distrustful of answering questions from strangers; giving them cameras and asking them to express themselves visually to some extent circumvented these barriers. It is also possible that providing the opportunity for respondents to gain new skills (in this case, through a 12 week photographic course that was an integral part of the research project) can increase reciprocity between researcher and researched. Back (2005) pursues a related argument, suggesting that the young people in his project were empowered, at least temporarily, by the opportunity to take photographs of places they considered dangerous. He notes that while many of the photos taken by respondents carried a history of dread and feeling threatened in these particular places, 'the act of photographic representation is itself an assertion of presence ... the "observational act" – controlled and conducted by the young person herself – becomes an assertion of belonging in an otherwise hostile place' (2005: 36). Thus, while youth researchers are certainly cognisant of the ethical concerns specific to visual research, they have also highlighted its potential for enhancing ethical practice.

Summary

In this chapter we have introduced readers to a range of different ways in which youth researchers can engage with visual research methods. We have identified three broad approaches – those based on the analysis of naturally occurring visual material, those which are produced by researchers, and those generated for the purposes of a research project by young people themselves – and have considered the strengths and weaknesses of these approaches as well as a range of practical and ethical issues associated with the use of visual methods. It is clear that visual methods are becoming increasingly popular research tools for youth researchers, not least as a generation of technologically capable young people themselves become social researchers. We further consider the use of new information and communication technologies in Chapter 10, when we explore the use of the internet for youth research.

Suggestions for further reading

Knowles, C. and Sweetman, P. (2004) *Picturing the Social Landscape: Visual Methods and the Sociological Imagination,* London, Routledge. This is an interesting edited collection bringing together a range of contributions from researchers working with visual methods.

Pink, S. (2001) *Doing Visual Ethnography: Images, Media and Representation in Research,* London, Sage. This is a very thorough introduction to a range of issues with which researchers need to engage when considering the use of visual methods in their research.

Prosser, J. (1998) *Image-based Research: A Resource for Qualitative Researchers,* London: Routledge. This is another edited collection providing insights into the use of visual methods by researchers from a range of backgrounds.

8 Surveys

Introduction

Notwithstanding the many benefits to be gained from undertaking in-depth, qualitative studies of young peoples' lives through the use of methods such as interviews, observation and visual approaches, it is often useful to gain some measure of the bigger picture. This is important for a number of reasons, including our general understanding of trends and patterns across different cohorts of young people, or between young people from different social groups and backgrounds, as well as for gathering evidence on which to base policies that directly impact on young people's lives. In order to gain this bigger picture, many researchers undertake social surveys, a method that Muijs (2004: 34) describes as 'probably the most popular (quantitative) research design in the social sciences'.

It is often argued that large scale quantitative investigations have traditionally rendered younger people invisible due to the predominant focus of surveys on households or family groupings (Scott, 2000), with adults invariably invited to respond on behalf of younger household members. However, in response to the increased emphasis within social research more generally on recognising young people as social actors (see Chapter 4), survey methodology has developed in a range of ways. For example, young people are increasingly asked to respond directly to surveys, in place of proxy-responses provided by their parents and carers. In addition, it is now commonplace to seek young people's formal consent for participation in survey research, to ask for their feedback during the instrument development stages of the process (de Leeuw et al., 2002), and to provide them with feedback of the research results (see for example Cleaver et al., 2005a; Nelson, 2006).

There is a wealth of literature available on the various technical aspects of the process of undertaking survey-based research: from face to face computer-assisted or telephone interview-based surveys to national and international self-completion surveys; from paper-based to online surveys; from quantitatively-measured observation of behaviour to content analysis (see for example de Vaus, 2002, 2007a, 2007b and 2007c; Groves et al., 2004; Kaplan, 2004; Rea and Parker, 2005; Sapsford, 2006). This literature explores the pros and cons associated with different types of surveys and the processes involved in developing theoretical frameworks and research questions; the challenges of selecting a sample and coping with non-response; the creation of questions and items; the process of piloting, pre-testing and gathering main survey data; undertaking coding and data entry; conducting data analysis using computer software; and reporting on statistical findings. This general literature will be of use to anyone considering undertaking survey research with young people.

What this more general literature does not do is to focus on some of the issues that are specific to survey research with young people. Borgers et al. (2000) concur, claiming that methodological knowledge on conducting surveys with younger respondents is scarce. While some advances in this knowledge base have taken place since this claim was initially made, much of it centres around addressing very specific technical issues, and is often focused on younger children rather than the older age group we are concerned with in this book. Some examples include information on young people's use of rating scales (Weng and Cheng, 2000); children's understanding of response options (Borgers et al., 2003); young people's understanding of negatively phrased items (Twist et al., 2004); and cultural differences in young people's responses to questions (Walker, 2006). De Leeuw et al. (2002) provide one of the most comprehensive accounts of the issues surrounding survey design for younger respondents. Whilst providing a wide ranging account of the evidence that can assist in the better production of survey instruments for children and young people, it does not consider some of the wider operational issues with regard to undertaking surveys with this age group.

This chapter therefore sets out to provide a wide-ranging discussion of six key questions relevant to the undertaking of surveys specifically with young people. Each of these questions takes as its focus some of the logistical, ethical and theoretical issues which arise specifically when surveying young people. Taken together with other more generic insights on the design and administration of surveys, an exploration of these questions should help readers wishing to undertake surveys with young people to adapt existing methods and processes. The key questions relate to: the choice of survey design; the framing of questions; locating respondents; maximising response rates; issues of informed consent; and the potential role of information and communications technology (ICT). Before addressing these questions, we outline what we mean by survey research, and why it is useful for the study of young people's lives.

What is survey research?

Surveys are widely used and accepted as research tools by both researchers and the general public. In essence, surveys are concerned with researching the views, attitudes and behaviours of a portion of the population (a sample) in order to extrapolate from the sample to the wider population. The constitution of the research sample is therefore key to the validity of survey research; ultimately a sample needs to be representative of the group about which claims are made, and there is a vast literature on how one might go about trying to ensure this. De Vaus (2002), for example, provides clear and useful guidance on sample selection, noting the importance of clearly defining the population from which the sample is to be drawn:

> For example, if we wanted to obtain a sample of university students, we would need to define the population of university students. Do we mean students from all universities or just one? Are we interested in universities in one country or a number of countries? Does it consist of current students only? ... Do we mean full-time students only? ... Once we had specified the population we would obtain a list of all population members. From this list we would use one of a number of sampling methods to select a representative sample of students. (2002: 70)

Most people are likely to have experienced taking part in some form of survey at some point in their lives, often in the guise of market research, and will almost certainly have read or heard about survey research through reports on the television and radio, in newspapers or the internet. Surveys are also widely used in the evaluation of government services and policies. As Rea and Parker (2005: 3) state, surveys are particularly accepted in democracies as they are 'perceived as a reflection of the attitudes, preferences and opinions of the very people from whom society's policy makers derive their mandate'. As we noted in Chapter 4, young people are no longer excluded from this evidence-based policy process. In order to construct relevant and useful policies for young people, governments are increasingly asking them about their attitudes and opinions and are then making the data available to researchers for further analysis (see Chapter 9).

There is also some evidence that young people themselves like surveys as a method of collecting their views. Stafford et al. (2003) talked to 200 children and young people between the ages of 9 and 16 about their views on a range of research and consultation methodologies. They found that young people viewed questionnaires and surveys positively for a number of reasons: self-completion questionnaires provided a way of taking part in research for those young people who might not speak out in interviews; they are confidential and anonymous (not everyone wants others to know what they think); and they are easy and convenient. Conversely, young people also stated that, when badly done, question-naires can be boring and inaccessible in style and language and that the answers given may be dishonest or simply what the young person feels they 'should' say. There are, then, many pros and cons associated with undertaking surveys with young people. The following discussion begins to address some of these in more detail by considering a number of key questions.

Capturing change over time or a snapshot in time?

There are a number of different strategies available to researchers wishing to carry out survey-based research, including whether to use a cross-sectional or a longitudinal research design. A cross-sectional design can be compared to a photographic snapshot, where data are collected at a single point in time, whilst a longitudinal design can be compared to the production of a series of snapshots, based on the use of repeat surveys at different points in time. For many purposes, a one-off cross-sectional design is perfectly adequate to meet the requirements of a particular researchproject. Cross-sectional surveys are also far less costly to administer than longitudinal surveys, both in terms of time and money. Where both might be in scarce supply, a researcher might have little choice but to use a cross-sectional research design. In practice, the majority of surveys are based on cross-sectional design.

There are three main types of longitudinal survey design. The first of these, the trend study, is based on a repeated cross-sectional design; in other words, the same questions are asked at different points in time, but each time with a different sample. The Young People's Social Attitudes Survey is a good example of a trend survey, providing invaluable data on how the attitudes of young people change over time. The second type of longitudinal survey design, the cohort study, is based on the tracking over time of a group of people who are united by their common age. A cohort may be tracked from birth, as in studies like the 1970 British Cohort Study (BCS70) which has followed a sample of all young people born in that year; from a particular point in their school-ing, as in studies like the Longitudinal Study of Young People in England, which is tracking a cohort consisting of a sample of all English school children who were in Year 9 in 2004; or from the point of first leaving school, as in studies like the Youth Cohort Study, which since the mid-1980s has tracked samples of successive cohorts of school leavers up until the age of 21. Cohort studies are particularly effective for exploring generational change, through, for example, comparing the experiences at age 16 of young people born in 1958 (the cohort included in the National

Child Development Study) and those born in 1970 (see, for example, Bynner et al., 2002). The third type of longitudinal design is the panel study, which asks questions of the same sample at different points in time. Unlike cohort studies, the sample will consist of individuals from a diverse range of ages. A good example of a youth orientated panel study is the British Youth Panel of the British Household Panel Survey (BHPS), which focuses on children aged 11 to 15 who are living in BHPS sample households. (Each of the surveys referred to above are described in greater detail in Chapter 9.)

As these examples suggest, there are particular benefits to be gained from using longitudinal methods to study young people's lives. Not only do they have the potential to provide important evidence of change over time, but in doing so they can feed into wider theoretical debates around the meaning and experience of young people as they move through the transitions from childhood to youth and from youth to adulthood. For this reason, there is a long tradition of longitudinal surveys being used in youth transitions research. Smith and McVie (2003), for example, discuss how the Edinburgh Study of Youth Transitions and Crime, based on a single cohort of around 4,000 young people who started secondary school in Edinburgh in the autumn of 1998, chose to adopt a longitudinal methodology in order to meet broad theoretical debates around how young people make sense of crime and the processes leading to involvement in crime as they undergo their transition to adulthood. While most of the examples provided so far are of very high profile, well-funded national surveys, it is equally possible to conduct much more modest longitudinal surveys of young people's lives, based on smaller, local samples (albeit bearing in mind that the type of analysis will necessitate a sample of a certain size) and rather more modest budgets. It is also important to note that respondents only need be re-contacted once to make a study longitudinal in nature; they do not need to be revisited with the same frequency as some of the examples provided above.

What are the right questions and how should they be asked?

One of the reasons why young people sometimes find surveys difficult and boring to take part in is because they may not be designed appropriately for the age group being targeted. Barker and Weller (2003) argue that the format of surveys is generally not renowned for being user-friendly to younger respondents. The choice of an interview-based or self-administered survey may be critical here; in the case of the former, an interviewer is on hand to read out the questions or guide a young person through a questionnaire, whilst in the case of the latter they are expected to navigate the questionnaire alone. When designing research instruments for young people, particularly those which are self-administered, it is therefore necessary to make sure not only that the layout and type of questions chosen are appropriate, but also that the language which is used relates to the target population's stage of cognitive development. As de Leeuw et al. (2002: 13) note, 'the wording of a question and the syntax are not only of importance for technical reading capacity (vocabulary, reading, decoding) but are of extreme importance for reading comprehension and interpretation as well'.

With this in mind, Borgers et al. (2000) provide a comprehensive overview of the types of questionnaires and questions that may be appropriate to use with different age groups up to the age of 16, when it is believed that young people are more or less cognitively able to take part in 'adult-level' surveys. Briefly, this includes a recognition that from 4 to 7 years children have limited language skills and are still very literal, with short attention spans. Consequently, any questionnaires used should be simple, short and clear. From 8 to 11 years, language and reading skills and the ability to distinguish between different points of view develop. At this stage, self-administered questionnaires become possible, although literacy skills are still developing. Questionnaires and specific questions designed for this age group therefore need to be simple, attractive and focused. Finally, between 12 to 16 years cognitive functioning becomes well developed (including formal thinking, negations and logic). Borgers et al. (2000) argue that standardised questionnaires similar to those designed for adults can be used with this age group, but that language should be appropriate and questionnaires should avoid ambiguity. Whilst this overview might be useful in terms of providing general guidance, it is nonetheless important to remember that young people develop at different rates and that young people of the same age may well respond very differently to a questionnaire supposedly targeted at their age group.

An example of the need to exercise caution in writing questions for young people is evidenced in the growing literature on the problems associated with 'negatively phrased' questionnaire survey items, for example asking respondents to agree or disagree with a statement such as 'I don't enjoy sports lessons at school'. Contrary to the general guidance on writing adult surveys, which commonly argues that a balance of positively and negatively phrased items in questionnaires can help to reduce response bias, evidence from research with young people suggests that they can find it difficult to indicate agreement by disagreeing with a negative statement or conversely to indicate disagreement by agreeing with a negative statement (Benson and Hocevar, 1985; Borgers et al., 2000 and see also Twist et al., 2004). In piloting a questionnaire which was to be used in the evaluation of younger adult users of Social Services provision, for example, it was noted by the researchers that some questions were designed as negatively phrased statements and these were sometimes interpreted incorrectly, by people with all levels of cognitive functioning. Service users would go to great lengths to discuss how they thought the statement was not a problem and then tick one of the agree boxes, indicating that there is a problem. It seems that negatively phrased statements may over-report problems in certain areas of services. (Personal Social Services Research Unit, 2006: 2)

If such questions are simply too difficult to understand, then this might negate any benefit they might bring to a survey, as well as potentially skewing results.

The best way to address the utility and appropriateness of question wording and format is to use one or more of a series of quality assurance procedures, which include expert review, cognitive interviewing and piloting, each of which we now consider. First, before questionnaires are piloted on a sample of young people, they can be subjected to expert review. By this, it is meant that those working with, and researching, young people review question items and suggest alternative language or phrasing options. Before piloting its research instruments for the International Civic and Citizenship Education Study (ICCS), for example, the International Association for the Advancement of Educational Achievement placed potential questions under expert scrutiny by international academics in the field and by the study's National Research Coordinators (an individual nominated by each participating country to coordinate and administer the research project at the national level) (International Association for the Advancement of Educational Achievement, 2007). This process allowed for the inclusion, exclusion and modification of specific items, drawing on the expert knowledge of those in the field. However, one might quite reasonably argue that the real experts on how a questionnaire will be received by young people are young people themselves, and that expert review procedures should therefore accord equal if not greater weight to the views of young people, which is possible with the next two quality assurance techniques (see Chapter 4 for a discussion of the potential involvement of young people in the early stages of the research process).

Cognitive interviewing is another increasingly common component of the question development stage of survey research, and a method which grew out of a systematic collaboration between cognitive scientists and survey researchers in the 1980s (Willis, 2004). As a variant of the in-depth qualitative interview, all of the rules of good qualitative interviewing discussed in Chapter 5 still apply. The key difference is the specific focus of the cognitive interview, which is concerned with respondents' thought processes when answering a survey question. Cognitive interviews are usually conducted on a one-to-one basis using a structured questionnaire and 'think aloud' methods, which consist of asking respondents to voice their thoughts while reading a particular piece of text. They have been used in a range of research with younger respondents, including studies of young people's understanding of text in the broadest sense, such as reading stories (see, for example, Sainsbury, 2003). They therefore provide a tried and tested method of investigating young people's understandings of what they read, including research questions and items.

During the cognitive interview it is necessary to train respondents to 'think aloud', as this is not something that they would normally do. One way of doing this is to play a brief recording of someone thinking aloud, to demonstrate the process, and then let the respondent practice with a sample question. Literature on cognitive interviewing also often suggests trying out an exercise in thinking aloud. One such exercise developed by Mingay to train adults and reported by Willis (1994), for example, asks respondents to 'try to visualise the place where you live, and think about how many windows there are in that place. As you count up the windows, tell me what you are seeing and thinking about' (Willis, 1994: 7). However, adapting such an exercise for young people may not be particularly beneficial. It has been noted that many young people can take the wording of questions very literally. For example, Scott et al. (1995) tell of how in the British Youth Panel survey (discussed further in Chapter 9) they wished respondents to answer as if on behalf of members of their own age group, using the phrase 'people of my own age' to indicate this. However, the pilot study showed that when presented with this option, some of the respondents tried to second guess the age of the interviewer, with the intention of answering the question on behalf of people of the interviewer's own age! Using abstract examples to help young people to understand the techniques of cognitive interviewing may, then, only confuse them about the task that lies ahead. As Presser et al. argue

> although there is now general agreement about the value of cognitive interviewing, no consensus has emerged about best practices, such as whether (or when) to use 'think-alouds' versus probes, whether to employ concurrent or retrospective reporting and how to analyse and evaluate results. In part this is due to the paucity of methodological research examining these issues, but it is also due to a lack of attention to the theoretical foundation for applying cognitive interviews to survey pre-testing. (2004: 113)

Nevertheless, a comprehensive discussion of cognitive interviewing and its relevance and usability for young people at various stages of cognitive development is provided by de Leeuw et al. (2002), who also discuss ideas as to how these methods can be optimised when used with young people.

A third quality control procedure in the development of question-naires is the careful piloting or pre-testing of research instruments with young people to gauge their reactions and to make any changes which might be deemed necessary. This is central to producing a research tool that will not only fulfil the aims of the research, but which is also user friendly. However, there is a surprisingly small literature on survey piloting of any kind, let alone more specifically on piloting inter-views with young people. As Presser et al. state:

> An examination of survey pre-testing reveals a paradox. On the one hand, pre-testing is the only way to evaluate in advance whether a questionnaire causes problems for interviewers or respondents. Consequently, both elementary textbooks and experienced researchers declare pre-testing indispensable. On the other hand, most textbooks offer minimal, if any guidance about pre-testing methods and pub-lished survey reports usually provide no information about whether questionnaires were pre-tested and, if so, how and with what results. (2004: 109)

De Leeuw et al. (2002: 26) concur with these observations, stating that 'there are few examples of systematic observation during pilot testing. Researchers mainly suffice with noting down the time it takes to fill in a test or questionnaire so they have data to better plan the major field-work'. They go on to provide a clear example of the benefits of pilot sur-veys, citing a survey of 15 to 16 year olds which used systematic observation during its pilot phase, and was subsequently able to adapt its methodology to suit the needs of its respondents. In the study which they cite, Helweg-Larsen and Larsen (2002) observed both mainstream students and students with special educational needs while they under-took a pilot version of a Danish health survey. During this process, it became apparent that students with special needs, along with a number of mainstream students, were experiencing problems. Based on this observation, the researchers adapted their data collection methods to use Audio-CASI (Computer Assisted Self-Interviewing) technology, a method discussed later in this chapter, in the main phase of the study.

Where can young people be found?

Having considered questions relating to overall research design and the creation of young-person friendly questionnaires, this section discusses finding and accessing potential sample members. As we have noted in previous chapters, educational establishments provide one of the key sites used by youth researchers from across a range of disciplines and traditions for gaining access to young people. This is particularly the case in relation to the conduct of large scale surveys where it is deemed important to capture large representative samples of young people under the age of 18. Administering questionnaires in schools, during the school day, means that a large number of young people can be located in the same place at the same time. This is a major practical advantage but, as we noted in both Chapters 2 and 3, youth researchers should be wary of viewing youth-orientated institutions such as schools as easy targets for seeking access to large age-stratified samples, especially in cases where the research topic may be of little or no relevance to the institutional setting in which the research is conducted. It should also be noted that the target population of a sample contacted through schools will necessarily be partial due to the fact that it does not include *all* young people of compulsory school age, including those who are home educated, or are in alternative provision, or for whatever reason are not on a school roll.

In light of this widespread reliance on schools for the gaining of large samples, it is noteworthy that a common discussion topic amongst those regularly commissioning and undertaking surveys in the UK is the perceived steady decline in the response rates of schools in recent years. In March 2005, the then Department for Education and Skills (DfES) commissioned research into the factors underlying the increasing difficulties that researchers face in achieving satisfactory response rates when attempting to conduct surveys in schools (Sturgis et al., 2005). This stemmed from a failure in 2003 to meet the benchmark response rate requirements for the reporting of England's results in two large and high profile international studies, the *Trends in International Mathematics and Science Study* (TIMSS) and the *Programme for International Student Assessment* (PISA). The research revealed that responses to school surveys in the UK have declined by approximately 2 per cent per annum between 1995 and 2004. The reasons for this decline were found to include the excessive number of requests received by schools to participate in research; a lack of time alongside excess workload; competing administrative and inspection requirements; a lack of relevance or benefit to the school; a lack of feedback from previous survey participation; and the information requested being already available elsewhere. Approaching a sample of young people through the school system may therefore no longer guarantee a high response rate.

If surveys with young people either cannot be undertaken or are unsuitable for administering in school settings, then it is likely that potential respondents will be approached in their homes. One of the key issues raised in the literature about home-based surveys is a lack of visibility and certainty about the involvement of younger respondents. Barker and Weller (2003), for example, found that when talking after the event to children who had purportedly taken part in a survey, it became clear that in some cases survey instruments had been completed by their parents on their behalf. However, this problem tends only to arise where surveys involve paper-based or online self-completion questionnaires. With this in mind, the most reliable method when surveying young people outside the school setting is to conduct face-to-face interviews.

However, paralleling the growing difficulties of gaining school-based samples, recruiting a home-based sample of young people may also be becoming increasingly difficult. While there is no specific literature on this issue with regard to young people, Sturgis et al. (2005) provide a good overview of the reasons why response rates to more general population home-based surveys are in decline. In particular they highlight the fact that it is now more difficult to find people at home and that, once contacted, it has become more difficult to persuade people to take part in interview surveys. This decline in cooperation has been linked to long term social trends such as social atomisation, increasing personal contact from a range of research organisations (social survey, market research and direct marketing organisations), and a general decline in people's willingness to participate for the greater good rather than for individual gain (Groves and Couper, 1998). Contacting potential respondents via internet-based surveys, and in particular via links from websites which they trust and use regularly, might then provide a more reliable method for achieving acceptable response rates. These and related issues are considered further in Chapter 10.

Will young people respond?

How can those administering surveys ensure that the maximum possible number of young people take part? This is a pertinent question in light of evidence outlined above on the increasing difficulties associated with gaining a research sample. When considering how to maximise survey responses the controversial issue of incentives, which we discussed in Chapter 2, often arises. In common with researchers working in other methodological traditions, there is now growing acceptance in the survey research community that, in order to generate a good response rate, some form of incentive may be necessary. Reasons for this trend are often connected to a range of social shifts that have taken place in recent years, including a significant decline in social and civic participation, but may also be associated with the sheer volume of unsolicited mail and telephone calls that have, for example, resulted in the growth of post- and phone-blocking technologies. In a discussion of research on the use of incentives in adult surveys, Ryu et al. (2005) found that both monetary and non-monetary rewards increase overall response rates, with the difference in response rates becoming even greater when the burden of the interview is increased. Their review of existing evidence suggests that non-monetary incentives are less effective than monetary ones and pre-paid incentives are more effective than deferred rewards. This study also sounds a note of caution, as little research has yet been done to address whether incentives affect sample composition by drawing on respondents with certain characteristics (i.e., those in greater need of whichever incentive is offered) or affect the reporting of certain opinions.

While ensuring a good level of initial participation is clearly important in a one-off cross-sectional study, recruitment and retention issues take on even greater significance in longitudinal studies with young people. In such circumstances, where respondent attrition needs to be minimised, the use of incentives can become a central part of the research strategy. If longitudinal surveys are administered via home addresses or telephone numbers then the survey can be severely compromised over time by loss of contact (moving house, for example, or simply choosing not to respond). Longitudinal studies with young people which are administered in schools can overcome some of the issues of respondent attrition. However, there are certain points in a student's school career when moving to different schools, or leaving school, may affect whether or not they continue to take part in a survey. In such circumstances 'end of project' incentives can be a useful way to ensure that young people stay in touch with and continue to participate in the study.

Boys et al's (2003) study of alcohol use amongst 540 15 and 16 year olds in England provides a good illustration of some of the strategies that can be adopted to minimise attrition. Their study was based on face-to-face survey interviews conducted with respondents at the end of the school day on school premises. Two follow-up postal surveys were planned. In order to make sure that the researchers could maintain contact with respondents, the young people were invited during the first face-to face interview to provide their current contact details, the address and phone number of a close friend or relative who would be able to help with locating them, and to nominate three school friends who might assist in locating them if contact was lost. As a result of these measures and a series of other strategies, only 3 per cent of participants were lost over the study period. These other strategies included telephone calls to verify that contact details were still correct; sending postcards to remind participants to expect a follow-up survey; sending reminder postcards if there was no response two weeks after receiving the questionnaire; telephone reminders; the option of a telephone interview; and high street vouchers sent as a thank you. The researchers conclude that 'rather than one particular strategy being the "magic bullet" responsible for high retention, it is likely that different strategies work well with different people and so a multi-method approach is most useful for ensuring minimum attrition' (2003: 372). Nonetheless, one might equally argue that a continued 'failure' to respond to reminders could and should be construed as the withdrawal of ongoing consent (see Chapter 2); there is arguably a fine line to be drawn between reducing sample attrition and making an unwelcome nuisance of oneself!

While it is clearly easier to track and maintain contact with cohorts of young people up until the age of 16 (and in some cases 18) through their schools, this is not without difficulty as schools may simply fail to respond to follow-up survey sweeps due to changes in key personnel and/or as a consequence of changing priorities. In such cases, incentives presented at the school level can help to reduce respondent attrition. In their study of methods for raising response rates in school surveys in England, Sturgis et al. (2005) found that – hardly surprisingly – head-teachers viewed monetary incentives as a good idea. However, the general view was that incentives are often too small to make a difference to a school and therefore do not necessarily have the desired effect, although what is deemed to be a large enough incentive is not clear. Moreover, the provision of incentives at an institutional level can add significant financial costs to a survey. If public money is being sought for research, then a very detailed rationale for incentive payments will be necessary and funds may not always be available or indeed forthcoming.

Often viewed as a cheaper option, the non-monetary incentive of 'feedback' is now regularly offered to schools or other institutions at the sampling stage of a research project. However, feedback was found by Sturgis et al. (2005) to be clearly linked to notions of relevance and benefit. Ultimately, if research was not perceived to be relevant to either individual learners or the school as a whole, then the incentive of feedback held no weight. Cleaver and Ireland's longitudinal survey research on citizenship education in secondary schools in England, the Citizenship Education Longitudinal Study (CELS) (Cleaver et al., 2005b; Ireland et al., 2006), has used feedback as one way of encouraging schools to administer surveys to their students. Schools are provided with a range of statistical tables which compare their students' answers to average national responses. Sample schools have indicated that this feedback is very useful, not least in helping them to feed directly into the management of citizenship education in the school and in completing inspection reports for the Office for Standards in Education (OFSTED). However, it should be noted that this form of incentive is not without cost: a significant amount of time is required to produce, format and administer the feedback to schools.

Providing feedback to young people themselves is also fairly common in survey research, although whether this is likely to provide sufficient incentive to participate and hence to boost response rates is debateable. A good example of this type of feedback is provided by the annual newsletters produced by the research team overseeing the Longitudinal Study of Young People in England, or 'Next Steps' as it is known to study participants (see Chapter 9 for a more detailed account of this survey). The glossy four page newsletters provide a digest of some of the findings which are presumably considered to be of particular interest to young people, including for example the most popular jobs amongst participants, their leisure pursuits outside of school, their views about school and teachers, and their relationships with parents. The newsletters also provide an important means of staying in touch with sample members, providing information on the next stage of the study (including a reminder that all respondents will each receive a gift token), and details of the study's email address and web site – which includes a wealth of information on the survey and its latest results – should young people require more information. A newsletter was also produced in the first year of the study which was specifically targeted at parents, who had also been interviewed as part of the survey's research design.

Who should give consent?

As in all forms of youth research, when involving young people in survey research – whether in schools, in the home, or elsewhere – it is always important to be aware of the existing power relations which structure the spaces that young people inhabit. As we have argued throughout this book, although attempts might be made to place young people at the centre of the research process, researchers should be acutely conscious of the contexts in which research is undertaken. Barker and Weller (2003: 51) note that in choosing approaches to researching younger respondents it is commonly assumed that the best way is to utilise 'legitimate forms of communication' is within the spaces in which they spend their time. Yet by so doing, many research projects simply reinforce existing power relations, which can limit young people's opportunities to have a say and in particular to give informed consent for their participation.

We noted in Chapter 2 that these concerns are particularly significant in the school setting where a number of spatial, temporal and power issues come into play. One example of this process in action is described by Denscombe and Aubrook (1992), who sought informed consent from 2,000 students who took part in a self-report study conducted in school time on their use of alcohol, tobacco and other drugs. From comments written on the questionnaires, and in follow-up interviews with participants, they found that participation was not always 'completely voluntary'. Their high response rate of 100 per cent, with an overall non-response rate per question of around 1 per cent, therefore raises wider issues about informed consent to survey research conducted within the school setting. If students in such settings are regarding research questionnaires as 'just another piece of schoolwork', then it is not surprising that completion rates are high once schools are recruited to a research project. In such circumstances, students will in all probability cooperate, and might be very well informed about the research, but their participation may not be entirely voluntary.

Strange et al. (2003) provide a useful overview of the structural, practical and interactional factors which can mediate how young people experience the completion of questionnaires in school time and whether they can truly give informed consent in such circumstances. These include school timetables; school sizes; the length of available lessons; the space available in classrooms; teachers' enthusiasm for the research; the relationships between researchers/teachers and students; and the way in which both the responses of students and the roles of researchers are constrained by the dominant cultural norms of the classroom. They conclude that 'it is the particular interaction between the setting (the school/classroom), the participants (young people) and the subject matter … that resulted in students responding to the questionnaire in particular ways' (2003: 345). This conclusion is further supported by the findings of David et al. (2001), who argue that the educational context of their research inevitably meant that children's and young people's involvement was almost guaranteed before formal consent was elicited. They conclude that 'a straightforward notion of children and young people's right or freedom to choose to participate in social research on the basis of the provision of adequate and appropriate information in the school setting especially seems naive' (2001: 364). Epstein (1998) also notes that any adults operating in a school setting can be positioned as 'another teacher' by both students *and* teachers, thereby affecting researcher objectivity and, we might add, the likely responses of young people.

Whilst such reflections are important, the reality of much survey research, especially that based on contract work, reflects a pressure to maximise response rates at the least possible cost. If administering surveys through schools gets a good rate of return, then researchers will often have little choice but to continue to seek access through these channels. One way that researchers are able to circumvent the issue of research becoming just another part of the school day is to include puzzles such as word searches and/or a space to draw a picture at the end of a questionnaire. As we noted in Chapter 2, this allows young people to appear to be taking part in the survey, whilst allowing them to choose how much or how little of the questionnaire they wish to complete. It might equally be the case that young people are perfectly capable of finding their own ways of expressing their disquiet at being used as 'questionnaire fodder'. This is certainly suggested by the fieldwork experience of two of the authors of this book. In a secondary school in England involved in a national survey, a whole class of students was asked to name and describe their parents' occupations. Answers from this particular school included pimp, porn-star and prostitute which, even with the most open mind in the world, were too many in number to reflect reality! In addition, the questionnaires were soiled with footprints. As students were provided with an envelope in which to seal their completed questionnaire to ensure confidentiality, any staff member returning to collect the questionnaires at the end of the session would not have been aware that this had taken place. The only course of action available to the researchers was to remove the school and the young people's responses from the survey – possibly an intended outcome for a group of respondents who did not appear to have given their consent to complete the questionnaire.

Can IT help?

Finally, we consider the contribution of information technologies and electronic communication in conducting surveys with young people. There is a wealth of literature available on the benefits and drawbacks of conducting online and computer-based surveys amongst the general population. As Denscombe (2006) states, research in this area has tended to concentrate on the positive impact of IT-based survey delivery on raising response rates and completion rates when compared to paper-based surveys, and the potential non-representativeness of respondents (i.e., those who have access to, or confidence in using, IT). Attention has also been drawn to issues such as privacy, the ethics of online data collection and concerns about personal information being transferred over the internet (see Nosek et al., 2002). Many of these issues are discussed in greater detail in Chapter 10, which focuses on the use of the internet in youth research, including the use of online surveys. Here, we focus on the use of IT in facilitating survey data collection through the use of offline technologies such as computer-assisted survey interviewing and the use of audio equipment to play questionnaires to the respondent through headphones (as is the case of interviews conducted as part of the British Youth Panel of the British Household Panel Survey).

Literature which specifically focuses on the role of IT in offline data collection among young people appears in the main to focus on two issues: the usefulness of computer-assisted surveys for addressing the needs of special groups of young people, such as those with low levels of literacy; and the role of IT in providing greater privacy for young people. One example of the benefits of using IT in survey data collection is provided by Gatward (2002), who discusses the use of Audio-CASI (Computer Assisted Self-Interviewing) technology during a pilot stage of a survey of the development and well-being of children and young people looked after by local authorities. Audio-CASI technology, which allows respondents to read or listen to each survey item on a computer screen and to then type in their own answers before being automatically routed by the computer to the next question, was chosen due to its positive effects on reporting on sensitive issues and risky behaviours (see also Davies and Morgan, 2005), alongside its utility in surveying those with learning difficulties, problems of concentration or low levels of literacy (see also Schneider and Edwards, 2000). This is achieved by providing clear guidance via onscreen and audio instructions, maintaining a balance between providing sufficient guidance and becoming too repetitive, introducing each section of the questionnaire 'step by step', and minimising the effort required from respondents (Gatward, 2002: 24).

The role of this technology for undertaking surveys on sensitive issues with special groups is further explored by de Leeuw et al. (1997), who make some useful recommendations for the adaptation of CASI technology with special populations. These include providing a user-friendly questionnaire, with a layout of which is easy to read on screen; involving respondents in the questionnaire design process; recognising that computer assisted questionnaires can take longer as they require special motor and IT skills; and providing a paper-based set of instructions as 'help' functions can often confuse respondents and hide the survey from view. Some CASI software packages are designed specifically for use with younger respondents, and include multimedia features such as graphics, speech, interactive elements and the use of animated virtual research assistants to guide young people through the survey. Some packages even include built-in computer game breaks!

The studies discussed so far focus on the potential for using CASI with specific sub-populations of young people, yet the effectiveness of the technique is premised on the assumption that younger generations are widely computer literate and that CASI surveys of the general population of young people will therefore be both preferred and be without technical difficulty. A word of caution is provided by Facer and Furlong, who note that some younger respondents can, contrary to expectations, be 'low and ambivalent' users of IT, highlighting the need to critique the perception of a homogeneous 'generation of digital children' (2001: 467). Young people who may be at a particular disadvantage when using such technology include those from lower social-economic groupings, those whose family cultures do not support the use of computers in daily life, and those whose parents do not have experience of and confidence in using IT. Moreover, lack of access to a home computer was not found to be compensated for by ready access to computers in other sites: those who have access to a computer at home are more likely to take advantage of opportunities to use computers at school and at friends' houses. This, in turn, can lead to certain young people gaining entrenched negative attitudes towards IT, opposing its penetration into their daily lives and identifying themselves as 'non-computer users'.

Summary

In this chapter we have introduced readers to a range of issues of particular relevance to conducting survey research with young people. Whilst there is a wealth of general literature on survey design, some of which we refer to below under 'further reading', there is a dearth of literature which addresses the specific needs of youth researchers, even though social surveys are widely used in youth research. It is our hope that this chapter will provide some useful pointers to the more effective use of survey methods in youth research. These themes continue in the next two chapters. In Chapter 9 we consider how secondary data sources, in particular those derived from large scale social surveys, can be used in youth research, whilst in Chapter 10 we include a focus on the growing use of internet-based surveys.

Suggestions for further reading

Czaja, R. and Blair, J. (2005) *Designing Surveys: A Guide to Decisions and Procedures,* second edition, London: Sage. This second edition reflects the impact on survey design of the increased use of information technologies.

De Vaus, D. (2002) *Surveys in Social Research,* fifth edition, London: Routledge. This is a classic introduction to all aspects of survey design.

Marsh, C. (1982) *The Survey Method: The Contribution of Surveys to Sociological Explaination,* London: George Allen and Unwin. This is another classic text on the survey method.

9 Using Secondary Data

Introduction

This chapter explores the use of secondary data in youth research: that is, the use of data that have already been collected by others, whether for administrative or research purposes. In the UK there is a wealth of data readily available for use and reuse by youth researchers, ranging from official statistics and research reports produced by government departments and various other agencies, through to an impressive array of data sets which have been deposited with the UK Data Archive, including an increasing number of qualitative data sets. With the growth of the internet, access to these various forms of data has never been easier, and by such means secondary data from other countries are also easily accessible, for example data from the US Census Bureau or the Australian Bureau of Statistics. Despite ready access for researchers to secondary data, it is probably fair to say that they are largely under-utilised, even though they have the potential to be of great benefit to youth researchers, whether used to provide contextual data, or to form the primary focus of a new study. Indeed, one of the major advantages of using secondary data sources is that in many cases the need to collect new data may be rendered superfluous. Secondary analysis also provides opportunities for researchers to conduct their own research using high quality data which might otherwise be extremely costly to generate.

This chapter outlines the possibilities of using secondary data in youth research, whether as a major focus of a study or as a supplement to other methods, including the growing opportunities for re-using qualitative data. An important distinction will be drawn in our discussion between the use of *aggregated* data and *microdata*. Aggregated data have already been subjected to preliminary analysis and are usually made available in the form of pre-specified tables of data, without access to individual records. This is the format in which most official statistical data are made available in the first instance. In contrast, microdata consist of records at the level of the individual case and therefore allow researchers to explore the original data for themselves. It would be inaccurate to refer to micro-data as 'raw data', as they will have been subject to some element of 'cleaning' and anonymising before being made available to the research community, but microdata nonetheless allow researchers to carry out their own analysis of the data, using variables and units of analysis of their choosing. We discuss the availability and use of both forms of data in this chapter.

It is not within the scope of this chapter to provide specific advice on techniques for secondary data analysis, and for guidance in this regard we refer readers to a range of excellent textbooks in the section on suggested further reading. Rather, the chapter will consider a series of important issues which need to be considered when using secondary sources, especially those generated for administrative purposes, and provides brief descriptions of some of the most useful sources of data for youth researchers.

Using official statistics in youth research

The term 'official statistics' is used to refer to data that are routinely collected by government agencies either for administrative purposes and/or to aid the development, implementation and monitoring of specific government policies. These data might be generated as by-products of administrative procedures, or might be collected specifically for the purpose of statistical analysis to inform government planning and decision-making. Throughout the calendar year, the UK's Office for National Statistics (ONS) and individual government departments regularly publish statistical releases and bulletins, in aggregated form, on a plethora of topics. Official statistics of specific relevance to youth researchers include, for example, regular updates on examination results, rates of participation in higher education, teenage pregnancy rates, and truancy rates. Beyond statistical sources focusing specifically on youth-related topics, a wealth of data sources are available on topics pertaining to the general population and which in their published format are usually disaggregated by broad age categories (e.g., 16 to 19 year olds, 20 to 25 year olds, and so on). This allows researchers to compare and contrast the experiences of young people relative to other groups. Sources of this nature include housing statistics, employment statistics, statistics on births, marriage and deaths (including suicides), and crime statistics.

Official statistics usually provide coverage of entire populations, so are not hampered by some of the difficulties associated with sample surveys, such as sample bias and non-response. It is possible, then, to use official statistics to build up a picture of patterns of behaviour at a national and, often, regional level, and also to explore these patterns over time, thus highlighting trends in behaviour. The ability to explore trends is important, as it is otherwise impossible to know whether what we are observing at any given point in time is typical or atypical, or represents an increase or a decrease in incidence or a maintenance of the status quo. The websites of various government departments, as well as the ONS, provide ready access to archived data. It is also useful to be able to draw comparisons between different sub-sections of the youth population. Official statistics are usually disaggregated by gender at the very least, whilst sometimes they are disaggregated by a variety of other variables, such as ethnicity or socio-economic status, allowing for a more detailed analysis of trends.

Official statistics relating to attainment in the General Certificate of Secondary Education (the GCSE, the qualification typically studied between the ages of 14 and 16 in England, Wales and Northern Ireland) provide a useful illustration of the richness of the data that are potentially available for use by youth researchers. The Department for Children, Schools and Families (DCSF) produces a series of statistical bulletins over the course of the year following the initial publication of examination results in August of each year, each successively providing a greater level of disaggregation. A 'Statistical First Release' in October of each year, for example, provides the first snapshot of national patterns of GCSE attainment analysed by gender, subject and type of school, and provisional analyses by gender at the level of Local Education Authority. Updates appear over the year, providing results further disaggregated by ethnicity, eligibility for free school meals, special educational needs, and English as an additional language. Additional bulletins on specific topics are also published from time to time; in 2005, for example, a special bulletin was published on the characteristics of low attaining pupils. All of these bulletins are easily accessible online via the DCSF Research and Statistics Gateway (www.dcsf.gov.uk/rsgateway/) which, in common with the websites of most government departments, acts as a portal for a vast array of statistical data and research reports.

When using official statistics, researchers are usually advised to exercise a healthy degree of caution. The validity and reliability of certain sources of official data have been subjected to heavy criticism over the years. This is particularly true of official statistics relating to crime rates, which are of great interest to many youth researchers, and we use this example by way of illustrating some of the issues of which researchers need to be aware in their use of official statistics. Crime statistics are the product of administrative procedures which by default place restrictions on what is likely to be measured as a crime. For a start, official crime statistics only measure *reported* crime, and even then only crime that has led to a charge and a conviction, with the police having considerable discretion in this respect. Youth researchers have more reasons than most to be cautious in their use of official crime statistics (Muncie, 2004). Official figures consistently point to much higher rates of crime amongst young people than among the general population, and it is widely argued that this says as much, if not more, about the heavy policing of young people's lives relative to other groups within society than it does about objective rates of crime. This is exemplified by the creation of new categories of offence in the Anti-Social Behaviour Act (2003), which are targeted specifically at young people and which effectively criminalise behaviours such as hanging around on the street with other young people, as well as in the disproportionate application of Anti-Social Behaviour Orders (ASBOs) to young people, which if breached have the potential to criminalise otherwise non-criminal forms of behaviour.

It is also widely argued that trends revealed by youth crime statistics reflect the extent to which the police operate on the basis of discriminatory assumptions concerning groups who are most likely to offend. These assumptions result not just in higher rates of arrest and conviction amongst young people as a whole in comparison with older populations, but in even higher rates amongst certain subsections of the youth population, such as ethnic minority youth (Muncie, 2004). So whilst a middle class white teenager might be let off without even a caution for underage public drunkenness and lying to the police about their identity (as was famously the case when Euan Blair, the son of former Prime Minister Tony Blair and Cherie Booth QC, celebrated his GCSE results back in 2000), it is extremely unlikely that a working class black teenager from Tower Hamlets would be so lucky if caught under the same circumstances – or even a middle class black teenager. For reasons such as these, radical critics of official crime statistics argue that their generation and subsequent use are associated with attempts to make visible and thus to control sub-sections of the population – in this case, young people.

It is also important to remember that administrative data are often used in highly strategic and politicised ways by policy makers and politicians alike, which should give us pause for thought before an uncritical use of official statistics. The way in which even the slightest increase or decrease in crime rates is heralded in the press is a case in point, but another example, this time drawn from the world of education statistics, illustrates this point equally well. Between 1990 and 1996 there was a dramatic four-fold increase in the number of permanent exclusions from English schools, rising from around 3,000 to over 12,000. Was this evidence that English schoolchildren had become four times more disruptive over this period? Whilst some observers might have been satisfied with such an explanation, more astute observers pointed to the effects of the 1988 Education Reform Bill and its emphasis on the marketisation of state schooling (Vulliamy and Webb, 2000). In other words, it had become increasingly important over the course of the 1990s for schools to wheedle out disruptive pupils in order to convince parents – prospective 'customers' in a system where education funding was linked to pupil numbers – of their intolerance of poor standards of behaviour. Numbers dropped off slightly after the mid-1990s, after these high rates of exclusion came in for criticism, although it was widely claimed that headteachers were instead resorting to exclusion by other means, for example by making greater use of fixed term exclusions, or by putting informal pressure on parents to move their children to an alternative school. Rates then rose again in the early 2000s with the introduction of new regulations which made it easier for headteachers to exclude pupils for particular categories of disruptive behaviour. So, in order to fully understand the messages conveyed by official statistics, it is essential that a researcher gains a thorough understanding of the broader political context of their production.

Despite these words of caution concerning the use of official statistics, we should be very careful not to throw out the baby with the bath water. Bryman (2004), amongst others, has argued that the problems specifically associated with official data on crime and deviance should not deter researchers from making use of other sources of official data, many of which are much less prone to the weaknesses associated with crime data. He argues that 'the flaws in many of the official statistics not concerned with crime and deviance are probably no worse than the errors that occur in much measurement deriving from methods like surveys based on questionnaires and structured interviews. Indeed, some forms of official statistics are probably very accurate by almost any set of criteria' (Bryman, 2004: 213). Whilst being wise to the potential problems associated with official statistics, the best advice is then to judge the strengths and weaknesses of any given source of official data entirely on its own merits.

Secondary analysis of large-scale survey data sets

We turn now to a consideration of the secondary use by youth researchers of quantitative data sets produced specifically for research purposes. Researchers in the UK are particularly fortunate in having access to a wide range of high quality data sources. Indeed, some of the more high profile amongst these, such as the UK's four birth cohort studies (based on cohorts born in the years 1946, 1958, 1970 and 2000), are frequently referred to as 'the crown jewels of UK social research'. In addition to a number of surveys targeted specifically at young people, which we discuss below, there are also many well regarded government-sponsored surveys which are of potential value to youth researchers. Surveys such as the General Household Survey, the Labour Force Survey and the Expenditure and Food Survey (created from the merger in 2001 of the Family Expenditure Survey and the National Food Survey) usually include young people aged 16 years and over as full sample members, and many household-based surveys may also include selected data pertaining to under-16 year olds living in the sampled households. Selected results from regular large scale surveys are available at an aggregated level in hard-copy or online formats, with published tables often disaggregated by different age bands. However, it is in their re-use as micro-data, providing researchers with access to individual-level records for their own analysis, that all of these data sets come into their own. In this section we will highlight some of the issues which researchers need to be aware of in their re-use, before introducing readers to a number of surveys which are conducted specifically amongst young people.

We noted in the introduction to this chapter that the use of secondary data sources by youth researchers can sometimes render the collection of new data redundant. Most of the surveys that are available for re-analysis have been conducted to very high standards and exacting specifications, both of which would be difficult to replicate without considerable financial investment, not to mention considerable technical skill. Moreover, existing survey data are often based on the use of tried and tested standardised questions which ensure that comparisons can more accurately be made over time or even between different surveys. Accordingly, researchers who might be considering the conduct of a new survey should always check first whether any relevant data have previously been collected and might therefore be suitable for re-use. In the UK, this can be done via a search of the online catalogue of the UK Data Archive based at the University of Essex (www.data-archive.ac.uk), a constituent part of the UK's Economic and Social Data Service (ESDS). The Archive has an international reputation as a centre of expertise in data acquisition, preservation, and dissemination, and hosts the largest collection of digital social science data in the UK. Researchers (including students) are able to register as users and gain free access to data held by the Archive (assuming these are being used for non-commercial purposes). Secondary data sets held by the Data Archive in most cases can be downloaded directly to a researcher's desktop via the internet, and in a variety of formats, including as SPSS data files. It is also possible to view frequencies, produce graphs, and conduct simple online tabulations for many of the major government surveys via the Nesstar service provided by ESDS (nesstar.esds.ac.uk/webview).

Before starting to work with an archived data set, it is essential that all relevant documentation is referred to in order to gain a good understanding of the conditions under which the data were originally collected and of the purposes which underpinned their collection. To facilitate an exploration of these sorts of issues, the Data Archive produces comprehensive documentation for the data sets which they supply, whilst it is also advisable to look at published studies and reports based on the data to find out more about the uses to which the data have already been put. It is very important to be aware that secondary analysis is dependent on data that may have been collected with quite different objectives to those of the secondary researcher, and to be aware of some of the limitations that this will inevitably impose on their re-use. This might mean, for instance, that the questions that were asked do not necessarily correspond with those in which a secondary researcher is primarily interested, that the range of potential responses that were originally presented to respondents might have been rather different to those which another researcher might have wanted to use, or that the survey may have omitted some areas of interest altogether. For example, one of the authors of this book has an interest in the pre-university gap year, in particular young people's participation in voluntary activity as part of a year out, and was aware that later cohorts of the Youth Cohort Study (see below) had been asked about gap year experiences. However, the range of potential responses pertaining to specific gap year activities did not include volunteering and only distinguished between overseas or UK-based travel and paid work. What at first sight appeared to be a potentially useful source unfortunately proved not to be so useful after all.

Having considered some of the pros and cons of secondary analysis, we now provide a necessarily brief introduction to a number of UK data sets which are either specifically concerned with the experiences and attitudes of young people, or which include a data collection phase targeted specifically at young people as part of their research design. What is striking about most of these surveys is their relatively narrow coverage: for the most part, focusing on aspects of education, training and work, or on various forms of risk behaviour. Existing surveys tend, then, to reflect some of the traditional preoccupations of transitions research, as well as the not uncommon focus in youth research on potentially problematic aspects of young people's lives (see our discussion of this pervasive discourse in Chapter 1). Roberts (2005), for example, has commented unfavourably on the neglect of young people's leisure activities in most surveys of young people's lives. However, it is important to remember that many surveys which are targeted at a general population sample, and which therefore include young people of 16 and over in their sampling, cover some of these neglected areas. Notwithstanding these preoccupations and omissions, it is clear that there is a richness of data available to researchers who are prepared to engage in secondary analysis. A brief introduction to a range of youth-related data sets is now provided, alongside some examples of published research which have drawn on these data sets.

The England and Wales Youth Cohort Study (YCS)

The YCS is sponsored by the Department for Children, Schools and Families and monitors the behaviour and decision-making of representative samples of school leavers as they make the transition from compulsory education to further or higher education or the labour market. Starting in 1985, YCS now extends to 12 cohorts, with the most recently archived data at the time of writing relating to Cohort 11. The frequency and timing of contact has varied over the life of the survey, although each cohort has been surveyed at least twice. Cohort 11 members have been contacted on four separate occasions between the ages of 16 and 20, with regular topics including experiences of education, training and employment; educational and career aspirations; and sources of advice and guidance, including questions for Cohort 11 specifically on their awareness of and views on the Connexions Service. The YCS is subject to high levels of attrition, especially amongst hard to reach groups of young people, and this particularly needs to be taken into account when using the data set (Croxford, 2006). YCS microdata are available from the UK Data Archive, whilst the Department for Children, Schools and Families regularly publishes statistical releases based on key YCS findings.

Burchardt (2004) used YCS data relating to 18 and 19 year olds in Cohorts 8 and 9 to explore the educational and occupational aspirations of disabled young people. She found, for example, that young disabled respondents not only expected to be offered lower earnings than their non-disabled peers, but that they were willing to accept these lower earnings. Moreover, disabled young people felt less confident and less well supported than their non-disabled peers. Burchardt nonetheless expressed surprise that, given societal discrimination against disabled people, the differences between disabled and non-disabled young people were as small as they were in relation to these particular indicators.

The Longitudinal Study of Young People in England ('Next Steps')

This survey is the new kid on the block, and the first wave of data, collected in 2004, was made available to researchers via the UK Data Archive at the end of 2006. Described as 'one of the largest and most challenging studies of young people that the DfES has ever commissioned', the Next Steps study is designed to provide evidence on the key factors affecting educational progression and attainment and subsequent transition following the end of compulsory education. The initial sampling frame, drawn in spring 2004, consisted of 21,000 Year 9 pupils from both state and independent schools in England, and achieved a response rate of 74 per cent. The sample deliberately includes an over-representation of pupils from ethnic minority backgrounds and from schools which score highly on key measures of deprivation. Since the first wave of data collection in 2004, sample members have been revisited on an annual basis up to and including 2007, with plans to continue data collection for further waves. The fieldwork involves face-to-face interviews with young people and their parents on a range of topics, including questions for young people on their attitudes towards schooling, their aspirations for the future, and how they spend their leisure time, and questions for parents on their involvement in their child's education, their views on education in general, their hopes for their children, and family activities. These data have been enhanced for state school pupils by the addition of data from the National Pupil Database, which include data on, for example, individual educational attainment, as well as the addition of data relating to the characteristics of each pupil's school and other geo-demographic variables, although these enhanced data are at present only available upon a direct request to the Department for Children, Schools and Families.

The first published report based on Next Steps data focused on the academic performance of ethnic minority pupils (Strand, 2007). The deliberate over-representation of ethnic minority pupils in LSYPE means that researchers at last have access to a rich source of data for exploring ethnic differences in educational outcomes. Previous data sources, such as the Youth Cohort Study, tended not to have sufficient numbers of ethnic minority sample members to be able to conduct statistically robust analyses. Strand's analysis highlighted that when attainment measures are controlled by a broader range of contextual variables, including not just social class but maternal education, entitlement to free school meals as an indicator of poverty, home ownership and family composition, the well-documented attainment gaps amongst pupils from most ethnic minority groups are substantially reduced. This is particularly dramatic amongst Pakistani pupils, where the gap in attainment between Pakistani and white pupils is reduced by four-fifths. However, the low attainment of Black-Caribbean pupils cannot be accounted for by such controls, leading Strand to conclude that explanations for unequal outcomes based solely on social class are not sufficient, and that researchers need to also take account of in-school factors such as teachers' perceptions and expectations relative to particular groups of pupils.

The Scottish School-leavers Survey (SSLS)

This survey is part of a series of cohort studies of Scottish school-leavers which dates back to the 1970s. In its current form, the SSLS targets leavers at three points in time: at 16/17, 18/19 and 22/23. The achieved sample at sweep 1 of Cohort 4 in 2003 consisted of just over 5,000 respondents out of a possible sample of 12,000 young people and at sweep 2 consisted of 3,200 respondents. The survey is carried out by means of a self-completion postal questionnaire, with questions covering experiences of schooling, decisions about staying on or leaving, experiences of employment and training, family circumstances and housing tenure. Funded by the Scottish Executive, one of the primary purposes of the SSLS is to provide data which will enable predictions to be made concerning the demand for higher education in Scotland.

However, broad use has been made of the data for secondary analysis. Microdata from SSLS are also available from the UK Data Archive, whilst the Scottish Executive regularly publishes research reports based on SSLS data.

Tinklin and Croxford (2000) used SSLS data to explore the experiences of high-attaining female school leavers in Scotland. They found that high attainment was related to having friends who took school seriously, and that this characteristic was more frequently found amongst young women's peer groups than those of young men. Despite current high profile concerns about male underachievement relative to girls, the researchers found that high-attaining young women were less likely to enter Higher Education than high-attaining young men, even though they were equally likely to apply for a place in HE. The authors suggested that this might be because young women were more likely to apply to over-subscribed courses, although unfortunately it was not possible to test this proposition within the available data.

The British Youth Panel of the British Household Panel Survey (BHPS)

The BHPS began life in 1991 with a panel of 10,300 individuals across approximately 5,500 households. Panel members have been followed up annually ever since, along with any new household members as and when they have entered into new living arrangements. Young people are included in the main sample in the year they turn 16, and are then eligible to participate fully in the study via an interview and a self-completion questionnaire on a range of topics including core themes such as household composition, employment, education and training, housing conditions, health, and political views. Since 1994, 11 to 15 year olds in BHPS households have been invited to complete a short self-completion questionnaire as part of the British Youth Panel, providing researchers with a growing pool of data on various aspects of youth transitions, which can then be linked to responses in the main survey once a respondent turns 16. The BYP questionnaire content varies slightly each year. In 2004, topics included young people's time use; relationships with parents and friends; their health, including drug and tobacco use, sport, exercise and diet; their feelings about school; experiences of paid work; their self-image and self-esteem; and an open-ended question about significant events in their lives over the previous 12 months.

Gayle has claimed that the BYP is a particularly important resource for youth researchers, 'because it is representative of Britain, now has a reasonably long run of data ... locates the young people's experiences within the household and tracks the young person into adult life' (2005: 34). It has also made use of youth-friendly research methods: a pre-recorded questionnaire is provided for young people to play on their personal sound systems. Young people can control the pace of the questionnaire and are ensured confidentiality even when other family members are present as the paper questionnaire only includes the response categories, and not the actual questions being asked. BYP data are available via the UK Data Archive.

The aptly-named Blow et al. (2005) used BYP data in conjunction with data from the main BHPS survey to explore the relationship between parental income and young people's smoking behaviour. The researchers point out that there is often a strong association between income and healthy behaviour. Their analysis of BHPS/BYP data found an inverse relationship between parental income and young people's smoking prevalence: in other words, the higher the income, the less likely a young person was to smoke. However, by looking at the smoking behaviour of younger siblings, they concluded that increases in household income led to an increased probability of *younger siblings* smoking.

The BHPS is soon to be superseded by the launch of a new household panel study to be known as the UK Household Longitudinal Study (UKHLS). The new study, which will incorporate the existing BHPS sample, will be the largest study of its kind in the world, with a target sample size of 40,000 households and approximately 100,000 individuals, including a booster sample of 3,000 ethnic minority households. Of particular relevance to youth researchers is the decision to conduct individual interviews with all household members aged ten and upwards. The UKHLS is also likely to include a qualitative element with a sub-sample of households. (See www.iser.essex.ac.uk/ukhls/ for further information.)

The Young People's Social Attitudes Survey (YPSA)

This survey has been conducted on three occasions as part of the British Social Attitudes Survey (BSA), an annual survey conducted by the National Centre for Social Research and part-funded by government. Each year, up to 3,600 respondents aged 18 and over from across England, Scotland and Wales are asked about their views on topics as diverse as newspaper readership, political parties and trust, health care, child care, poverty, the workplace, charitable giving, the countryside, transport, the environment, race, religion, civil liberties, fear of crime, and the portrayal of sex and violence in the media. In 1994, around 600 12 to 19 year olds who lived in the households of BSA respondents participated in the first Young People's Social Attitudes Survey, designed in collaboration with the charity Barnado's. About half of the questions asked in the YPSA were identical to those asked of over-18 year olds, allowing comparisons not only between parents and children but also between younger and older siblings in the same household. In addition, the face-to-face interview covered topics such as gender differences, problems at school, views about education and work, prejudice and morality, friendships, and household tasks. The YPSA was repeated in 1998 and 2003. Data from the 2004 survey demonstrated a number of discernible trends since the original survey in 1994, including a decline in young people's interest and knowledge in politics, increased support for the view that one parent can raise a child just as well as two, and a decline in young people's perceptions of the degree of racial prejudice in Britain (see Park et al., 2004, for a full report on the 2003 findings). Microdata from YPSA are available from the UK Data Archive. In addition, pre-specified tables of data from the main annual survey are accessible via an interactive online database (www.Britsocat.com), which allows users to view survey findings disaggregated by seven age categories, including 18 to 24 year olds as a separate category.

The Young Life and Times Survey (YLT)

This survey originated as a companion survey to the Northern Ireland Life and Times Survey (NILT), the Northern Ireland equivalent to the British Social Attitudes Survey. Between 1998 and 2000, all 12 to 17 year olds in sampled households were invited to participate in a parallel survey. In 2003 the YLT was re-launched with an entirely distinct methodology, no longer linked to the adult NILT sample. The new survey, sampled via Child Benefit Records, is targeted at all 16 year olds who celebrate their sixteenth birthday in February of the survey year. In 2007, the YLT achieved a sample of 627 respondents out of a potential sample of 1,900 young people. A few questions are included in both the YLT and the NILT, but for the most part the YLT covers separate topics, including community relations, identity, cross-community contact, social contact, politics, mental health, and education. One of the avowed aims of the survey is to give young people in Northern Ireland a voice, and as part of this process young people are invited to nominate topics for inclusion. The YLT website (www.ark.ac.uk/ylt/) provides interactive access to results in tabular form, with the option of disaggregation either by gender or by different religion, whilst microdata from the study are available via both the YLT website and the UK Data Archive.

Data from the YLT 2005 were used by Burns (2006) to explore the incidence and nature of school-based bullying in Northern Ireland. The study revealed that the incidence of bullying was lowest in schools with an even mix of Catholic and Protestant students. The survey also found that young people from poorer families were more likely to have experienced bullying, whilst young men with experience of same-sex attraction were almost three times as likely to have been bullied at school than young men claiming only heterosexual attraction.

The 1970 British Cohort Study (BCS70)

The BCS70 is an ongoing longitudinal study of a group of individuals who were all born in the same week in April 1970. Following initial data collection at birth, contact has been made with the sample members at ages 5, 10, 16, 26, 29 and 34. With each successive contact, the scope of enquiry has broadened, embracing physical, educational, social and economic development. Now in their late thirties, the sample members hardly constitute 'the youth of today', yet the study remains an important source of data on the changing nature of youth transitions amongst 'Thatcher's children', and provides a useful benchmark for comparison with other cohort studies, notably the 1958 National Child Development Study (NCDS) which went before it and, in time, data which will hopefully be collected on youth transitions from the Millennium Cohort Study of children born in 2000. Microdata from all of these studies are available via the UK Data Archive. Numerous research publications have drawn upon data from the BCS70, including Bynner et al's (2002) comparison of the experiences of sample members in the BCS70 and NCDS, a study which confirms the dramatic generational shift in young people's experiences of transitions to adulthood.

The Youth Lifestyles Survey (YLS)

This survey has been carried out twice: first in 1992–1993 and again in 1998–1999. Funded by the Home Office, this rather innocuously titled survey aims to investigate offending amongst young people and how patterns of offending differ by age, lifestyle and other demographic factors. The survey consists of a sample of around 5,000 young people in England and Wales in the 18 to 30 age range, generated from households included in the sample for the British Crime Survey (BCS). The survey had two elements. The first was a face-to-face interview, which investigated respondents' experiences of schooling; work, training and unemployment; income, financial hardship and expenditure; family life; housing experiences; leisure; worries about crime, world affairs and personal events; feelings of safety in various settings; victimisation; attitudes to crime and punishment; and contact with the police. In a separate computer-assisted self-completion questionnaire, respondents were asked about substance use and their own criminal records. The YLS is a useful complement to data from the BCS, a self-report victimisation survey which includes young people aged 16 and over in the main sample.

Richardson and Budd (2006) used 1998–1999 YLS data to explore the relationship between drinking and offending. They found a strong association between binge drinking and criminal and disorderly behaviour, and concluded that the frequency of *drunkenness* specifically is a better predictor of likely offending than the frequency of drinking per se. They also noted a particular association between binge drinking and crimes of violence. Microdata from both the YLS and the BCS are available via the UK Data Archive.

Other youth-related survey data sets held by the UK Data Archive

In addition to the high profile surveys already mentioned, the UK Data Archive provides access to a wealth of other survey data sets relevant to youth research. These include a variety of data sets collected as part of the ESRC's two major youth research programmes, the 16–19 Initiative of the 1980s and the Youth, Citizenship and Social Change programme of the 1990s, as well as other studies funded by a variety of sponsors which have focused on different aspects of young people's lives. Examples of youth-related studies contained within the UK Data Archive include: Under-16s and the National Lottery; Civil Rights in Schools: School Students' Views; Young People's Involvement in Sport; Smoking, Drinking and Drug Use amongst Young People (a regular survey conducted by the Department of Health); Young People's Representations of Conflicting Roles in Child Development (a study investigating young people's experiences of work, especially work that is commonly assumed to be inappropriate for children); Young People's Use of Places and Views on their Local Environment; and the Home Office Citizenship Survey (focusing on community cohesion, race and faith, volunteering and civil renewal). Browsing through the UK Data Archive will reveal many other fascinating data sets of potential use to youth researchers. There is a wealth of data available!

Secondary analysis of qualitative data

Secondary analysis is probably associated in the minds of most researchers with *quantitative* sources of data. However, there is a growing emphasis in the UK as well as elsewhere on the re-use of *qualitative* data. This represents something of a seismic shift in more qualitatively-orientated circles, not least because the feasibility and desirability of re-using qualitative data is a hotly contested topic (see Parry and Mauthner, 2004; Bishop, 2005; Moore, 2006). Nonetheless, for some time now qualitative researchers seeking funding from the UK's Economic and Social Research Council (ESRC) have been required to offer their data for potential archiving in the 'Qualidata' division of the UK Data Archive (www.qualidata.essex.ac.uk). Qualidata's focus is on acquiring digital data from purely qualitative as well as mixed methods contemporary research, as well as the acquisition of paper-based archives from some classic UK-based studies. These classic studies currently include Stan Cohen's 'Folk Devils and Moral Panics' study, which famously focused on the genesis and development of the 'moral panic' surrounding the widely reported clashes between Mods and Rockers at British seaside resorts in the 1960s. In all of these cases, great attention is paid to the importance of the context in which a study has been conducted, and in the case of classic studies such as Cohen's, extensive interviews have been carried out with the original researchers to provide as much contextual information as possible. Critics of the re-use of qualitative data argue that it is impossible to gain a full understanding of context when using data collected by other researchers and that this in itself renders re-use problematic (Parry and Mauthner, 2004). Others have refuted these claims, arguing that the reuse of qualitative data should be viewed more in terms of a process of the *re*contextualisation of data, something that even the original researchers would need to bear in mind in reanalysing their 'own' data (Moore, 2006), and a process which can actually enhance secondary analysis.

An interesting example of the importance of context is provided by Goodwin and O'Connor's (2005) restudy of a previously little known project directed by Norbert Elias in the early 1960s, entitled 'Adjustment of Young Workers to Work Situations and Adult Roles'. The original study included nearly 900 face-to-face interviews with young people who had left school in 1960, yet the bulk of these interviews had until recently never been fully analysed. Goodwin and O'Connor's own recent analysis of the data reveals the complexity of youth transitions during this period, even though the received wisdom in this area often assumes that youth transitions in the 1960s and 1970s tended to be linear, smooth and relatively uncomplicated relative to youth transitions of the 1980s and beyond. Their argument is that the broader sociological focus of transitions research during this time tended to highlight more macro-level concerns such as class and gender; and that the same data, if viewed from a more contemporary perspective which includes a focus on individual(ised) biographies, reveal the individual-level complexity of transitions that was part of the story in the 1960s and 1970s. This example suggests that re-analysing qualitative data with a different set of theoretical and conceptual concerns in mind to the original researchers can indeed be a very fruitful and insightful exercise. It also flags up the benefits of comparing contemporary research with older, historically-situated studies of youth experience.

As the secondary analysis of qualitative data has become increasingly well established, so there has been a sustained focus in recent years on developing forms of good practice in relation to archiving, most recently through 'QUADS', the ESRC's Qualitative Archiving and Data

Sharing Initiative (Corti, 2006). One of the projects funded under QUADS revolved around the development of good practice in the archiving and re-use of existing data from the *Inventing Adulthoods* project, which we have referred to throughout this book, a qualitative longitudinal study of young people growing up in England and Northern Ireland at the turn of the twenty-first century (Henderson et al., 2006b). With QUADs funding, the project team have been able to focus in particular on some of the practical and ethical problems associated with the secondary analysis of data from an existing study. The team have been working on the production of a range of resources to aid this process, including researchers' own thoughts about the young people at each re-visit, accounts of the specific places in which the research was based, and broader reflections on the research process, all by way of providing important contextual information for secondary analysts. The team have also involved a small number of young people from the study in this process, exploring their perspectives on how best to overcome problems of confidentiality, privacy and ownership, including their views on the best ways of conveying their changing stories over time. Full details of the project – including a fascinating clip from an Open University-produced DVD about the project's longitudinal research process – can be found at the *Inventing Adulthoods* website (www.lsbu.ac.uk/inventingadulthoods).

Summary

In this chapter we have introduced readers to the potential uses of secondary data sources in youth research. We have highlighted some of the issues of which secondary analysts need to be aware, focusing in particular on an understanding of the importance of context – a consideration of equal importance to the re-use of both quantitative and qualitative data. We have introduced readers to youth-related data sets with the highest profile and provided illustrations of the kinds of analyses which are possible with such data. In addition to the potential these data sets offer for complex statistical or qualitative analysis, youth researchers might equally want to draw upon these data sets to provide important contextual and descriptive accounts of young people's experiences – in most cases, these data are only a click of the mouse away.

Suggestions for further reading

Field, A. (2005) *Discovering Statistics using SPSS*, London: Sage. This is a user-friendly introductory text.

Heaton, J. (2004) *Reworking Qualitative Data: The Possibility of Secondary Analysis*, London: Sage. This is an introduction to the secondary analysis of qualitative data.

Levitas, R. and Guy, W. (eds) (1996) *Interpreting Official Statistics*, London: Routledge. This is a useful edited collection on some of the challenges of using official statistics.

Rose, D. and Sullivan, O. (1996) *Introducing Data Analysis for Social Scientists*, Buckingham: Open University Press. This is a widely used introductory text on quantitative secondary analysis.

10 Using the Internet for Youth Research

Introduction

The use of the internet for purposes of youth research has become increasingly commonplace. Nowadays, it is hard to imagine conducting a piece of research without at least some recourse to the internet, even if only to download the latest government policy document, the latest statistical release, or to locate an elusive research paper. However, the internet has created the potential for a much broader and exciting range of uses by researchers, both as a research tool and as a source of data in its own right. Researchers interested in young people's lives in particular have much to gain from internet-based research, as young people constitute the highest users of web-based technologies. A quick Google search for official statistics on internet usage reveals that, in 2007, only 4 per cent of the UK's 16 to 24 year olds claimed never to have accessed the internet, compared with 27 per cent of the population as a whole, with 70 per cent of 16 to 24 year olds stating that they accessed the internet either every day or nearly every day, a rise from 60 per cent of the age group in 2006 (Office of National Statistics, 2007). Accessing websites such as YouTube, MySpace, Facebook, iTunes, and an ever changing array of websites that move in and out of favour on an almost daily basis has become a standard feature of young people's everyday life. Conducting youth research via the medium of the internet has the potential, then, to be a very fruitful path to pursue.

This chapter focuses first on ways in which youth researchers can capitalise on new technologies in their research. The chapter starts with a consideration of some of the advantages of conducting research online, as well as some of the drawbacks. It then goes on to consider the ways in which the internet is increasingly being used as a forum for the deployment of well-established research methods such as surveys and interviews in new contexts, and then moves on to consider the potential for using websites, blogs and chat rooms as sources of research data in their own right.

Advantages of online research

In one of the earliest texts produced on internet research methods – or what the authors refer to as 'computer-mediated communication' – Mann and Stewart (2000) argue that the internet offers huge potential for extending the scope of traditional methods for accessing participants, thereby extending social research to topics which might previously have been rather difficult, if not impossible, to explore. In particular, they note that internet-based research has the potential to transcend geographical limitations, allows relative ease of access to groups of people with shared interests and/or shared demographic characteristics, including hard to reach populations, and facilitates research on sensitive topics. These are all major strengths of internet research, especially in the context of youth studies, and we consider each in turn.

Transcending geographical limitations

A major advantage of using the internet as the basis for research is that its scope is not limited by geographical constraints. In cyberspace, young people are only a click of the mouse away from an invitation to participate in research, regardless of their geographical location. This is a huge advantage given that much youth research – particularly of a qualitative nature – tends to be limited to geographically-restricted samples, often due to the high costs involved in travelling to multiple research sites. Internet-based research therefore facilitates relative ease of access to young people based not only in one's home country, but also provides unparalleled opportunities to engage in comparative research. This is particularly so of research embracing users of the internet in areas where rates of internet access are high, such as Europe, North America and Australasia, but potentially provides access to young people in other parts of the globe as well.

Greener and Hollands (2006), for example, conducted research on the global subculture of 'virtual psytrance', embracing young people who enjoy computer-generated 'psychedelic trance' music and who participate in online psytrance discussion forums. Through links to an online questionnaire posted on every psytrance forum found on the internet by the researchers, responses were eventually obtained from nearly 600 young people from over 40 different countries, demonstrating not only the effectiveness of their method but also reinforcing the researchers' empirical findings concerning the global nature of this subculture. It is hard to imagine how they might have succeeded in attaining such a geographically-dispersed sample through other means.

The use of the internet as a medium for conducting research also facilitates ongoing access with young people who are geographically mobile. For example, researchers interested in youth travel are able to stay in touch with respondents throughout their time overseas for as long as they have access to the internet, either via email, instant messaging, social networking sites or via entries posted in online travel diaries, allowing for the collection of 'real time' rather than retrospective data on young people's travel experiences (Binder, 2004).

Accessing distinct population sub-groups

Greener and Hollands' (2006) study of psytrance also illustrates one of the most extraordinary features of the evolution of the internet to date, namely its ability to bring together like-minded people within virtual communities. These communities consist of individuals, often drawn from many parts of the globe, with a common interest, whether a shared hobby or subcultural identity, a shared set of beliefs or values, shared demographic characteristics, or a shared life experience. Support groups in particular seem to thrive in cyberspace. For example, when one of us recently sustained a knee injury she was intrigued to discover the existence of an online support group going by the name of 'Knee Geeks', providing information and a message board facility for similarly-afflicted individuals – it really does seem as if there is a website for everybody out there somewhere!

The internet has the capacity, therefore, to facilitate access to groups of individuals who in all probability would never otherwise have come together and would almost certainly be much harder to trace. In many cases, these virtual communities effectively provide access to sampling frames of members of hard to reach groups, for whom such a resource is not ordinarily readily available, or not readily available within the public realm (see our earlier discussion of accessing hard to reach groups in Chapter 3). Wood (2003), for example, was able to gain access to a sample of young people involved in the 'straightedge' subculture in the USA and Canada (an offshoot of hardcore punk characterised by abstinence from alcohol, smoking and illegal drugs) via appeals for participants on straightedge websites and online message boards, 20 of whom he subsequently interviewed face to face. He notes that the subculture's 'relative obscurity' would have made it difficult for him to access this number of young people through other means.

Mann and Stewart (2000) also note that the internet allows potential access to individuals located within closed sites or within sites where physical access is often limited. In the context of youth research, these might include, for example, young offender institutions, care homes, boarding schools and hospitals. Using the internet as a means of conducting research in sites such as these might also do away with the need to otherwise work through gatekeepers, concerns about informed consent notwithstanding.

Researching sensitive topics

A further advantage of internet-based research is its potential for conducting research on sensitive topics (again, see our earlier discussion in Chapter 3). Online research participants can choose to remain anonymous throughout the research process, without the researcher ever meeting them in person or possibly having access to any details concerning their specific whereabouts. This might be a particularly valuable feature if researching potentially sensitive subjects, including research on illegal or high-risk activities, for example, or research on potentially embarrassing topics. For many young people, the ability to remain anonymous throughout the research process, and not just within the subsequent analysis, may make the difference in choosing whether or not to take part in a research project in the first place. Commenting on their research on young lesbians and gay men, for example, Valentine et al. note that 'the cloak of anonymity provided by the disembodied nature of online forms of communication can provide a closeted young person with the self-confidence and security necessary to overcome their fears about talking about sexuality' (2001: 122).

In a similar vein, Farrow and Arnold (2003) carried out research on sexual activity and alcohol consumption amongst university students by means of an anonymised online survey. Respondents were recruited via two routes: emails were sent to all students registered at the institution in question, and requests for participation were posted on student-orientated websites. According to the researchers, the study generated 'frank and honest' answers, leading them to conclude that the use of an online survey did not appear to have inhibited young people's responses. Joinson (2005) also highlights research that suggests that the degree of self-disclosure is actually higher in online surveys than in paper equivalents, and that respondents to online surveys are less likely to provide socially desirable responses than respondents to paper surveys. He concludes that the internet offers the potential to preserve privacy whilst encouraging openness, which is clearly desirable in any form of research, but especially when conducting research on sensitive topics.

Cost savings

A further set of advantages relates to cost and time savings. Internet-based research methods are relatively inexpensive compared with the costs of travelling extensively to engage in face-to-face fieldwork, for example, or the costs of a large postal survey. Instead, most of the data collection costs are transferred onto research participants, in terms of their own costs for internet access and usage. Csipke and Horne (2007), for example, noted that their decision to use internet-based methods of data collection in researching the views of mainly young and almost exclusively female users of pro-anorexia websites was in part informed by their limited access to research funding. The researchers worked for the mental health charity SANE and chose to host a questionnaire on the charity's website, alongside postings on the websites of other relevant organisations.

In addition to cutting the amount of time spent by researchers both on the road and in the field, internet-based research can also lead to considerable savings in the amount of time spent in coding and/or transcribing data. Survey responses can be entered directly into a data base, whilst text-based data can be simply cut and pasted, word for word, into a word processing package and/or into a computer-assisted qualitative data analysis package such as NVivo, ATLAS-ti or similar (see Lewins and Silver, 2007). This in particular represents a huge saving of both time and money. Moreover, the resulting data will be free from data entry or transcription errors and, in the case of interview data, from transcribers' well-meaning efforts to 'tidy up' participants' responses.

Drawbacks of internet research

Having outlined some of the major gains to be made by using the internet for research, it is important to consider some of the drawbacks. Many of these relate to inequalities in access to the internet and to the potential sources of bias that might creep into youth research (survey-based research in particular) if these are ignored. Although young people are heavy users of the internet, it is nonetheless the case that certain groups of young people are more likely to make use of it than others, and a small minority may rarely if ever do so. A key variable relates to whether a young person has internet access at home, and Park et al. (2004) note that whilst 93 per cent of young people with home access regularly use the internet, only 59 per cent of those without home access do so. Not surprisingly, they also note a marked difference in household income between households with or without internet access, alongside differences in the level of parental education. If a researcher is seeking a representative sample of young people in general, rather than a representative sample of young people who use the internet, then these differences are important to bear in mind.

Moreover, it is important to be aware that those who choose to participate in online research are a self-selecting group of internet users, and if they have been invited to participate in a research project via user groups and support groups are also unlikely to be 'typical' of the groups from which they are drawn in as much as they represent those who have taken the effort to join a user group in the first place. They may, therefore, feel more strongly about their shared interest than those who have either not made the effort or do not have the resources to join. Relying solely on internet-based research methods to conduct research amongst young people will then almost invariably introduce a source of bias into one's sampling, and depending on the topic a researcher might need to supplement internet-based methods with more conventional offline methods.

Another potential problem relates to the issue of trust in cyberspace. If a participant states that she is a 17 year old woman, we have to take this on trust, although that person may actually be a 50 year old man. The same is applicable of course to other forms of research where researchers do not have direct access to participants, such as research based on postal surveys, although the use where possible of relevant sampling frames might act as a damage limitation measure in this regard. Nonetheless, internet-based research is particularly susceptible to the problem of identification verification. Neither is it possible in most cases to know the geographical location of a potential research participant from their email address alone, and this too needs to be taken at face value: we might think that we are conducting research with British young people, or American young people, when in practice our sample includes young people from all over the world. A related point is the extent to which a sample may be so geographically dispersed as to render our research meaningless. Whilst a nationally (or internationally) distributed sample might be regarded as a good thing for certain forms of research, for others a dispersed sample might not be very helpful, and might result in a rather weak and watered down set of conclusions, from which it is impossible to generalise.

The internet as a forum for new ways of using well-established research methods

Having considered some of the pros and cons of internet-based research, we turn now to a consideration of the ways in which the internet can be used as a means of generating original data in youth research through the use of well-established research methods in new contexts. This section explores the use of internet surveys and internet interviewing, and briefly refers to the growing practice amongst researchers of creating websites specifically for research purposes. Subsequent sections explore the potential of using the internet as a source of naturally-occurring data in its own right.

Internet-based surveys

Internet-based surveys have become an extremely common phenome-non. Many websites include regular quizzes and opinion polls on their homepages just for the fun of it, user surveys often appear as pop-ups when accessing many sites, and there are numerous specialist websites, such as UK Survey Panel.com and YouGov.com, which have been created to provide a one-stop-shop for people who have a particular penchant for completing internet-based surveys! Some of these sites also provide a small payment for each survey completed. Internet-based surveys seem, then, to have become as ubiquitous as 'off-line' surveys – if not more so – and are arguably much quicker and easier to complete than their paper-based equivalents.

Internet-based surveys take a number of different forms (Sue and Ritter, 2007). Some are conducted via targeted emails, with a question-naire either attached to the email or included as part of the message itself. Potential respondents are invited to complete the survey and to then email their responses back to the researcher. It is increasingly com-mon, however, for internet-based surveys to be hosted on dedicated websites, with respondents able to complete the survey online, either in response to a targeted email or via some other form of promotion, including through invitations to participate posted on relevant websites. The deployment of surveys which are promoted via targeted emails is of course premised on prior access to a relevant mailing list. A researcher might, for example, post an email to all members of a user group or discussion forum. Alternatively, an email may be sent out on a researcher's behalf by the owner of an emailing list or the adminis-trator of an institution such as a school, university or workplace.

Holdsworth (2006), for example, gained access to a large sample of university students in her research on student living arrangements through the cooperation of four higher education institutions in and around Greater Merseyside in the UK. Institutional gatekeepers granted access to students via emails and postings on electronic bulletin boards, and by such means all young people eligible for inclusion in the study were invited to complete a web-based questionnaire. The response rate varied between institutions but the researchers nonethe-less achieved a sample of over 3,000 students. Chesney (2006), how-ever, sounds a note of caution concerning the effectiveness of using email communication as the means of inviting students to participate in research. He compared the effectiveness of oral requests in lecture halls versus email requests, and concluded that the sending of imper-sonal emails to a student mailing list 'is the worst way researchers can approach students to request participation'; requests via personalised emails or oral requests in lecture halls proved to be the most effective methods.

Where surveys are promoted via established websites, such sites might include links to a selection of surveys of direct relevance to the specific topic of the website or of relevance to the demographic characteristics of the website's target audience. Many youth-oriented websites regularly include links to online surveys and at the time of writing, for example, the website of the National Union of Students contained a link to a survey on the impact of different teaching approaches on students' learning; the British Youth Council website (www.byc.org.uk) included links to surveys on voting and politics, and on young people and sexual health; and The Site website (an advice and information site for young people, www.thesite.org) included a survey on work and study on its pages. Where links to online surveys are located on publicly-accessible websites such as these, respondents may come across the survey entirely by chance. In such cases, researchers have little control over who might respond, such that the eventual sample might well include individuals who are not really eligible to participate or who lie outside of the target audience. Yet this will not always be apparent, especially if filter questions which might help researchers to detect respondents who are outside of the study's remit are not included within a survey. Nor indeed in some cases might researchers have control over how many times the same person might respond, although Csipke and Horne (2007) provide examples of how this particular problem might be minimised, including through the scrutiny of 'free text' sections of surveys to ensure suspected repeat responders are eliminated.

A further valuable feature of conducting surveys via online methods is their capacity to be completed at a time which is convenient to respondents and at respondents' own pace, with increasing numbers of online surveys now also designed to facilitate completion in several sittings rather than having to be completed in one go. Although these particular features are equally true of postal surveys, internet-based surveys have the further advantage of 'arriving' relatively unannounced, via a personal email or through an individual coming across information about a survey online, rather than in the form of a questionnaire falling onto the doormat. This might be particularly important in relation to sensitive topics; a young person might, for example, be reluctant to complete an unsolicited postal survey on drug use or criminal activity if those with whom they live – especially their parents, perhaps – also know about it and might want to know how they responded. This does nonetheless raise the issue of whether parental consent should be sought before inviting under-16 year olds to participate in online research, as is often the case in more traditional forms of research. As discussed in Chapter 2, the solution to this dilemma is undoubtedly dependent on the specific topic and its context, although internet researchers should perhaps be particularly wary of conducting online surveys with under-16 year olds on sensitive subjects such as sexual behaviour and attitudes, given broader public concerns regarding internet 'grooming'.

Internet-based interviewing

The concept of an internet-based interview may initially seem somewhat incongruous, given that interviews are usually associated with face-to-face contact. The strengths of the traditional face-to-face interview include the ability to interact on a personal level, to incorporate an awareness of body language and non-verbal cues into the encounter, and hence to develop a rapport between interviewers and respondents in as naturalistic a way as possible. Nonetheless, researchers are making increasing use of text-based interactions in cyberspace as proxies for spoken interviews. Reflecting on this trend, and the questions it raises about what counts as a 'real' interview, Hine (2005: 10) argues that researchers are thus encouraged to 'think more deeply about what it is that we valued about [face-to-face] interviews as a methodological stance'. Early theories of online behaviour tended to focus on what was lost during internet-based interaction, for example the lack of visual cues which are ordinarily present in a face-to-face interview. Yet the experiences of researchers who have used online text-based interviewing suggest that a skilled researcher can still generate a rich level of social interaction. Joinson (2005) argues that it is possible to achieve an even greater level of intimacy in online interviewing than in face-to-face interviewing, given the heightened sense of anonymity generated by remote rather than direct contact. However, this sense of rapport and freedom of disclosure may take some time to develop, and is very much dependent on the interactional skills of the researcher: as Hine (2005: 18) pithily observes, 'clearly, there is far more to conducting effective qualitative research online than the ability to send email'.

Internet-based interviews can be either synchronous or asynchronous. In the case of synchronous (or near synchronous) interviewing, the researcher and the participant conduct the interview in real time, via technologies such as instant messaging, private chat room facilities or via a fast email link. In the case of asynchronous interviewing, the interview is conducted via a series of email exchanges over an extended period of time, and does not require both parties to be online simultaneously. There are pros and cons to both approaches. Synchronous interviewing is more like chat and is likely to consist of relatively short, punctuated interactions, but shares something of the immediacy of a face-to-face encounter. In contrast, asynchronous interviewing allows participants to develop detailed and nuanced responses, but can be a rather more disconnected experience, lacking the spontaneity of synchronous interviewing, but nonetheless benefiting from the gradual building up of rapport over time (Kivits, 2005).

Kendall (2000) used near synchronous interviewing as part of her research on the users of 'BlueSky', an interactive forum used largely by 'sophisticated computer users' in their mid to late twenties, many of whom were also professionally engaged within the IT industry.

Commenting on the absence of face-to-face interaction usually experienced in interviewing, she notes that 'whilst I was not able to observe facial and bodily gestures … I did learn the social contexts for the text produced on BlueSky and also learned BlueSky participants' own methods for compensating for the lack of physical contact and "given off" information' (2000: 257–8). Kendall's sustained exposure to BlueSky – between 10 and 20 hours a week for over two years – revealed to her the 'elaborate subculture' and system of communication that had emerged in the absence of face-to-face contact in the forum: 'now fully acclimatised to the medium, they experience their online conversations as very similar to face-to-face interaction' (2000: 259). This example reinforces the importance, then, of acclimatising oneself to the specific subcultural practices associated with different online communities. This is an important element in all forms of research, but is particularly salient in the absence of direct physical contact.

So far in this section we have focused on forms of online interviewing which are based on the exchange of text-based messages. However, Fielding and MacIntyre (2006) describe the potential of internet-based technologies which allow for more conventional forms of interviewing. 'Access Grid Node' technologies (AGN) facilitate what might best be described as 'an enhanced form of video teleconferencing', allowing 'projected images and sound to be exchanged in real time between different computers' (Fielding and MacIntyre, 2006: section 1.1). It is then possible to undertake real-time interviewing across geographical distance, with research participants travelling to their nearest AGN site in order to participate. AGN technology also makes it possible to convene focus groups consisting of individuals situated in several different countries (notwithstanding potential scheduling challenges arising from the existence of different time zones!). Given the requirement for participants to travel to an AGN site, and therefore assuming the means to do so as well as a high level of motivation to participate, it is perhaps questionable whether AGN-based fieldwork will take off in relation to much youth research. Fielding and MacIntyre's own AGN-based fieldwork includes interviews with criminal trial judges from the UK and the USA, whom they describe as 'elite respondents', although their initial piloting of the technology involved a convenience sample of university students. The potential application of AGN-interviewing to student-based research is perhaps more apparent, then, given that increasing numbers of universities have at least one AGN site. Nonetheless, it is important for youth researchers to at least be aware of the potential of new technologies in this regard.

Project websites

Many research projects now establish an online presence with the creation of a project website, typically providing background information on a project, access to working papers, and other useful links. Individuals who are invited to take part in a research project may be referred to the website to find out more about the project. In the case of internet-based research, this may also be used as a way of directly recruiting participants. An internet survey or a dedicated chat room facility might be included on the website, or an email link directly to the project's researchers allowing individuals to signal their interest in other forms of involvement. A project website might also include links to other websites of relevance to the project, including for example websites of related self-help groups, websites providing further information on a topic, or a link to a dedicated discussion forum. Examples of project websites which have included pages dedicated to the young people involved in the research include the *Inventing Adulthoods* project website based at London South Bank University (www.lsbu.ac.uk/inventingadulthoods/), the website of the 'Next Steps' longitudinal study which we discussed in Chapter 9 (www.nextstepsstudy.org.uk), and the 'Project Reaction' website based at De Montfort University (www.youthactionnetwork.org.uk/index.php?option=com_content&task=view&id=22).

Using the internet as a source of naturally occurring data: 'virtual ethnography'

The final part of this chapter considers the potential for youth research of using the internet as a rich source of naturally occurring data: data that are 'out there' in the social world and accessible to researchers without the need to generate these for ourselves through the deployment of methods such as interviews, surveys and focus groups. According to Hine (2000), the internet is simultaneously both a cultural context and a cultural artefact. It is possible, for example, to observe real-time chat between groups of individuals engaged in the building of virtual communities in cyberspace. One can eavesdrop on the 'private' thoughts of individuals in online diaries and 'blogs'. Photograph albums, historical records and many other 'documents of life' (Plummer, 2001) are also increasingly accessible online. There is, then, considerable scope for imaginative uses of these various data sources, and this section explores the possibilities that exist under the broad umbrella of 'virtual ethnography' (Hine, 2000), including online observation and the content analysis of bulletin boards, blogs and websites more generally.

In Chapter 6 we explored the use of observation as a method for youth research, highlighting the strong tradition of ethnographic studies within the field. Youth researchers have long been interested in exploring the ways in which young people make sense of the social world, not least through their engagement with youth-based institutions, policy arenas, leisure activities and subcultures. Direct involvement with such contexts through participant or non-participant observation has led to rich insights into young people's worlds. In the context of the internet, researchers have ready access to a huge wealth of youth orientated settings, allowing for the detailed exploration of online communities and the 'identity work' which goes on within them. Bennett (2004), for example, argues that the internet might usefully be regarded as a loose collection of virtual youth subcultures. As such, he notes, the internet offers youth researchers new ways of conceptualising subculture, 'based around the relative exclusivity offered by membership of an internet-based fan site or chatline, where "inclusion" is achieved, for example, through the demonstration of "specialist" knowledge and expertise in relation to music, film, sport or a variety of other forms of youth leisure' (2004: 163). The internet thus provides an abundance of opportunities to explore new youth subcultural formations, and to consider the ways in which identity might be constructed and (re)negotiated within these spaces. Indeed, many of the examples already discussed in this chapter have included an element of online observation or content analysis, and have been all the more insightful as a consequence.

Virtual ethnography nonetheless raises some challenging methodological issues, some of which are discussed by Richman (2007) in the specific context of youth research. Amongst the issues she considers, the ethics of online 'lurking' by researchers emerges as a particular concern, and one which we raised briefly in Chapter 6. Online lurking refers to the practice of reading messages on discussion forums, message boards, chat rooms and other online forums, but without any first hand participation. In research terms, this is effectively a variant of non-participant observation, but with the added dimension of virtual invisibility. Such a practice on the part of a researcher best equates with the adoption of a covert research role, which in most 'non-virtual' settings is regarded as ethically dubious, especially in the context of research involving young people (see Chapter 2 for more on this). But is the internet a special case? Many researchers argue that it is, and that as these sites are publicly accessible they are fair game for researchers. Moreover, given the many hundreds – if not thousands – of users attached to many sites, many argue that it would be impossible to secure any meaningful sense of informed consent. A parallel might be a traditional ethnography of a shopping mall, a night club or a football ground, where it might be considered somewhat unreasonable to be expected to secure the consent of all potential participants. Mulveen and Hepworth, for example, argue that

> the non-reactive study of public message boards contained on pro-anorexia websites can be compared to naturalistic observation of a public space ... As public message boards are open to anyone with internet access, the study of this internet medium does not raise concerns of invading privacy, which the study of more private forms of internet communication, such as email, might. (2006: 287)

Smyres (1999) carried out research into young women and their body image via qualitative analysis of the interactions of members of 'gURL', an online community for young women in their teens. Her research was based solely on an analysis of postings by site users to the bulletin boards, which she considered to be 'the topics adolescent girls would discuss in their own space and without the intervention of adults'. Her decision to focus on gURL was informed by her view that it would have been nigh-on impossible to study teenagers' 'off-line' naturally-occurring interactions in relation to the theme of body image, short of 'eavesdropping in the dressing rooms of teen clothing stores', and that gURL provided not only unobtrusive and easy access for her as a researcher but also offered anonymity and safety to those who used the site. So, rather than lurking in changing rooms, Smyres chose to lurk in cyberspace:

> I simply added my name to the list of site subscribers, obtained a username and password, and was free to log onto the site at any time. Because this is not a real-time part of the site, it was easy to remain anonymous. Quite simply, no one even knew I was there. (Smyres, 1999)

According to Smyres, an unobtrusive approach was both ethically and analytically appropriate: ethically, as the girls were not harmed by her lurking, and analytically, as 'I did not need to clarify information or probe into why the girls felt this way. Instead, the data found on the site were sufficient for this initial study' (1999). She would no doubt agree with Mann and Stewart's assessment that lurking is not only a common practice amongst internet users, but can be regarded as 'ethical and sometimes wise' (2000: 14).

Although Richman (2007) adopted a similar methodology for much of her own research on young people's chat rooms, she is open about her own misgivings in relation to adopting a lurker role in the context of youth research. One of her concerns arises from the way in which lurking perpetuates 'adult–youth power inequalities', with young people's supposedly autonomous spaces being subjected to the adult gaze without the knowledge of participants. She is clearly troubled by this, but defends her practice by pointing to the public nature of her research spaces and the fact that bulletin board postings are designed with the intention of being read and responded to: 'although this does not directly constitute consent for research or participation, it does make the analysis of their contents less ethically ambiguous. Just as researchers may analyse newspaper or magazine articles, I have chosen to collect and analyse online publications' (2007: 197).

However, one might reasonably argue that most young people do not consider their online postings to share much in common with newspaper or magazine articles, and neither do they expect them to be read and responded to by researchers. Online sites may well blur the divide between public and private, but they nonetheless provide an important autonomous space for many of their members. This is illustrated well by a study of the home pages on one social networking site of over 200 young black women in their mid-teens, all from southern US states (Stokes, 2007). Stokes was interested in the ways in which their home pages were used as sites of sexual self-expression, the nature of the 'sexual scripts' which existed in these home pages, and how these scripts related to dominant discourses within hip-hop culture. Her work highlights the importance to these young women of the safe space created by the internet to 'try on' different sexual identities without the risk or embarrassment of face-to-face encounters, and she demonstrates some awareness of the tension that exists between respecting the parameters of this space and conducting research into the practices that occur in this space.

Other researchers exploring youth-dominated websites have nonetheless felt it ethically necessary or important to seek permission for their online observations. Williams and Reid (2007), for example, conducted an analysis of communication between users of three pro-anorexic websites, and sought permission to do so from each of the website administrators, whilst Mulveen and Hepworth notified the users of another pro-anorexia website that they would be observing the site 'in order to avoid any possible perceptions on the part of this web community that they had been observed for research purposes covertly' (2006: 287). They also sought informed consent from all participants who were directly quoted in their study, and ensured that their quotations could not be traced back to the originating website via search engines. Williams and Reid (2007) also argued that users of the site could always resort to private messaging options if they wanted to ensure that their postings were not subject to public scrutiny, although whether the users of a website should be expected to change their practices to avoid the 'researcher gaze' is questionable. As these examples suggest, there is a divergence of opinion within the research community regarding the ethics of seeking permission to observe online, but all seem to agree on the importance of protecting one's sources in any subsequent dissemination of research findings.

If message board postings might be seen as aspects of a quasi-private world, and not therefore directly equivalent to newspaper or magazine articles, it might be argued that the same cannot be said of web logs – or 'blogs' as they are more commonly known. The last few years have witnessed an explosion of blogs, covering all manner of topics and specialist interests, and young people are at the forefront in the take-up of this new technology. In a study of 70 randomly selected teenage bloggers, Huffaker and Calvert (2005) found that around a fifth of bloggers included their full name on their home page, and that three fifths provided contact information in the form of an email address, an instant messenger user name, or a link to a personal web page. They conclude that unlike other forms of computer mediated communications, where some form of anonymity is the norm, teenage blogs provide

> a space for self-expression, usually in the form of long, personal, and thoughtful entries ... The online presentations of teenagers demonstrate that blogs are an extension of the real world, rather than a place where people like to pretend. (Huffaker and Calvert, 2005)

These conclusions might suggest that blogs – in contrast to discussion board postings – could legitimately be treated as analogous to magazine and newspaper articles, and that researchers need feel no qualms about not only analysing their content but revealing their online location. Not all bloggers operate directly in the public realm in this way, however, as many blogging platforms allow their users to restrict access to specified readers, rather than providing open access to all comers. Hodkinson and Lincoln (2008) draw an interesting analogy between young people's use of online journals and the use of their bedrooms, regarding both as individually owned and controlled spaces, rather than spaces open to public scrutiny.

Hodkinson (2007) analyses the role of online journals in the Goth subculture, where he notes that postings to collective discussion groups have in recent years been replaced by communication via blogs on the LiveJournal platform. Hodkinson engaged in participant observation of this platform, setting up and regularly contributing to his own Goth blog as well as regularly reading the entries of around 50 other bloggers, most of whom were in their twenties. He notes that he made no secret of his dual researcher/blogger role, and from time to time referred to his research interests within his blog. Although two bloggers gave permission for short sections of their blogs to be published in Hodkinson's research, he chose to use pseudonyms for all other research participants, thus protecting their identities. This is significant, as many of these bloggers were operating with restricted reader access to their journals.

Richman's (2007) study of chat rooms also incorporated an element of direct interaction, through posting a request for information about young people's use of message boards on one of the research sites. Once a researcher makes his or her presence known online, however, a further set of issues come into play in relation to the degree of self-disclosure that is appropriate. In traditional ethnography, researchers may often find that various of their characteristics – not least their age, but also for example their gender, sexuality or ethnicity – mark them out as different to those whom they seek to observe, which often hinders the process of acceptance into a research setting (see Chapters 3 and 6). Virtual ethnography, in contrast, has the potential to mask the physical and socially-ascribed characteristics of the researcher. As Rutter notes

In the field the ethnographer may make considerable efforts to mask and make redundant the research role. Those around are encouraged to 'forget' that the ethnographer is in the setting as a researcher, and to begin instead to see him or her as a person. For the online ethnographer the problem is transfigured: how to be seen as a person or a researcher when you cannot be seen at all? (2005: 88)

There are, however, significant ethical issues raised by the possibility of deliberate – or even unintended – deceit on the part of a researcher seeking to minimise the impact of their individual characteristics (Mann and Stewart, 2000). The experience of many internet researchers suggests that potential participants in internet research are often suspicious of those claiming to be researchers, regardless of who they are, and might demand some form of evidence of their credibility before agreeing to participate (see, for example, research by Sanders, 2005, on sex workers). This is particularly likely to be the case among groups of young people with marginalised identities. For example, young people using gay and lesbian chat rooms might be understandably suspicious of the motivations of someone claiming to be a researcher and might seek assurances that a researcher shares their sexual identity or, if straight, will be sensitive to their worlds. Conversely, in the absence of visual cues it may be harder for a researcher to prove their genuine insider status. Hodkinson (2002) found this to be the case in his study of goth identity, style and subculture, noting that it was more difficult to gain advantage from his insider status when conducting online interviews in comparison with face-to-face interviews, where his appearance made it obvious that he was himself part of the goth subculture.

Summary

In this chapter we have sought to demonstrate the potential of using the internet for conducting youth research. We have highlighted some of the ways in which well established methods can be adapted for use in virtual environments and have also considered the wealth of publicly accessible data which the internet offers to researchers interested in young people's engagement in ICTs and online communities. Throughout, we have highlighted both the pros and cons of using the internet for research purposes, including unprecedented access to geographically dispersed and often hard to reach populations and communities of like-minded young people. We find ourselves in agreement with Hine's assessment of the value of internet research: 'New media seem to offer the hope of reaching different populations of research subjects in new ways, but their promise is tinged with anxiety' (2005: 1). We hope, however, that these anxieties do not prevent youth researchers from exploring the rich possibilities afforded by internet-based research.

Suggestions for further reading

Hine, C. (ed.) (2005) *Virtual Methods: Issues in Social Research on the Internet*, Oxford: Berg. This is an edited collection highlighting many of the issues touched upon in this chapter.

Mann, C. and Stewart, F. (2000) *Internet Communication and Qualitative Research: A Handbook for Researching Qualitative*, London: Sage. This was one of the first texts on internet-based research methods. Although technologies have moved on since it was first published, the book still contains many important insights.

Sue, V. and Ritter, L. (2007) *Conducting Online Surveys*, London: Sage. This provides an overview of the main challenges and opportunities presented by online surveys.

Association of Internet Researchers Ethics Committee (2002) 'Ethical decision making and internet research'. Recommendations for good practice www.aoir.org/reports/ethics.pdf

'Exploring online research methods': This is an online training resource for internet-based research: www.geog.le.ac.uk/orm/

Appendix: A compendium of web-based resources for youth researchers

In addition to the more conventional text-based resources listed in the bibliography, we thought it would be helpful to provide a guide to some of the web-based resources of potential use to youth researchers. This list is not exhaustive, and the inclusion of specific websites in this appendix should not necessarily be taken as an endorsement of their content or of the quality of the information contained within them. Nonetheless, these resources provide useful gateways into the international youth research community, and most contain links pages of their own. The name and url of each source is followed by a short description taken from each organisation's website. At the time of writing, the links listed below were accurate, but these may of course change over time: a search for the name of the organisation/resource should hopefully locate any 'missing' organisations if this is the case.

Youth research organisations and networks

This first section provides links to a range of youth research networks across the globe. Many of these organisations organise regular conferences and seminars on youth research, and details of these will usually be found on their websites, often alongside links to working papers, publications, directories of researchers and other useful resources. Some sites also have linked blogs.

American Youth Policy Forum: www.aypf.org/ AYPF is 'a non-profit, nonpartisan professional development organisation, provides learning opportunities for policy leaders, practitioners, and researchers working on youth and education issues at the national, state and local levels'.

Australian Clearinghouse for Youth Studies: www.acys.info/home ACYS is a not-for-profit project funded by the Australian Government. It 'provides information on the complex and wide-ranging issues that affect young people today, from early adolescence to the early adult years ... The information provided is interdisciplinary, acknowledging the overlapping nature, or inter-connectedness, of youth issues'.

Australian Youth Research Centre: www.edfac.unimelb.edu.au/yrc/ The AYRC is based at the University of Melbourne. Its aims include the following: to 'identify local, national and international research issues relevant to young people', to 'conduct appropriate, relevant and useful research that addresses these issues', to 'facilitate communication between educators, researchers, policy makers and people working in the youth sector', and to 'strengthen international research links and scholarship in the area of youth policy'.

British Sociological Association Youth Study Group: www. britsoc.co.uk/specialisms/Youth.htm The BSA's Youth Study Group 'intends to provide a forum for all those interested in researching young people. The group hopes to attract existing BSA members as well as to promote links with other disciplines and agencies involved in youth work and research'.

Center for Youth Development and Policy Research, Washington DC: cydpr.aed.org/index.cfm CYDPR 'is a national capacity building intermediary. The mission of the Center is to create and strengthen the infrastructures that support the positive development of all youth'.

Centre for the Study of Childhood and Youth, University of Sheffield, UK: cscy.group.shef.ac.uk/index.htm CSCY is 'a multi-disciplinary Research Centre committed to contributing to the improvement of children and young people's lives. Through research and dissemination it is actively involved in gaining a greater understanding of the lives of children and young people in modern society and in helping to develop and shape local, national and international policies that improve their everyday lives'.

European Association for Research on Adolescence: www.earaonline. org/ 'EARA concerns itself with a broad array of topics within the area of psychological research on adolescence', topics which are 'of interest to psychologists, but also to those working in disciplines such as Sociology, Psychiatry, Biology, and Education'. The Association's aims include: 'to promote and safeguard high quality basic and applied psychological research in Europe on all aspects of adolescence' and 'to create a forum for bringing together European researchers who are engaged in any aspect of psychological research on adolescence'.

European Sociological Association Youth and Generation Research Network: www.youthandgeneration.org/ 'Youth and Generation is a research network of European Sociological Association that is open for participation from youth researchers from all over Europe and abroad. It covers all aspects of sociological and cultural youth research … Youth and Generation facilitates internet communication and hosts the discussion list ESA-Youth'.

European Youth Observatory: www.diba.es/eyo/ EYO is a European network, 'having as its objective research into the youth condition, in order to promote the exchange of data and experiences, reflection and cooperation between local administrations, on one hand, and the creation of the conditions for the elaboration and the implementation of common projects, on the other'.

The Finnish Youth Research Society: www.nuorisotutkimus seura.fi/index.php?lk_id=4 'The purpose of the Youth Research Society is to promote multi-disciplinary youth research in Finland. To this end we organize national and international seminars, maintain a registry of youth researchers, publish the journal *Nuorisotutkimus* [Youth Research], and produce a series of youth research publications. Through the Finnish Youth Research Network, founded in the beginning of 1999, the society carries out and funds various research activities'.

Hong Kong Youth Research Centre: www.hkfyg.org.hk/yrc/english/yr-yrc.html The aims and objectives of the YRC are 'to conduct and encourage youth research into all areas of social, political and economic life, on which the values, behaviors, needs and problems encountered by the young people in Hong Kong are then able to be ascertained; to provide the public information on young people through timely and quality youth studies; and to maximize and share research resources by cooperation or joint ventures with local or overseas youth research institutions or agencies'.

International Sociological Association Research Committee on Sociology of Youth (RC34): www.isa-sociology.org/rc34.htm The aim of RC34 is 'to contribute to the development of theory and practice of youth sociology and youth research on an international level, uniting professional knowledge, scientific consciousness, and social commitment of its members to work on problems and issues of youth on a local, regional, and international level'.

Society for Research on Adolescence: www.s-r-a.org/ The SRA is 'a rapidly growing, dynamic society focused on the theoretical, empirical, and policy research issues of adolescence. Through its biennial meetings and publishing efforts, SRA promotes the dissemination of research on adolescents and serves as a network and forum for its members'.

Trust for the Study of Adolescence: www.studyofadolescence. org.uk/ TSA is a UK-based applied research and training organisation. 'TSA's primary commitment is to improving the lives of young people. We believe that there is a lack of knowledge and understanding about adolescence and young adulthood. We are working to close this gap by: undertaking applied research; providing training and conferences for professionals; carrying out practice-development projects; producing and marketing publications; influencing policy-makers, service providers and public opinion'.

UP2YOUTH: www.up2youth.org/home/ 'UP2YOUTH is an EU-funded research project concerned with the agency of young people in the context of social change … The UP2YOUTH Internet Portal not only serves to document the structure, progress and results of the project, but also to provide the European youth research community a platform for information and networking'.

Welsh Assembly's Children and Young People Research Network: www.link-wales.org.uk/ Link's aims include 'encouraging and developing all aspects of research for the benefit of children and young people in Wales', 'providing advice and expertise in research work with children, young people and their families' and 'promoting Wales in the UK, European and Global research communities'.

Youth Research Forum: youthresearchforum.com/ 'YRF is a Think Tank, with an agenda for action, servicing public, corporate and voluntary sectors that share a common need to effectively address issues facing young people today'.

National and international youth organisations

This section provides links to official state-sponsored youth organisations across the globe, including participatory forums such as youth councils. These websites contain useful links relating to topics such as youth work, youth policy and a very wide range of issues affecting young people.

British Youth Council: www.byc.org.uk/ BYC is 'led by young people for young people, aged 26 and under, across the UK. We connect with our community of member organisations and network of Local Youth Councils, to empower all of us, wherever we're from, to have a say and be heard. Our fresh take on training and volunteering and our lively campaigns – both local and global – inspire young people to have a positive impact and make their voices count'.

European Youth Forum: www.youthforum.org/en/ 'The European Youth Forum works to empower young people to participate actively in the shaping of Europe and the societies in which they live, and in improving the living conditions of young people as European citizens in today's world. The European Youth Forum defends the interests of all young people in Europe. As a platform, it is the representative body of its member organisations towards institutions and partners active in the youth field'.

European Youth Parliament: www.eypej.org/ The European Youth Parliament 'is a unique forum designed to actively engage young people in the moulding of their future society. The EYP represents a non-partisan and independent educational project which is tailored entirely to the needs of the young European citizen … Today the EYP is one of the largest European platforms for political debate, intercultural encounters, political educational work and the exchange of ideas among young people in Europe'.

International Youth Foundation: www.iyfnet.org/ IYF 'works around the world in strengthening children and youth, including education, health, and work, as well as providing organization building resources'.

National Youth Agency: www.nya.org.uk/ The UK's National Youth Agency 'supports those involved in young people's personal and social development and works to enable all young people to fulfil their potential within a just society'. The home page includes a link to the NYA's 'Young Researcher Network', which aims to 'value, support and encourage research led by young people. It will empower young people and raise their voice and influence on matters that affect their lives'.

National Youth Agency's 'Youth Information' website: www. youthinformation.com/ 'Youthinformation.com is the National Youth Agency's online information toolkit for young people and all those working with them. Youthinformation.com was one of the first FREE information resources for young people available on the internet. The site includes over 1000 information topics and holds contact details for more than 1200 national organisations'.

UK Youth Parliament: www.ukyouthparliament.org.uk/4598.html 'The UK Youth Parliament enables young people to use their energy and passion to change the world for the better. Run by young people for young people, UKYP gives the young people of the UK, between the age of 11 and 18 a voice, which is heard and listened to by local and national government, providers of services for young people and other agencies who have an interest in the views and needs of young people'.

Youth at the United Nations: www.un.org/esa/socdev/unyin/ This is the website of the United Nation's Programme on Youth, which aims to 'enhance awareness of the global situation of youth and increase recognition of the rights and aspirations of youth; promote national youth policies, national youth coordinating mechanisms and national youth programmes of action as integral parts of social and economic development, in cooperation with both governmental and non-governmental organizations; and strengthen the participation of youth in decision-making processes at all levels in order to increase their impact on national development and international cooperation'.

Sources of statistical data

As outlined in Chapter 9, a wide range of statistical information is now readily accessible via the internet. The list below provides access to searchable websites linked to a variety of secondary data services, including access to downloadable data sets from the UK Data Archive.

Australian Bureau of Statistics: www.abs.gov.au/ This is the main gateway for official statistics on all aspects of Australian society, including statistical releases specifically focusing on young people.

Department for Children, Schools and Families research and statistics gateway: www.dcsf.gov.uk/rsgateway/ This is an invaluable resource for UK researchers, providing access to up to the minute statistical information on all aspects of young people's lives covered by the remit of the DCSF, including statistics on educational attainment, truancy and school exclusions, post-16 destinations, and various aspects of child protection.

The Economic and Social Data Service (includes the UK Data Archive and Qualidata): www.esds.ac.uk/ As referred to in Chapter 9, the ESDS 'is a national data service providing access and support for an extensive range of key economic and social data, both quantitative and qualitative, spanning many disciplines and themes. ESDS provides an integrated service offering enhanced support for the secondary use of data across the research, learning and teaching communities'. This includes access both to qualitative and quantitative data.

Eurostat: epp.eurostat.ec.europa.eu/ This is the main gateway for statistical information relating to member states of the European Union, including statistics on various aspects of young people's lives.

National Data Network's Children and Youth Statistical Portal:
www.central.nationaldatanetwork.org/NDNPortal/portal/portal.do
The National Data Network is an Australian venture which provides 'a
national platform for acquiring, sharing, and integrating data relevant to
policy and research in Australia'. As part of the venture, NDN has developed a portal focusing specifically on statistical information relating to
childhood and youth.

Office for National Statistics: www.statistics.gov.uk/default.asp
This is the main gateway for statistical information relating to UK society, and contains a wealth of information.

US Census Bureau: www.census.gov/   This is the main gateway for
statistical information relating to the United States of America.

Ethical guidelines for social research

This section provides links to the ethical research guidelines and codes
of practice of a selection of organisations, including learned societies as
well as commercial and voluntary sector organisations.

British Educational Research Association's Ethical Guidelines:
www.bera.ac.uk/publications/pdfs/ETHICA1.PDF   'The underpinning aim of the guidelines is to enable educational researchers to weigh
up all aspects of the process of conducting educational research within
any context (from student research projects to large-scale funded projects)
and to reach an ethically acceptable position in which their actions are
considered justifiable and sound'.

British Psychological Society Guidelines for Minimum
Standards of Ethical Approval in Psychological Research:
www.bps.org.uk/downloadfile.cfm?file_uuid=2B522636-1143-
DFD0-7E3D-E2B3AEFCACDE&ext=pdf   'The following Guidelines
For Minimum Standards of Ethical Approval in Psychological Research
have been approved by the British Psychological Society's Research
Board and Ethics Committee as current best practice for research gov-
ernance in psychological research'.

British Psychological Society Guidelines for Ethical Practice in
Psychological Research Online: www.bps.org.uk/downloadfile.
cfm?file_uuid=2B3429B3-1143-DFD0-7E5A-4BE3FDD763CC&ext=pdf
'The term Internet Mediated Research (IMR) covers a wide range of
research activities ranging from purely observational studies to surveys
and *in vivo* quantitative studies to highly structured and well controlled
experiments. These guidelines supplement, rather than replace, the general ethical principles of the British Psychological Society (BPS, 2006), to
allow for the additional ethical and practical issues inherent in IMR'.

British Sociological Association Statement of Ethical Practice: www.britsoc.co.uk/equality/Statement+Ethical+Practice.htm 'The purpose of the statement is to make members aware of the ethical issues that may arise throughout the research process and to encourage them to take responsibility for their own ethical practice. The Association encourages members to use the Statement to help educate themselves and their colleagues to behave ethically'.

Market Research Society guidelines for Conducting Ethical Research with Children and Young People: www.mrs.org.uk/standards/ downloads/revised/active/children_young_people_mar06.pdf 'These guidelines cover any research directly involving people under the age of 18 whether carried out independently or in conjunction with a parent, guardian, carer or other responsible adult'.

Social Research Association Ethical Guidelines: www.the-sra. org.uk/ethical.htm 'The origins of the SRA's concern to maintain an up-to-date set of ethical guidelines and be proactive in the discussion of social research ethics lies in our sense of responsibility for standard-setting in the profession of social research … (T)he key responsibility for ethical awareness and for the status of the profession rests with each individual social researcher and funder, as the actions of each affect us all'.

And finally …

If you are interested in finding out about training opportunities in relation to any of the research methods referred to in this book, then you are advised to check out the website of the ESRC National Centre for Research Methods: www.ncrm.ac.uk/. The NCRM provides a focal point for methodological research, training and capacity building activities among the UK social science community. The NCRM website includes access to a searchable data base of research methods training opportunities in the UK, as well as information on methods-related seminars, conferences and online training resources.

Bibliography

Aggleton, P. (1987) *Rebels Without a Cause? Middle Class Youth and the Transition from School to Work*. London: Falmer Press.

Alderson, P. (1995) *Listening to Children: Children, Ethics and Social Research*. Ilford: Barnardo's.

Alderson, P. (2001) 'Research by children', *International Journal of Social Research Methodology*, 4(2): 139–53.

Alderson, P. (2004) 'Ethics', in S. Fraser, V. Lewis, S. Ding, M. Kellett and C. Robinson (eds), *Doing Research with Children and Young People*. London: Sage.

Alderson, P. and Morrow, V. (2004) *Ethics, Social Research and Consulting with Children and Young People*. Barkingside: Barnardo's.

Alexander, C. (2000) *The Asian Gang: Ethnicity, Identity, Masculinity*. Oxford: Berg.

Alldred, P. and Gillies, V. (2002) 'Eliciting research accounts: re/producing modern subjects?', in M. Mauthner, M. Birch, J. Jessop and T. Miller (eds), *Ethics in Qualitative Research*. London: Sage.

Allen, C. (2001) 'On the social consequences (and social conscience) of "the foyer industry": a critical ethnography', *Journal of Youth Studies*, 4(4): 471–94.

Allen, L. (2005) 'Managing masculinity: young men's identity work in focus groups', *Qualitative Research*, 5(1): 35–7.

Allen, L. (2006) 'Trying not to think "straight": conducting focus groups with lesbian and gay youth', *International Journal of Qualitative Studies in Education*, 19(2): 163–76.

Andes, L. (1998) 'Growing up Punk: meaning and commitment careers in a contemporary youth subculture', in: J. Epstein (ed.), *Youth Culture: Identity in a Postmodern World*. Malden, MA: Blackwell.

Apter, T. (2001) *The Myth of Maturity: From Adolescence to Adulthood*. London: W.W. Norton.

Arnett, J. (2004) *Emerging Adulthood: The Winding Road from Late Teens through the Twenties*. Oxford: Oxford University Press.

Arnstein, S. (1969) 'A ladder of citizen participation', *Journal of the American Institute of Planners*, 35(4): 216–24.

Atkinson, P. and Silverman, D. (1997) 'Kundera's *Immortality*: the interview society and the invention of self', *Qualitative Inquiry*, 3(3): 342–5.

Atkinson, P., Coffey, A. and Delamont, S. (2003) *Key Themes in Qualitative Research: Continuities and Changes*. Lanham, MA: AltaMira Press.

Aune, K. (2006) 'Marriage in a British evangelical congregation: practising post-feminist partnership?' *The Sociological Review*, 54(4): 638–57.

Back, L. (2005) '"Home from home": youth, belonging and place', in C. Alexander and C. Knowles (eds), *Making Race Matter*. Basingstoke: Palgrave.

Badham, B. (2004) 'Participation for a change: disabled young people lead the way', *Children and Society*, 18(2): 143–54.

Bagnoli, A. (2004) 'Researching identities with multi-method autobiographies', *Sociological Research Online*, 9(2): available at www.socresonline.org.uk/9/2/Bagnoli.html>

Ball, S. (1981) *Beachside Comprehensive*. Cambridge: Cambridge University Press.

Ball, S., Maguire, M. and Mcrae, S. (2000) *Choices, Pathways and Transitions Post-16: New Youth, New Economies in the Global City*. London: Routledge.

Barber, T. (2007) 'Young people and civic participation: a review', *Youth and Policy*, 96: 19–39.

Barker, J. and Weller, S. (2003) 'Is it fun? Developing children-centred research methods', *International Journal of Sociology and Social Policy*, 23(1/2): 33–58.

Barnes, J. (1979) *Who Should Know What? Social Science, Privacy and Ethics*. Harmondsworth: Penguin.

Beck, U. (1992) *Risk Society: Towards a New Modernity*. London: Sage.

Becker, H. (1998) *Tricks of the Trade: How to Think about Your Research While You're Doing It*. Chicago: University of Chicago Press.

Becker, H., Greer, B., Hughes, E. C. and Strauss, A. (1961) *Boys in White*. Chicago: University of Chicago Press.

Bennett, A. (2002) 'Researching youth culture and popular music: a methodological critique', *British Journal of Sociology*, 53(3): 451–66.

Bennett, A. (2003) 'The use of "insider" knowledge in ethnographic research on contemporary youth music scenes', in A. Bennett, M. Cieslik and S. Miles (eds), *Researching Youth*. Basingstoke: Palgrave.

Bennett, A. (2004) 'Virtual subculture? Youth, identity and the internet', in A. Bennett and K. Kahn-Harris (eds), *After Subculture: Critical Studies in Contemporary Youth Culture*. Basingstoke: Palgrave.

Bennett, A. and Kahn-Harris, K. (eds) (2004) *After Subculture: Critical Studies in Contemporary Youth Culture*. Basingstoke: Palgrave.

Bennett, A., Cieslik, M. and Miles, S. (2003) *Researching Youth*. Basingstoke: Palgrave.

Benson, J. and Hocevar, D. (1985) 'The impact of item phrasing on the validity of attitude scales for elementary school children', *Journal of Educational Measurement*, 22(3): 231–40.

Best, A. (2000) *Prom Night: Youth, Schools and Popular Culture*. London: Routledge.

Best, A. (2006) *Fast Cars, Cool Rides: The Accelerating World of Youth and their Cars*. New York: NYU Press.

Best, A. (2007) *Representing Youth: Methodological Issues in Critical Youth Studies*. New York: New York University Press.

Biehal, N., Clayden, J., Stein, M. and Wade, J. (1995) *Moving On: Young People and Leaving Care Schemes*. London: HMSO.

Biesta, G. and Lawy, R. (2006) 'From teaching citizenship to learning democracy: overcoming individualism in research, policy and practice', *Cambridge Journal of Education*, 36(1): 63–79.

Biklen, S. (2007) 'Trouble on memory lane. Adults and self-retrospection in researching youth', in A. Best (ed), *Representing Youth: Methodological Issues in Critical Youth Studies*. New York: New York University Press.

Binder, J. (2004) 'The whole point of backpacking: anthropological perspectives on the characteristics of backpacking', in G. Richards and J. Wilson (eds), *The Global Nomad: Backpacker Travel in Theory and Practice*. Clevedon: Channel View Publications.

Bishop, L. (2005) 'Protecting respondents and enabling data sharing: reply to Parry and Mauthner', *Sociology*, 39(2): 333–6.

Bloustein, G. (2004) 'Buffy Night at the Seven Stars: a "subcultural" happening at the "glocal" level', in A. Bennett and K. Kahn-Harris (eds), *After Subculture: Critical Studies in Contemporary Youth Culture*. Basingstoke: Palgrave.

Blow, L., Leicester, A. and Windmeijer, F. (2005) *Parental Income and Children's Smoking Behaviour: Evidence from the British Household Panel Survey*. London: Institute for Fiscal Studies.

du Bois-Reymond, M. (1998) '"I don't want to commit myself yet": young people's life concepts', *Journal of Youth Studies,* 1(1): 63–79.

Bolton, A., Pole, C. and Mizen, P. (2001) 'Picture this: researching child workers', *Sociology*, 35(2): 501–19.

Borgers, N., de Leeuw, E. and Hox, J. (2000) 'Children as respondents in survey research: cognitive development and response quality', *Bulletin de Methodologie Sociologique,* 66: 60–75.

Borgers, N., Hox, J. and Sikel, D. (2003) 'Response quality in survey research with children and adolescents: the effect of labelled response option and vague quantifiers', *International Journal of Public Opinion Research,* 15(1): 83–94.

Boys, A., Marsden, J., Stillwell, G., Hatchings, K., Griffiths, P. and Farrell, M. (2003) 'Minimizing respondent attrition in longitudinal research: practical implications from a cohort study of adolescent drinking', *Journal of Adolescence,* 26(3): 363–73.

Bradford Brown, B., Larson, R. and Saraswathi, T. (2002) *The World's Youth: Adolescence in Eight Regions of the Globe*. Cambridge: Cambridge University Press.

Brewer, J. (2000) *Ethnography*. Buckingham: Open University Press.

British Educational Research Association (BERA) (2004) *Revised Ethical Guidelines for Educational Research*. Southwell: British Educational Research Association, www.bera.ac.uk/publications/guides.php

British Sociological Association (BSA) (2002) *Statement of Ethical Practice for the British Sociological Association*. Durham: British Sociological Association, www.britsoc. co.uk/equality/Statement+Ethical+Practice.htm

British Youth Council (2000) *Youth Agenda: Involving Young People in Research*, Discussion Paper No. 11, www.invo.org.uk/pdfs/Involving_Young_People_in_Research_151104_FINAL.pdf

Brooks, R. (2005) *Friendship and Educational Choice: Peer Influence and Planning for the Future*. Basingstoke: Palgrave.

Browning, S. (2005) *Engaging Young People in Evaluation and Consultation*. Big Lottery Fund Research: Issue 10. London: Big Lottery Fund.

Brownlie, J., Anderson, S. and Ormston, R. (2006) *Children as Researchers*. Edinburgh: Scottish Executive Education Department.

Bryman, A. (1988) *Quantity and Quality in Social Research*. London: Routledge.

Bryman, A. (2004) *Social Research Methods*. Oxford: Oxford University Press.

Bryman, A. (2006) *Mixed Methods Research: Four Volume Set*. London: Sage.

Burgess, R. (1984) *In the Field: An Introduction to Field Research*. London: Allen and Unwin.

Burns, S. (2006) *School Bullying in Northern Ireland – It Hasn't Gone Away, You Know*. ARK Research Update 48. Belfast: ARK. www.ark.ac.uk/publications/updates/update48.pdf

Burchardt, T. (2004) 'Aiming high: the educational and occupational aspirations of disabled young people', *Support for Learning*, 19(4): 181–6.

Bynner, J., Elias, P., McKnight, A., Pan, H. and Pierre, G. (2002) *Young People's Changing Routes to Independence*. York: Joseph Rowntree Foundation.

Calenda, T., Rodgers, J. and Tyler, C. (2005) *Findings and Recommendations from the Youth Empowerment Team (YET)*. San Francisco, CA: The San Francisco Lesbian,

Gay, Bisexual, Transgender Community Center, www.sfcenter.org/pdf/YET_survey.pdf

Camic, P., Rhodes, J. and Yardley, L. (eds) (2003) *Qualitative Research in Psychology: Expanding Perspectives in Methodology and Design*. Washington, DC: American Psychological Association.

Carter, J. (2004) 'Research note: reflections on interviewing across the ethnic divide', *International Journal of Social Research Methodology*, 7(4): 345–53.

Chamberlayne, P., Bornat, J. and Wengraf, T. (2000) *The Turn to Biographical Methods in Social Science: Comparative Issues and Examples*. London: Routledge.

Chatterton, P. and Hollands, R. (2003) *Urban Nightscapes: Youth Cultures, Pleasure Spaces and Corporate Power*. London: Routledge.

Chesney, T. (2006) 'The effect of communication medium on research participation decisions', *Journal of Computer-Mediated Communication*, 11(3): article 10, jcmc.indiana.edu/vol11/issue3/chesney.html

Christiansen, P. and James, A. (eds) (2000) *Conducting Research with Children*. London: Falmer Press.

Christiansen, P. and Prout, A. (2002) 'Working with ethical symmetry in social research with children', *Childhood*, 9(4): 477–97.

Cieslik, M. (2001) 'Researching youth cultures: some problems with the cultural turn in British youth studies', *Scottish Youth Issues Journal*, 2: 27–47.

Clarke, J. (2005) 'New Labour's citizens: activated, empowered, responsibilized, abandoned?' *Critical Social Policy*, 25(4): 447–63.

Cleaver, E., Ireland, E., Kerr, D. and Lopes, J. (2005a) *Listening to Young People: The Citizenship Education Longitudinal Study 2005. The Views of Young People* (Broadsheet). Slough: NFER.

Cleaver, E., Ireland, E., Kerr, D. and Lopes, J. (2005b) *Citizenship Education Longitudinal Study: Second Cross-sectional Survey 2004. Listening to Young People: Citizenship Education in England*. Department for Education and Skills Research Report 626. London: Department for Education and Skills.

Coffey, A., Lashua, B. and Hall, T. (2007) 'Interludes, intermissions and transitions: young people's 'everyday' biographical work'. Paper presented to the British Sociological Association Annual Conference, 13 April.

Cohen, L., Manion, L. and Morrison, K. (2007) *Research Methods in Education*. London: Routledge.

Cohen, P. (1996) *Rethinking the Youth Question: Education, Labour and Cultural Studies*. London: Macmillan.

Coles, B. (1995) *Youth and Social Policy: Youth Citizenship and Young Careers*. London: UCL Press.

Corti, L. (2006) Editorial, *Methodological Innovations Online*, 1, 2: erdt.plymouth.ac.uk/mionline/public_html/viewarticle.php?id=33&layout=html

Côté, J. (2000) *Arrested Adulthood: The Changing Nature of Maturity and Identity*. New York: New York University Press.

Creswell, J. and Plano Clark, V. (2006) *Designing and Conducting Mixed Methods Research*. London: Sage.

Croxford, L. (2006) 'The Youth Cohort Surveys – how good is the evidence?', *Special CES Briefing No. 38*, Edinburgh: Centre for Educational Sociology.

Csipke, E. and Horne, O. (2007) 'Pro-eating disorder websites: users' opinions', *European Eating Disorders Review*, 15(3): 196–206.

Curtis, R. (2002) 'Co-existing in the real world: the problems, surprises and delights of being an ethnographer on a multidisciplinary research project', *International Journal of Drug Policy*, 13(4): 297–300.

Czarniawska, B. (2004) *Narratives in Social Science Research*. London: Sage.

David, M., Edwards, R. and Aldred, P. (2001) 'Children and school-based research: "informed consent" or "educated consent"?', *British Educational Research Journal*, 27(3): 347–65.

Davies, M. and Morgan, A. (2005) 'Using Computer-Assisted Self-Interviewing (CASI) questionnaires to facilitate consultation and participation with vulnerable young people', *Child Abuse Review*, 14(6): 389–406.

Delamont, S. and Atkinson, P. (1995) *Fighting Familiarity: Essays on Education and Ethnography*. Cresskill, NJ: Hampton Press.

Delgado, M. (2005) *Designs and Methods for Youth-led Research*. London: Sage.

Denscombe, M. (2006) 'Web-based questionnaires and the mode effect: an evaluation based on completion rates and data contents of near-identical questionnaires delivered in different modes', *Social Science Computer Review*. 24(2): 246–54.

Denscombe, M. and Aubrook, L. (1992) '"It's just another piece of schoolwork": the ethics of questionnaire research on pupils in schools', *British Educational Research Journal*, 18(2): 113–31.

Denzin, N. (1989) *Interpretive Interactionism*. Newbury Park, CA: Sage.

Denzin, N. (1997) *Interpretive Ethnography: Ethnographic Practices for the Twenty-First Century*. Thousand Oaks, CA: Sage.

Denzin, N. (2003) *Performance Ethnography: Critical Pedagogy and the Politics of Culture*. Newbury Park, CA: Sage.

Department for Education and Skills (2004) *Working Together: Giving Children and Young People a Say*. publications. teachernet.gov.uk/default.aspx? PageFunction= productdetails&PageMode=publications&ProductId=DfES+0134+2004

Department for Education and Skills (2005) *Youth Matters*, Cm6629. Norwich: The Stationery Office.

Department for Children, Schools and Families (2007) *Aiming High for Young People: A Ten Year Strategy for Positive Activities*. London: HM Treasury/DCSF.

Devine, F. and Heath, S. (1999) *Sociological Research Methods in Context*. Basingstoke: Macmillan.

Driver, S. (2007) 'Beyond "straight" interpretations: researching queer youth digital video', in A. Best (ed.) *Representing Youth: Methodological Issues in Critical Youth Studies*. New York: New York University Press.

Dunne, G., Prendergast, S. and Telford, S. (2002) 'Young, gay, homeless and invisible: a growing population?', *Culture, Health & Sexuality: An International Journal for Research, Intervention and Care*. 4 (1): 103–15.

Dwyer, P. and Wyn, J. (2001) *Youth, Education and Risk: Facing the Future*. London: Routledge.

Dyson, A. and Meagher, N. (2001) 'Reflections on the case studies: towards a rationale for participation?', in J. Clark, A. Dyson, N. Meagher, E. Robson and M. Wootten (eds), *Young People as Researchers: Possibilities, Problems and Politics*. Leicester: Youth Work Press.

Economic and Social Research Council (1997) *Children 5–16: Growing into the 21st Century*. Programme Information Pack. Swindon: ESRC.

Eder, D. and Fingerson, L. (2003) 'Interviewing children and adolescents', in J. Holstein and J. Gubrium (eds), *Inside Interviewing: New Lenses, New Concerns*. Thousand Oaks, CA: Sage.

Edwards, R. and Alldred, P. (1999) 'Children and young people's views of social research: the case of research on home–school relations', *Childhood*, 6(2): 261–81.

Elsley, S. (2004) 'Children's experience of public space, *Children and Society*, 18: 155–64.

Emond, R. (2003) 'Ethnography in practice: a case study illustration', in A. Bennett., M. Cieslik and S. Miles (eds), *Researching Youth*. Basingstoke: Palgrave.

Epstein, D. (1998) '"Are you a girl or are you a teacher?" The 'least adult' role in research about gender and sexuality in a primary school', in G. Walford (ed.), *Doing Research About Education*. London: Falmer Press.

Facer, K. and Furlong, R. (2001) 'Beyond the myth of the "cyberkid": young people at the margins of the information revolution', *Journal of Youth Studies,* 4(4): 451–69.

Farrow, R. and Arnold, P. (2003) 'Changes in female student sexual behaviour during the transition to university', *Journal of Youth Studies,* 6(4): 339–55.

Faulks, K. (2006) 'Education for citizenship in England's secondary schools: a critique of current principle and practice', *Journal of Education Policy*, 21(1): 59–74.

Fay, B. (1996) *Contemporary Philosophy of Social Science: A Multicultural Approach*. Oxford: WileyBlackwell

Feldman, M., Bell, J. and Berger, M. (2003) *Gaining Access: A Practical and Theoretical Guide for Qualitative Researchers*. Walnut Creek: AltaMira Press.

Fielding, M. (2007) 'Beyond "voice": new roles, relations, and contexts in researching with young people', *Discourse: Studies in the Cultural Politics of Education*, 28(3): 301–10.

Fielding, M. and Bragg, S. (2003) *Students as Researchers: Making a Difference*. Cambridge: Pearson Publishing.

Fielding, M. and McIntyre, M. (2006) 'Access Grid Nodes in field research', *Sociological Research Online*, 11, 2 www.socresonline.org.uk/11/2/fielding.html

Fine, M. and Weiss, L. (1998) *The Unknown City: The Lives of Poor and Working-Class Young Adults*. Boston, MA: Beacon Press.

Fingerson, L. (1999) 'Active viewing: girls' interpretations of family television programs', *Journal of Contemporary Ethnography*, 28(4): 389–418.

Finney, N. and Rishbeth, C. (2006) 'Engaging with marginalized groups in public open space research: the potential of collaboration and combined methods', *Planning Theory and Practice*, 7(1): 27–46.

Flory, R. and Miller, D. (2000) *GenX Religion*. London: Routledge.

Flutter, J. and Rudduck, J. (2004) *Consulting Pupils: What's in it for Schools*. London: RoutledgeFalmer.

France, A. (2000) *Youth Researching Youth: The Triumph and Success Peer Research Project*. Leicester: Youth Work Press.

France, A. (2004) 'Young people', in S. Fraser, V. Lewis, S. Ding, M. Kellett and C. Robinson (eds), *Doing Research with Children and Young People*. London: Sage.

Franks, M. (2006) *Count Us In: Young Refugees in the Education System*. Leeds: The Children's Society.

Fraser, S., Lewis, V., Ding, S. and Kellett, M. (eds) (2003) *Doing Research with Children and Young People*. London: Sage.

Frosh, S., Phoenix, A. and Pattman, R. (2002) *Young Masculinities: Understanding Boys in Contemporary Society*. Basingstoke: Palgrave.

Frost, L. (2003) 'Researching young women's bodies: values, dilemmas and contradictions', in A. Bennett, M. Cieslik and S. Miles (eds), *Researching Youth*. Basingstoke: Palgrave.

Furlong, A. and Cartmel, F. (2007) *Young People and Social Change: New Perspectives,* second edition. Buckingham: Open University Press.

Gatward, R. (2002) 'Interviewing children using audio-CASI', *Social Survey Methodology Bulletin,* 50: 16–26.

Gauntlett, D. and Holzwarth, P. (2006) 'Creative and visual methods for exploring identity', *Visual Studies*, 21(1): 82–91.

Gayle, V. (2005) 'Youth transitions', in *Changing Scotland: Evidence from the British Household Panel Survey*. Bristol: The Policy Press.

Giddens, A. (1991) *Modernity and Self Identity: Self and Society in the Late Modern Age*. Cambridge: Polity.

Gillard, S. (2001) 'Winning the peace: youth, identity and peacebuilding in Bosnia and Herzegovina', *International Peacekeeping*, 8(1): 77–98.

Glen, S. (2000) 'The dark side of purity or the virtues of double-mindedness?', in H. Simons and R. Usher (eds), *Situated Ethics in Educational Research*. London: RoutledgeFalmer.

Glesne, C. (1989) 'Rapport and friendship in ethnographic research', *Qualitative Studies in Education*, 2(1): 45–54.

Gold, R. (1958) 'Roles in sociological fieldwork observation', *Social Forces*, 36(3): 217–33.

Goodenough, T., Williamson, E., Kent, J. and Ashcroft, R. (2003) '"What did you think about that?" Researching children's perceptions of participation in a longitudinal genetic epidemiological study', *Children and Society*, 17(2): 113–25.

Goodwin, J. and O'Connor, H. (2005) 'Exploring complex transitions: looking back at the "Golden Age" of from school to work', *Sociology*, 39(2): 201–20.

Gordon, T. and Lahelma, E. (2003) 'From ethnography to life history: tracing transitions of school students', *International Journal of Social Research Methodology*, 6(3): 245–54.

Gordon, T., Holland, J. and Lahelma, E. (2000) *Making Spaces: Citizenship and Difference in Schools*. Basingstoke: Macmillan.

Gordon, T., Holland, J. and Lahelma, E. (2001) 'Ethnographic research in educational settings', in P. Atkinson, A. Coffey and S. Delamont (eds), *Handbook of Ethnography*. London: Sage.

Greener, T. and Hollands, R. (2006) 'Beyond subculture and post-subculture? The case of virtual psytrance', *Journal of Youth Studies*, 9(4): 393–418.

Griffin, C. (1985) *Typical Girls? Young Women from School to the Job Market*. London: Routledge and Kegan Paul.

Griffin, C. (1993) *Representations of Youth: The Study of Youth and Adolescence in Britain and America*. Cambridge: Polity Press.

Griffin, C. (2001) 'Imagining new narratives of youth: youth research, the "new Europe" and global youth culture', *Childhood*, 8(2): 147–66.

Groves, R. and Couper, M. (1998) *Nonresponse in Household Interview Surveys*. New York: Wiley.

Groves, R., Floyd, J., Couper, M., Lepkowski, J. Singer, E. and Tourangeau, R. (2004) *Survey Methodology*. New York: Wiley.

Groves, R., Singer, E. and Corning, A. (2000) 'Leverage–salience theory of survey participation: description and an illustration', *Public Opinion Quarterly*, 64: 299–308.

Hall, S. and Jefferson, T. (eds) (1976) *Resistance Through Rituals: Youth Subcultures in Post-war Britain*. London: Hutchinson.

Hall, T., Lashua, B. and Coffey, A. (2006) 'Stories as sorties', *Qualitative Researcher*, 3: 2–4 www.cf.ac.uk/socsi/qualiti/QualitativeResearcher/QR_Issue3_06.pdf

Hall, T., Williamson, H. and Coffey, A. (1998) 'Conceptualising citizenship: young people and the transition to adulthood', *Journal of Education Policy*, 13(3): 301–15.

Hammersley, M. (1992) *What's Wrong with Ethnography?* London: Routledge.

Hammersley, M. (1998) *Reading Ethnographic Research: A Critical Guide*, second edition. London: Longman.

Harden, J., Scott, S. and Backett-Milburn, K. (2000) 'Can't talk, won't talk?: methodological issues in researching children', *Sociological Research Online*, 5(2): www.socresonline.org.uk/5/2/harden.html

Hargreaves, D. (1967) *Social Relations in a Secondary School*. London: Routledge.

Harpham, T., Huong, N., Long, T. and Tuan, T. (2005) 'Participatory child poverty assessment in rural Vietnam, *Children and Society*, 19: 27–41.

Harris, A. (2004) *Future Girl: Young Women in the Twenty First Century*. London: Routledge.

Harrison, L. (2000) 'Representing sexual hegemony: focus groups and governmentality', in J. McLeod and K. Malone (eds), *Researching Youth*. Hobart: Australian Clearinghouse for Youth Studies.

Hart, R. (1992) *Children's Participation: From Tokenism to Citizenship*, Florence: UNICEF International Child Development Centre.

Hart, R. (1997) *Children's Participation: The Theory and Practice of Involving Young Citizens in Community Development and Environmental Care*. London: Earthscan Publications.

Heath, S. (1999) 'Watching the backlash: the problematisation of young women's academic success in 1990s Britain', *Discourse: Studies in the Cultural Politics of Education*, 20(2): 249–66.

Heath, S. and Cleaver, E. (2003) *Young, Free and Single? Twenty-Somethings and Household Change*. Basingstoke: Palgrave.

Heath, S. and Cleaver, E. (2004) 'Mapping the spatial in shared household life: a missed opportunity?', in C. Knowles and P. Sweetman (eds), *Picturing the Social Landscape: Visual Methods and the Sociological Imagination*. London: Routledge.

Heath, S., Charles, V., Crow, G. and Wiles, R. (2007) 'Informed consent, gatekeepers and go-betweens: negotiating consent in child- and youth-orientated institutions', *British Educational Research Journal*, 33(3): 403–17.

Helwig-Larsen, K. and Larsen, H.B. (2002) *A nation-wide survey conducted among 15–16 year-old Danish school children that included questions an sensitive topics*. Paper presented at the International Conference on Improving Surveys. (ICIS, 2002). August 2002: Copenhagen.

Henderson, S., Holland, J., McGrellis, S., Sharpe, S. and Thomson, R. (2006a) *Inventing Adulthoods: A Biographical Approach to Youth Transitions*. London: Sage/Open University Press.

Henderson, S., Holland, J. and Thomson, R. (2006b) 'Making the Long View: Perspectives on context from a qualitative longitudinal (QL) study', *Methodological Innovations Online*, 1(2): erdt.plymouth.ac.uk/mionline/public_html/viewarticle.php?id=29&layout=html

Herring, S.C., Scheidt, L.A., Bonus, S. and Wright, E. (2004) 'Bridging the gap: A genre analysis of weblogs', *Proceedings of the 37th Hawaii International Conference on System Sciences*. csdl.computer.org/comp/proceedings/hicss/2004/2056/04/2056 40101b.pdf

Hey, V. (1997) *The Company She Keeps: An Ethnography of Girls' Friendship*. Buckingham: Open University Press.

Hine, C. (2000) *Virtual Ethnography*. London: Sage.

Hine, C. (2005a) 'Virtual methods and the sociology of cyber-social-scientific knowledge', in C. Hine (ed.), *Virtual Methods: Issues in Social Research on the Internet*. Oxford: Berg.

Hine, C. (2005b) *Virtual Methods: Issues in Social Research on the Internet*. Oxford: Berg.

HM Government (2004) *Every Child Matters: Change for Children*, www.every childmatters.gov.uk/_files/F9E3F941DC8D4580539EE4C743E9371D.pdf

Hodkinson, P. (1998) 'Career decision making and the transition from school to work', in M. Grenfell and D. James (eds), *Bourdieu and Education*. London: Falmer Press.

Hodkinson, P. (2002) *Goth: Identity, Style and Subculture*. Oxford: Berg.

Hodkinson, P. (2004) 'The Goth scene and (sub)cultural substance', in A. Bennett and K. Kahn-Harris (eds), *After Subculture. Critical Studies in Contemporary Youth Culture*. Basingstoke: Palgrave.

Hodkinson, P. (2007) 'Interactive online journals and individualisation', *New Media and Society*, 9(4): 625–50.

Hodkinson, P. and Lincoln, S. (2008), 'Online journals as virtual bedrooms: young people, identity and personal space', *Young*, 16(1): 27–46.

Hodkinson, P. and Sparks, A. (1997) 'Careership: a sociological theory of career decision-making', *British Journal of Sociology of Education*, 18(1): 29–44.

Hogan, D. and Greene, S. (2004) *Researching Children's Experiences: Approaches and Methods*. London: Sage.

Holdsworth, C. (2006) '"Don't you think you're missing out, living at home?" Student experiences and residential transitions', *Sociological Review* 54(3): 495–519.

Holland, J., Bell, R., Henderson, S., McGrellis, S., Sharpe, S. and Thomson, R. (2001) 'Youth values and transitions: young people's participation in the research process', in J. Clark, A. Dyson, N. Meagher, E. Robson, E. and M. Wootten (eds), *Young People as Researchers: Possibilities, Problems and Politics*. Leicester: Youth Work Press.

Hollands, R. (2003) 'Double exposure: exploring the social and political relations of ethnographic youth research', in A. Bennett, M. Cieslik and S. Miles (eds), *Researching Youth*. Basingstoke: Palgrave.

Holloway, S. and Valentine, G. (eds) (2000) *Children's Geographies: Playing, Living, Learning*. London: Routledge.

Hollway, W. and Jefferson, T. (2000) *Doing Qualitative Research Differently: Free Association, Narrative and the Interview Method*. London: Sage.

Homan, R. (1991) *The Ethics of Social Research*. Harlow: Longman.

Homan, R. (2001) 'The principle of assumed consent: the ethics of gatekeeping', *Journal of Philosophy of Education*, 35(3): 329–43.

Hopkins, P. (2008) 'Ethical issues in research with unaccompanied asylum-seeking children', *Children's Geographies*, 6 (1): 37–48.

Horrocks, C. and Blyth, E. (2003) 'Service user evaluations: young people, participation and client-centredness', *Youth and Policy*, 82: 16–26.

Huffaker, D.A. and Calvert, S.L. (2005) 'Gender, identity, and language use in teenage blogs', *Journal of Computer-mediated Communication*, 10(2): http://jcmc.indiana.edu/vol10/issue2/huffaker.html

Humphreys, L. (1975) *The Tea Room Trade: Impersonal Sex in Public Places*. New York: Aldine de Gruyter.

International Association for the Advancement of Educational Achievement (2007) International Civic and Citizenship Education Study: http://iccs.acer.edu.au/

Ireland, E., Kerr, D., Lopes, J. and Nelson, J., with Cleaver, E. (2006) *Active Citizenship and Young People: Opportunities, Experiences and Challenges in and Beyond School, Citizenship Education Longitudinal Study: Fourth Annual Report*. Department for Education and Skills Research Report 732. London: Department for Education and Skills.

Jackson, S., Ajayi, S. and Quigley, M. (2005) *Going to University from Care*. London: Institute of Education.

Jacobson, Y. and Luzzatto, D. (2004) 'Israeli youth body adornments: between protest and conformity', *Young*, 12(2): 155–74.

James, A., Jenks, C. and Prout, A. (1998) *Theorizing Childhood*. Cambridge: Polity.

Jewitt, C. (1997) 'Images of men: male sexuality in sexual health leaflets and posters for young people', *Sociological Research Online*, 2(2): www.socresonline.org.uk/2/2/6.html

Johnson, K. and White, K. (2004) 'Binge-drinking in female university students: a theory of planned behaviour perspective', *Youth Studies Australia*, 23(2): 20–2.

Joinson, A. (2005) 'Internet behaviour and the design of virtual methods', in C. Hine (ed.), *Virtual Methods: Issues in Social Research on the Internet*. Oxford: Berg.

Jones, A. (2004) 'Involving children and young people as researchers', in S. Fraser, V. Lewis, S. Ding, M. Kellett and C. Robinson (eds), *Doing Research with Children and Young People*. London: Sage.

Jones, G. and Wallace, C. (1992) *Youth, Family and Citizenship*. Buckingham: Open University Press.

Jordan, S. and Yeomans, D. (1995) 'Critical ethnography: problems in contemporary theory and practice', *British Journal of Sociology of Education*, 16(3): 389–408.

Jossellson, K. (ed.) (1996) *Ethics and Process in the Narrative Study of Lives*. Thousand Oaks, CA: Sage.

Kaplan, D.W. (2004) *The Sage Handbook of Quantitative Methodology for the Social Science*. London: Sage

Kehily, M.-J. (2002) *Sexuality, Gender and Schooling: Shifting Agendas in Social Learning*. London: RoutledgeFalmer.

Kellett, M. (2005) *How to Develop Children as Researchers: A Step-by-Step Guide to Teaching the Research Process*. London: Paul Chapman.

Kellett, M., Lewis, V., Robinson, C. and Fraser, S. (eds) (2003) *The Reality of Research with Children and Young People*. London: Sage.

Kelly, P. (2003) 'Growing up as a risky business? Risks, surveillance and the institutionalized mistrust of youth', *Journal of Youth Studies*, 6(2): 165–80.

Kelly, P. (2006) 'The entrepreneurial self and youth at-risk: exploring the horizons of identity in the 21st Century', *Journal of Youth Studies*, 9(1): 17–32.

Kendall, L. (2000) '"Oh no! I'm a nerd!" Hegemonic masculinity on an on-line forum', *Gender and Society*, 14(2): 256–74.

Kirby, P. (2004) *A Guide to Actively Involving Young People in Research: For Researchers, Research Commissioners and Managers*. Eastleigh: INVOLVE. www.invo.org.uk/pdfs/Involving_Young_People_in_Research_151104_FINAL.pdf

Kirby, P., HAYS Young Researchers, Wubner, K. and Lewis, M. (2001) 'The HAYS project: Young people in control?', in J. Clark, A. Dyson, N. Meagher, E. Robson and M. Wooten (eds), *Young People as Researchers: Possibilities, Problems and Politics*. Leicester: Youth Work Press.

Kirby, P., Lanyon, C., Cronin, K. and Sinclair, R. (2003). *Building a Culture of Participation: Involving Children and Young People in Policy, Service Planning, Delivery and Evaluation. Handbook*. London: Department for Education and Skills.

Kivits, J. (2005) 'Online interviewing and the research relationship', in C. Hine (ed.), *Virtual Methods: Issues in Social Research on the Internet*. Oxford: Berg.

Lacey, C. (1970) *Hightown Grammar: The School as a Social System*. Manchester: Manchester University Press.

Lather, P. (1991) *Getting Smart: Feminist Research and Pedagogy with/in the Postmodern*. London: Routledge.

Lee, R. (1996) *Doing Research on Sensitive Topics*. London: Sage.

de Leeuw, E., Borgers, N. and Strijbos-Smits, A. (2002) 'Children as respondents: developing, evaluating and testing questionnaires for children'. Paper presented at the *International Conference on Questionnaire Development, Evaluation and Testing Methods*. Charleston, South Carolina, November.

de Leeuw, E., Hox, J., Kef, S. and Van Hattum, M. (1997) 'Overcoming the problems of special interviews on sensitive topics: computer assisted self-interviewing tailored for young children and adolescents', *Proceedings of the 1997 Sawtooth Software Conference*. Sequim, WA. USA.

Leonard, M. (1998) 'Paper planes: travelling the New Grrrl geographies', in T. Skelton and G. Valentine (eds), *Cool Places: Geographies of Youth Cultures*. London: Routledge.

Leonard, M. (2006) 'Teenagers telling sectarian stories', *Sociology* 40(6): 1117–33.

Leonard, M. (2007) 'With a capital "G": gatekeepers and gatekeeping in research with children', in A. Best (ed.), *Representing Youth: Methodological Issues in Critical Youth Studies*. New York: New York University Press.

Lewins, A. and Silver, C. (2007) *Using Software in Qualitative Research: A Step-by-Step Guide*. London: Sage.

Lewis, A. and Lindsay, G. (2000) *Researching Children's Perspectives*. Buckingham: Open University Press.

Lewis, V., Kellett, M., Robinson, C., Fraser, S. and Ding, S. (2004) *The Reality of Research with Children and Young People*. London: Sage.

Leyshon, M. (2002) 'On being "in the field": practice, progress and problems in research with young people in rural areas', *Journal of Rural Studies*, 18(2): 179–91.

Lieblich, A., Tuval-Mashiach, R. and Zilber, T. (1998) *Narrative Research*. London: Sage.

Lincoln, S. (2004) 'Teenage girls' "bedroom culture": codes versus zones', in A. Bennett and K. Kahn-Harris (eds), *After Subculture. Critical Studies in Contemporary Youth Culture*. Basingstoke: Palgrave.

Lincoln, S. (2005) 'Feeling the noise: teenagers, bedrooms and music', *Leisure Studies*, 24(4): 399–414.

Lincoln, Y. and Guba, E. (1985) *Naturalistic Inquiry*. Thousand Oaks, CA: Sage.

Lindsey, J. (2004) 'Gender and class in the lives of young hairdressers: from serious to spectacular', *Journal of Youth Studies*, 7(3): 259–77.

Lofland, J. and Lofland, L. (1994) *Analysing Social Settings: A Guide to Qualitative Observation and Analysis*. Florence: Wadsworth Publishing.

Luzzatto, D. and Jacobson, Y. (2001) 'Youth graffiti as an existential coping device: the case of Rabin's assassination', *Journal of Youth Studies*, 4(3): 351–65.

Mac an Ghaill, M. (1993) 'Beyond the white norm: the use of qualitative methods in the study of black youths' schooling in England', in P. Woods and M. Hammersley (eds), *Gender and Ethnicity in Schools: Ethnographic Accounts*. London: Routledge.

Mac an Ghaill, M. (1994) *The Making of Men: Masculinities, Sexualities and Schooling*. Buckingham: Open University Press.

MacDonald, R. and Marsh, J. (2005) *Disconnected Youth? Growing Up in Britain's Poor Neighbourhoods*. Basingstoke: Palgrave.

MacDonald, R., Mason, P., Shildrick, T., Webster, C., Johnston, L. and Ridley, L. (2001) 'Snakes and ladders: in defence of studies of youth transition', *Sociological Research Online*, 5(4) www.socresonline.org.uk/5/4/macdonald.html

Madsen, U. (2006) 'Imagining selves: school narratives from girls in Eritrea, Denmark and Nepal: ethnographic comparisons of globalization and schooling', *Young*, 14(3): 219–233.

Malbon, B. (1999) *Clubbing: Dancing, Ecstacy and Vitality*. London: Routledge.

Mann, C. and Stewart, F. (2000) *Internet Communication and Qualitative Research: A Handbook for Researching Online*. London: Sage.

Marsh, D., O'Toole, T. and Jones, S. (2007) *Young People and Politics in the UK. Apathy or Alienation?* Basingstoke: Palgrave.

Martino, W. and Pallotta-Chiarolli, M. (2003) *So What's a Boy? Addressing Issues of Masculinity and Schooling*. Maidenhead: McGraw Hill/Open University Press.

Mason, J. (2006) 'Six strategies for mixing methods and linking data in social science research', *NCRM Working Paper Series*, 4/06. ESRC National Centre for Research Methods: http://www.ncrm.ac.uk/research/outputs/publications/WorkingPapers/2006/0406_six_strategies_for_mixing_methods.pdf

Masson, J. (2004) 'The legal context', in S. Fraser, V. Lewis, S. Ding, M. Kellett and C. Robinson (eds), *Doing Research with Children and Young People*. London: Sage.

Matthews, H. (2001) 'Power games and moral territories: ethical dilemmas when working with children and young people', *Ethics, Place and Environment: A Journal of Philosophy and Geography*, 4(2): 117–8.

Mauthner, M. and Douchet, A. (1997) 'Reflections on a voice-centred relational method: analysing maternal and domestic voices', in J. Ribbens and R. Edwards (eds), *Feminist Dilemmas in Qualitative Research: Public Knowledge and Private Lives*. London: Sage.

Mauthner, M., Birch, M., Jessop, J. and Miller, T. (eds) (2002) *Ethics in Qualitative Research*. London: Sage.

May, T. (2001) *Social Research: Issues, Methods and Process*. Buckingham: Open University Press.

McDowell, L. (2001) '"It's that Linda again": ethical, practical and political issues involved in longitudinal research', *Ethics, Place and Environment: A Journal of Philosophy and Geography*, 4(2): 87–100.

McLeod, J. (2000) 'Metaphors of the self: searching for young people's identities through interviews', in J. McLeod and K. Malone (eds), *Researching Youth*. Hobart: Australian Clearinghouse for Youth Studies.

McLeod. J. and Malone, K. (eds) (2000) *Researching Youth*. Hobart: Australian Clearinghouse for Youth Studies.

McRobbie, A. (2000) *Feminism and Youth Culture*, second edition. Basingstoke: Macmillan.

McRobbie, A. and Garber, J. (1976) 'Girls and subcultures: an explanation', in S. Hall and T. Jefferson (eds), *Resistance Through Rituals: Youth Subcultures in Post-war Britain*. London: Hutchinson.

Miles, S. (1996) 'The cultural capital of consumption: understanding "postmodern" identities in a cultural context', *Culture and Psychology*, 2(2): 139–58.

Miller, T. and Bell, L. (2002) Consenting to what? Issues of access, gatekeeping and "informed" consent', in M. Mauthner, M. Birch, J. Jessop and T. Miller (eds), *Ethics in Qualitative Research*. London: Sage.

Mizen, P. (2003) *The Changing State of Youth*. Basingstoke: Palgrave.

Mizen, P. (2005) 'A little "light work"? Children's images of their labour', *Visual Studies*, 20(2): 124–39.

Moore, K. (2003) 'E-heads versus beer monsters: researching young people's music and drug consumption in dance club settings', in A. Bennett, M. Cieslik and S. Miles (eds), *Researching Youth*. Basingstoke: Palgrave.

Moore, N. (2006) 'The contexts of context: broadening perspectives in the (re)use of qualitative data', *Methodological Innovations Online*, 1, 2: http://erdt.plymouth. ac.uk/mionline/public_html/viewarticle.php?id=27&layout=html

Morris-Roberts, K. (2001) 'Intervening in friendship exclusion? The politics of doing feminist research with teenage girls', *Ethics, Place and Environment: A Journal of Philosophy and Geography*, 4(2): 147–53.

Morris-Roberts, K. (2004) 'Colluding in "compulsory heterosexuality"? Doing research with young women at school', in A. Harris (ed.), *All About the Girl: Culture, Power and Identity*. London: Routledge.

Morrow, V. (2001) 'Using qualitative methods to elicit young people's perspectives on their environments: some ideas for community health initiatives', *Health Education Research*, 16(3): 255–68.

Mortimer, J. and Larson, R. (eds) (2002) *The Changing Adolescent Experience: Societal Trends and the Transition to Adulthood*. New York: Cambridge University Press.

Muijs, D. (2004) *Doing Quantitative Research in Education with SPSS*. London: Sage.

Mulveen, R. and Hepworth, J. (2006) 'An interpretative phenomenological analysis of participation in a pro-anorexia Internet site and its relationship with disordered eating', *Journal of Health Psychology*, 11(2): 283–96.

Muncie, J. (2004) *Youth and Crime*, second edition. London: Sage.

Murray, C. (2006) 'Peer led focus groups and young people', *Children and Society*, 20: 273–86.

Nairn, K., Munro, J. and Smith, A. (2005) 'A counter-narrative of a "failed" interview', *Qualitative Research*, 5(2): 221–44.

National Youth Agency (NYA) (2005) Involving Children and Young People: An Introduction. www.nya.org.uk/Templates/internal.asp?NodeID=93062

National Youth Agency (NYA) (2007a) Hear By Right website: www.nya.org.uk/hearbyright/ home.asp?cid=180&cats=215

National Youth Agency (NYA) (2007b) What's Changed – Every Child Matters Outcomes Example: www.nya.org.uk/Templates/internal.asp?NodeID=92145

Nayak, A. (2003) '"Ivory lives": economic restructuring and the making of white-ness in a post-industrial youth community', *European Journal of Cultural Studies*, 6(3): 305–25.

Nelson, J. (2006) *Active Citizenship and Young People: The Citizenship Education Longitudinal Study 2006. The Views of Young People*. Slough: NFER.

Newman, M., Woodcock, A. and Dunham, P. (2006) '"Playtime in the borderlands": children's representations of school, gender and bullying through photographs and interviews', *Children's Geographies*, 4(3): 289–302.

Nosek, B., Banjani, M. and Greenwald, A. (2002) 'E-research: ethics, security, design and control in psychological research on the internet', *Journal of Social Issues*, 58(1): 161–76.

Noy, C. (2004) '"This trip really changed me": backpackers' narratives of self-change', *Annals of Tourism Research*, 31(1): 78–102.

Noyes, A. (2004) 'Video diary: a method for exploring learning dispositions', *Cambridge Journal of Education*, 34(2): 193–209.

Office for National Statistics (2007) *Internet Access 2007: Households and Individuals*. National Statistics First Release. London: National Statistics.

Office for Standards in Education (OFSTED) (2005) *Every Child Matters. Framework for the Inspection of Schools in England from September 2005*. London: Office for Standards in Education: www.ofsted.gov.uk/publications/index.cfm?fuseaction=pubs.summary&id=3861

O'Neill, T. (2003) 'Anti-child labour rhetoric, child protection and young carpet weavers in Kathmandu, Nepal', *Journal of Youth Studies*, 6(4): 413–31.

Owen, P. (2007) 'Blair: shooting not a metaphor for British youth', article available at www.guardian.co.uk/politics/2007/feb/16/immigrantpolicy/ukcrime

Padfield, M. and Proctor, I. (1996) 'The effect of interviewer's gender on the inter-viewing process: a comparative enquiry', *Sociology*, 30(2): 355–66.

Panelli, R., Punch, S. and Robson, E. (eds) (2007) *Global Perspectives on Rural Childhood and Youth: Young Rural Lives*. London and New York: Routledge.

Park, A., Phillips, M. and Johnson, M. (2004) *Young People in Britain: The Attitudes and Experiences of 12 to 19 Year Olds*. Department for Education and Skills Research Report RR564. London: NatCen/Department for Education and Skills.

Parry, O. and Mauthner, M. (2004) 'Whose data are they anyway? Practical, legal and ethical issues in archiving qualitative data', *Sociology*, 38(1): 139–52.

Pascoe, C. (2007) *Dude, You're a Fag: Masculinity and Sexuality in High School*. Berkeley: University of California Press.

Pattman, R. and Kehily, M.J. (2004) 'Memories of youth and interviewing young people', in C. Horrocks, N. Kelly, B. Roberts and D. Robinson (eds), *Narrative, Memory and Identity*. Huddersfield: Huddersfield University Press.

Perry, C., Thurston, M. and Green, K. (2004) 'Involvement and detachment in researching sexuality: reflections on the process of semi-structured interviewing', *Qualitative Health Research,* 14(1): 135–48.

Personal Social Services Research Unit (2006) *Younger Adults' Understandings of Questions for a Service User Experience Survey,* Research Summary 41, November Canterbury: University of Kent.

Pink, S. (2001) *Doing Visual Ethnography.* London: Sage.

Plummer, K. (2001) *Documents of Life 2: An Invitation to a Critical Humanism.* London: Sage.

Pole, C., Mizen, P. and Bolton, A. (1999) 'Realising children's agency in research: partners and participants?' *International Journal of Social Research Methodology,* 2(1): 39–54.

Polkinghorne, D. (1995) 'Narrative configuration in qualitative analysis', in J. Hatch and R. Wisniewski (eds), *Life History and Narrative.* London: Falmer Press.

Presser, S., Couper, M., Lessler, J., Martin, E., Martin, J., Rothgeb, J. and Singer E. (2004) 'Methods for testing and evaluating survey questions', *Public Opinion Quarterly,* 68(1): 109–130.

Prieto, L. (2000) 'An urban mosaic in Shangri-La', in R. Flory and D. Miller (eds), *GenX Religion.* London: Routledge.

Prosser, J. (2007) 'Visual methods and the visual culture of schools', *Visual Studies,* 22(1): 13–30.

Proweller, A. (1998) *Constructing Female Identities. Meaning Making in an Upper Middle Class Youth Culture.* Albany: State University of New York Press.

Punch, S. (2002) 'Interviewing strategies with young people: the 'secret box', stimulus material and task-based activities', *Children and Society,* 16(1): 45–56.

Putnam, R. (2000) *Bowling Alone: The Collapse and Revival of American Community.* New York: Simon & Schuster.

Raby, R. (2007) 'Across a great gulf? Conducting research with adolescents', in A. Best (ed.), *Representing Youth: Methodological Issues in Critical Youth Studies.* New York: New York University Press.

Ramcharan, P. and Cutcliffe, J. (2001) 'Judging the ethics of qualitative research: considering the "ethics as process" model', *Health and Social Care in the Community,* 9(6): 358–66.

Rea, L. and Parker, R. (2005) *Designing and Conducting Survey Research,* third edition. San Francisco, CA: Jossey-Bass.

Reay, D. and Lucey, H. (2000) '"I don't really like it here but I don't want to be anywhere else": children and inner city council estates', *Antipode,* 32(4): 410–28.

Reeves, J. (2007) '"Tell me your story": applied ethics in narrative research with young fathers', *Children's Geographies,* 5(3): 253–65.

Richardson, A. and Budd, T. (2006) 'Young adults, alcohol, crime and disorder', *Criminal Behaviour and Mental Health,* 13(1): 5–16.

Richardson, J. (ed.) (2002) *Handbook of Qualitative Research Methods for Psychology and the Social Sciences.* Oxford: Blackwell.

Richman, A. (2007) 'The outsider lurking online: adults researching youth cybercultures', in A. Best (ed.), *Representing Youth: Methodological Issues in Critical Youth Studies.* New York: New York University Press.

Roberts, B. (2002) *Biographical Research.* Buckingham: Open University Press.

Roberts, K. (2005) Review of *Young People's Changing Routes to Independence,* by Bynner, J., Elias, P., McKnight, A., Pan, H. and Pierre, G. *Leisure Studies,* 24(1): 99–100.

Robson, E. (2001) 'The Routes project: disadvantaged young people interviewing their peers', in J. Clark, A. Dyson, N. Meagher, E. Robson and M. Wooten (eds), *Young People as Researchers: Possibilities, Problems and Politics.* Leicester: Youth Work Press.

Roker, D. (1993) 'Gaining the edge: girls at a private school', in I. Bates and G. Riseborough (eds), *Youth and Inequality*. Buckingham: Open University Press.

Russell, I. (2005) *A National Framework for Youth Action and Engagement: Report of the Russell Commission*. Norwich: HMSO.

Rutter, J. (2005) 'Ethnographic presence in a nebulous setting', in C. Hine (ed.), *Virtual Methods: Issues in Social Research on the Internet*. Oxford: Berg.

Ryu, E., Couper, M. and Marans, R. (2005) 'Survey incentives: cash vs in-kind; face-to-face vs mail; response rates vs nonresponse error', *International Journal of Public Opinion Research*, 18(1): 89–106.

Sainsbury, M. (2003) 'Thinking aloud: children's interactions with text'. *Reading*, 37(3): 131–35.

Saldana, J. (ed.) (2005) *Ethnodrama: An Anthology of Reality Theatre*. Lanham, MA: AltaMira Press.

Saldanha, A. (2002) 'Music, space, identity: geographies of youth culture in Bangalore', *Cultural Studies*, 16(3): 337–50.

Sanders, B. (2005) 'In the club: ecstasy use and supply in a London nightclub', *Sociology*, 39(2): 241–58.

Sanders, T. (2005) 'Researching the online sex work community', in C. Hine (ed.), *Virtual Methods: Issues in Social Research on the Internet*. Oxford: Berg.

Sapsford, R. (2006) *Survey Research*, second edition. London: Sage.

Schneider, S. and Edwards, B. (2000) 'Developing usability guidelines for Audio-CASI respondents with limited literacy skills', *Journal of Official Statistics*, 16(3): 255–71.

Scott, J. (2000) 'Children as respondents: the challenge for quantitative research', in P. Christensen and A. James (eds), *Research with Children: Perspectives and Practices*. London: Falmer Press.

Scott, J., Brynin, M. and Smith, R. (1995) 'Interviewing children in the British Household Panel Survey', in J. Hox, B. van der Meulen, J. Janssens, J. ter Laak and L. Tavecchio (eds), *Advances in Family Research*. Amsterdam: Thesis Publishers.

Shaw, C. (1930) *The Jackroller*. Chicago: University of Chicago Press.

Simpson, K. (2007) '"Knowing me, knowing you": critical pedagogy, international volunteering and the gap year', *Paper presented to BSA Youth Study Group Seminar on (Re)minding the Gap: Young People and the Gap Year in Contemporary Society*, University of Surrey, 10 January.

Skeggs, B. (1994) 'Situating the production of feminist ethnography', in J. Purvis and M. Maynard (eds), *Researching Women's Lives from a Feminist Perspective*. London: Taylor and Francis.

Skeggs, B. (1995) 'Theorising, ethics and representation in feminist ethnography', in B. Skeggs (ed.), *Feminist Cultural Theory: Process and Production*. Manchester: Manchester University Press.

Skeggs, B. (2005) 'The making of class and gender through visualizing moral subject formation', *Sociology*, 39(5): 965–82.

Skelton, T. and Valentine, G. (1998) *Cool Places: Geographies of Youth Cultures*. London: Routledge.

Smalley, N., Scourfield, J., Greenland, K. and Prior, L. (2004) 'Services for suicidal young people: qualitative research on lay and professional perspectives', *Youth and Policy*, 83: 1–18.

Smith, D. and McVie, S. (2003) 'Theory and method in the Edinburgh Study of Youth Transitions and Crime', *British Journal of Criminology*, 43(1): 169–195.

Smyres, K. (1999) 'Virtual corporeality: adolescent girls and their bodies in cyber-space', *Cybersociology,* Issue Six: Research Methodology Online, www.cybersociology.com/files/6_2_ethicsinonlineethnog.html

Smythe, W. and Murray, M. (2000) 'Owning the story: ethical considerations in narrative research', *Ethics and Behaviour*, 10(4): 311–36.

Solberg, A. (1996) 'The challenge in child research: from "being" to "doing"', in J. Brannen and M. O'Brien (eds), *Children in Families: Research and Policy.* London: Falmer.

Sparrman, A. (2006) 'Film as a political and educational device: talk about men, male sexuality and gender among Swedish youth', *Visual Studies*, 21(2): 167–82.

Stacey, J. (1988) 'Can there be a feminist ethnography?' *Women's Studies International Forum*, 11(1): 21–7.

Stafford, A., Laybourn, A. and Hill, M. (2003) 'Having a say: children and young people talk about consultation', *Children and Society,* 17: 361–73.

Stanley, L. and Wise, S. (1993) *Breaking Out Again: Feminist Ontology and Epistemology.* Routledge: London.

Stephen, D. and Squires, P. (2003) '"Adults don't realise how sheltered they are": a contribution to the debate on youth transitions from some voices on the margins', *Journal of Youth Studies*, 6(2): 145–64.

Stokes, C. (2007) 'Representin' in cyberspace: sexual scripts, self-definition, and hip hop culture in Black American adolescent girls' home pages', *Culture, Health and Sexuality*, 9(2): 169–84.

Strand, S. (2007) *Minority Ethnic Pupils in the Longitudinal Study of Young People in England,* Research Report No. DCSF-RR002, London: Department for Children, Schools and Families.

Strange, V., Forest, S., Oakley, A. and the Ripple Study Team (2003) 'Using research questionnaires with young people in schools: the influence of the social context', *International Journal of Social Research Methodology,* 6(4): 337–46.

Sturgis, P., Smith, P. and Hughes, G. (2005) *A Study of Suitable Methods for Raising Response Rates in School Surveys,* Research Report 721. London: Department for Education and Skills.

Sue, V. and Ritter, L. (2007) *Conducting Online Surveys.* London: Sage.

Taft, J. (2007) 'Racing age: reflections on anti-racist research with teenage girls', in A. Best (ed.), *Representing Youth: Methodological Issues in Critical Youth Studies.* New York: New York University Press.

Thomas, N. and O' Kane, C. (1998) 'The ethics of participatory research with children', *Children and Society.* 12(5): 336–48.

Thomas, S. and Byford, S. (2003) 'Research with unaccompanied children seeking asylum – ethical issues', *British Medical Journal*, Dec 13, 327(7428): 1400–2.

Thomson, P. and Gunter, H. (2007) 'The methodology of students-as-researchers: valuing and using experience and expertise to develop methods', *Discourse: Studies in the Cultural Politics of Education*, 28(3): 327–42.

Thomson, R. and Holland, J. (2003) 'Hindsight, foresight and insight: the challenges of longitudinal qualitative research', *International Journal of Social Research Methodology*, 6(3): 233–44.

Thomson, R. and Holland, J. (2005) '"Thanks for the memory": memory books as a methodological resource in biographical research', *Qualitative Research*, 5(2): 201–19.

Thomson R., Holland, J., Henderson, S., McGrellis, S., and Sharpe, S. (2002) 'Critical moments: choice, chance and opportunity in young people's narratives of transition', *Sociology*, 36(2): 335–54.

Thrasher, F. (1927) *The Gang: A Study of 1,313 Gangs in Chicago*. Chicago: University of Chicago Press.

Tinklin, T. and Croxford, L. (2000) *Scottish School Leavers Survey Special Report No.3: High-Attaining Female School Leavers*, Report for Scottish Executive, Edinburgh. Scottish Executive.

Twist, L., Gnaldi, M., Schagen, I. and Morrison, J. (2004) 'Good readers but at a cost? Attitudes to reading in England', *Journal of Research in Reading*, 27(4): 387–400.

Tyler, P., Turner, C. and Mills, H. (2006) *Involving Young People in Research*. Barnardo's: www.barnardos.org.uk/involving_young_people_in_research_pdf

United Nations (1989) *Convention of the Rights of the Child*. New York: United Nations.

Valentine, G. (1999) 'Being seen and heard? The ethical complexities of working with children and young people at home and school', *Children's Geographies Conference*, Liverpool, November.

Valentine, G. (2004) *Public Space and the Culture of Childhood*. Aldershot: Ashgate.

Valentine, G., Butler, R. and Skelton, T. (2001) 'The ethical and methodological complexities of doing research with "vulnerable" young people', *Ethics, Place and Environment: A Journal of Philosophy and Geography*, 4(2), 119–25.

de Vaus, D. (2002) *Surveys in Social Research*, fifth edition. London: Routledge.

de Vaus, D. (ed.) (2007a) *Social Surveys II Volume 1: History, Ethics and Criticisms*. London: Sage.

de Vaus, D. (ed.) (2007b) *Social Surveys II Volume 2: Survey Instruments and Data Sources*. London: Sage.

de Vaus, D. (ed.) (2007c) *Social Surveys II Volume 3: Survey Applications*. London: Sage.

de Vaus, D. (ed.) (2007d) *Social Surveys II Volume 4: Survey Quality*. London: Sage.

Vulliamy, G. and Webb, R. (2000) 'Stemming the tide of rising school exclusions: problems and possibilities', *British Journal of Educational Studies*, 48(2): 119–33.

Walker, M. (2006) 'Ameliorating culturally based extreme response tendencies to attitude items'. Paper presented to the *Australian Consortium for Social and Political Research Incorporated (ACSPRI) Social Science Methodology Conference*, Sydney, December, www.acspri.org.au/conference2006//proceedings/

Walkerdine, V., Lucey, H. and Melody, J. (2000) *Growing Up Girl: Gender and Class in the 21st Century*. Basingstoke: Macmillan.

Ward, J. and Henderson, Z. (2003) 'Some practical and ethical issues encountered while conducting tracking research with young people leaving the "care" system', *International Journal of Social Research Methodology*, 6(3): 255–9.

Ward, J., Henderson, Z. and Pearson, G. (2003) *One Problem among Many: Drug Use among Care Leavers in Transition to Independent Living*. Home Office Research Study 260. London: Home Office.

Weller, S. (2007) *Teenagers' Citizenship: Experiences and Education*. London: Routledge.

Weng, L. and Cheng, C. (2000) 'Effects of response order on Likert-type scales', *Educational and Psychological Measurement*, 60(6): 908–24.

Wengraf, T. (2001) *Qualitative Research Interviewing: Biographic Narrative and Semi-Structured Methods*. London: Sage.

Whyte, W. (1943) *Street Corner Society: The Social Structure of an Italian Slum*. Chicago: University of Chicago Press.

Wierda-Boer, H. and Ronka, A. (2004) '"I wished my mother enjoyed her work": adolescents' perceptions of parents' work and their links to adolescent psychological well-being', *Young: Nordic Journal of Youth Research*, 12(4): 317–35.

Wiles, R., Crow, G., Charles, V. and Heath, S. (2007) 'Informed consent and the research process: following rules or striking balances', *Sociological Research Online,* 12(2), www.socresonline.org.uk/12/2/wiles.html

Williams, M., Dicks, B., Coffey, A. and Mason, B. (2006) *Qualitative Data Archiving and Re-use: Mapping the Ethical Terrain,* Methodological Issues in Qualitative Archiving and Data Sharing: Briefing Paper 2. Cardiff: University of Cardiff.

Williams, S. and Reid, M. (2007) 'A grounded theory approach to the phenomenon of pro-anorexia', *Addictions Research and Theory*, 15(2): 141–52.

Williamson, H. (2004) *The Milltown Boys Revisited.* Oxford: Berg.

Willis, G. (1994) *Cognitive Interviewing and Questionnaire Design: A Training Manual.* Working Paper 7, National Center for Health Statistics. Washington, DC: Office for Research Methodology.

Willis, G. (2004) *Cognitive Interviewing: A Tool for Improving Questionnaire Design.* London: Sage.

Willis, P. (1977) *Learning to Labour: How Working Class Kids get Working Class Jobs.* Farnborough: Saxon House.

Wood, R. (2003) 'The straightedge youth sub-culture: observations on the complexity of sub-cultural identity', *Journal of Youth Studies*, 6(1): 33–52.

Wyn, J. and White, P. (1997) *Rethinking Youth.* Sydney: Allen and Unwin.

Author Index

Subject Index